Teaching Comparative Education:
trends and issues informing practice

Teaching Comparative Education:
trends and issues informing practice

Edited by
Patricia K. Kubow & Allison H. Blosser

Oxford Studies in Comparative Education
Series Editor: David Phillips

SYMPOSIUM
BOOKS

Symposium Books
PO Box 204, Didcot, Oxford OX11 9ZQ, United Kingdom
www.symposium-books.co.uk

Published in the United Kingdom, 2016

ISBN 978-1-873927-82-3

This publication is also available on a subscription basis
as Volume 25 Number 2 of *Oxford Studies in Comparative Education*
(ISSN 0961-2149)

Printed and bound in the United Kingdom by Hobbs the Printers, Southampton
www.hobbs.uk.com

Contents

INTRODUCTION

Framing the Teaching Comparative Education Terrain: the need for critical agency in teacher education

PATRICIA K. KUBOW & ALLISON H. BLOSSER

This book, *Teaching Comparative Education: trends and issues informing practice*, has emerged from our concern to give greater attention to how comparative education is being taught, or advocated for, in teacher education within higher education institutions. We are pleased that it was of immediate interest to Symposium Books for the Oxford Studies in Comparative Education series. In this volume, we, along with a host of seminal scholars in the field of comparative and international education (CIE), explore the conceptual, normative and practical ways in which the field is being taught. The goal of the book is to consider the ideological and conceptual landscape – both the social and the political spaces in which CIE is situated – and what these changes mean for the teaching of CIE. The intellectual and social aims and purposes of CIE are also examined, as are the sociopolitical issues and trends influencing its practice. The contributing authors explore the philosophical, sociological, political and cultural aspects of teaching CIE, drawing upon their own particular epistemological leanings and professional convictions.

A unifying conviction on the part of most of the book's contributors is that comparative education enables comparativists and practitioners alike to question totalizing narratives, including that influencing teacher education. Across the chapters, there is an anxiety about the position of CIE in the academy and the desire for CIE to play a more central role in both undergraduate and graduate education. A particular concern raised by many of the authors – in locations as diverse as Germany, Singapore, the United Kingdom and the United States – is with the technicist or utilitarian impulse in teacher education. The societal turn toward utilitarian educational purposes and aims is especially apparent in the performance-based standards movement worldwide and its attendant impact on teacher education curriculum, course offerings and accreditation processes. Various contributors to this volume (i.e. Michael Crossley, Carlos Alberto Torres, Irving Epstein, and Marcelo Parreira do Amaral and Sabine Hornberg) see teaching students to critique neoliberal policies and practices as one of the central responsibilities of CIE instructors both now and in the future. In response, some of these comparativists have sought to emphasize the benefits of the intellectual and social aims of CIE and to argue for, or expend effort on, integrating CIE into teacher education at the preservice and advanced levels.

As editors of this volume, we argue that comparative educators must give greater attention (and soon) to how the field might better position itself to have a more secure place in teacher education at universities in the United States and elsewhere. At this particular historic juncture, this means that we must emphasize CIE's practical benefits – that is, how the study of CIE can better enable teachers to instruct students. While comparativists in the field have given great attention over time to the age-old identity debate about the meanings of comparative education and international education, and the question of whether CIE is a field or fields (Erwin H. Epstein), much less attention has been given to what the field hopes to become and the implications of this for the teaching of CIE. For many comparative educators, the field's identity issue is an old debate and no longer among the most pressing issues for the field; most comparativists have moved on. Moreover, while it is easy for those in the field to recognize the value of CIE, there is doubt by those outside the field about CIE's place in teacher education. This discrepancy between comparativists and non-comparativists over the value of CIE, therefore, should be of great concern to the field. In our view, the increasing marginalization of comparative education in teacher education programs deserves immediate attention, leading us to ask how we, as comparative educators, are going to act on our convictions to help CIE secure its place in teacher education.

Toward that end, this volume seeks to frame the teaching comparative education terrain. As the volume's editors, we argue for *agentic practice* on the part of comparative educators to mirror the field's agentic perspective. Albert Bandura (2001) uses the term 'agentic perspective' to refer to one's capabilities aligned with the purpose of one's life pursuits. We contend that the agency-oriented perspective that underlies much of the theory applied to understanding educational policies and practices must be harnessed and applied to successfully advocate for CIE as essential to teacher education. Within this book, there is an overwhelming sense that now is the time to do something new within the field of CIE – for example, reconceptualize it (Michael Crossley); adopt a new narrative (Carlos Alberto Torres); problematize the nation-state (Noah W. Sobe); and advocate for CIE in teacher education (Patricia K. Kubow and Allison Blosser). Robert

F. Arnove and Barry L. Bull, Karen L. Biraimah, and Marcelo Parreira do Amaral and Sabine Hornberg offer useful models or ideas that could be incorporated in CIE courses, and their chapters provide rich descriptions of CIE courses, concepts and activities.

However, the chapters within this volume also suggest paradoxes for the field to consider. For example, while international tests (e.g. the Program for International Student Assessment [PISA] and Trends in International Mathematics and Science Study [TIMSS]) bring the importance of CIE to the forefront of educational policy and allow the field an opportunity to assert its relevance and utility, comparativists also see, and importantly so, a pressing need to critique the very practices that such tests have helped to usher in (e.g. accountability, uncritical educational policy borrowing, and so on). Because CIE is also concerned with the normative, we, as comparative educators, have a duty to critique educational policies and practices that further exacerbate inequalities. Toward that end, contributors Maria Manzon, Irving Epstein, and Robert F. Arnove and Barry L. Bull emphasize the moral or normative dimension of the field and believe that CIE practitioners must not lose sight of such ends.

While we do not want to lose the epistemological and philosophical nature of the field and its contributions in this regard, we also recognize the need for attention at the practical level for the development of agency on the part of CIE instructors so that they, and the students they teach, can challenge the totalizing narratives influencing teacher education. For a field that has contributed greatly to defining and applying critical theory in the comparative study of educational phenomena, it is paradoxical that the very agency that critical theory seeks to cultivate has had rather limited success in positioning CIE as required and essential to teacher education. Though many in the field have studied the potentialities and challenges of globalization and its implications for education, much less effort has been given to how CIE can draw upon that knowledge to counter the parochialism or narrowing of the conceptual terrain in teacher education. While it would seem that globalization might present an opening for CIE to position itself as essential in teacher education, there is limited evidence to suggest that comparative educators have been particularly successful in making their field relevant to teacher education. Many of the authors in this volume have experienced success through dissemination and/or implementation of CIE in teacher education, though they recognize as well the threats and challenges to, or dilemmas involved in, CIE's integration.

The main questions therefore posed in, and by, this book include: What are the challenges and opportunities for CIE, and its practice, now and in the future? And what does and should the teaching of CIE look like going forward? To investigate these questions, the book is organized into three sections: Part 1 – Ideological and Conceptual Landscape of CIE; Part 2 – Aims and Purposes of CIE; and Part 3 – Sociopolitical Trends and Issues Influencing Practice of CIE. The implications for what CIE should be taught, and how, are examined in light of the ideological, sociocultural, political and economic trends influencing education worldwide.

In the first section of the book focused on the ideological and conceptual landscape of comparative and international education, Robert F. Arnove and Barry L. Bull consider the roles of the social sciences and philosophy in teaching comparative education as a way to explore the ideological and epistemological landscape of CIE. They maintain that empirical issues in CIE are intricately bound to normative ones and thereby propose an approach to teaching CIE wherein students apply philosophical and social science perspectives to case studies. Arnove and Bull identify several philosophical and social science perspectives that are useful for analyzing educational policies and practices internationally. They find the universal but non-comprehensive philosophies of Rawls, Sen and Nussbaum and the social science perspectives of anthropology, sociology, and political science to be particularly apt for helping CIE students normatively evaluate case studies in education. Further, Arnove and Bull offer criteria for selecting good case studies to analyze. Then, to illustrate the usefulness of the philosophical and social scientific perspectives they advocate, the authors offer an illustrative case (that of South Africa) and demonstrate how as a professor of CIE one might help students analyze the case from various perspectives. Overall, Arnove and Bull's chapter not only makes an important ideological argument about the normative dimension of CIE, but it also offers many useful ideas for CIE instructors to help students understand the moral judgments that are an inherent part of educational decision-making.

This chapter is followed by the contribution of Michael Crossley, who argues that the reconceptualization of the teaching of CIE must include critical attention to, and interrogation of, three trends in education: (1) the impact of cross-national tests on international policy transfer; (2) the hegemony of the 'big data' movement; and (3) the 'uncritical international transfer of the expensive, large-scale and big science modalities for educational and social research'. Crossley grounds his argument in a conceptual discussion of CIE's development in the UK, and particularly at the University of Bristol. He highlights challenges to the field, such as the neoliberal remodeling of teacher preparation to focus on skills and competencies – a trend many other contributors to this volume have also observed – and methodological debates among scholars in the field. Crossley also explains how, upon the creation of the British Association for International and Comparative Education, the field was reconceptualized to support postgraduate research training. To demonstrate how CIE has been reconceptualized in practice, Crossley offers a detailed description of recent programmatic developments at the University of Bristol. He discusses how Bristol's EdD program emphasizing Learning, Leadership and Policy integrates CIE perspectives into its units *and* has a specialized comparative research unit, which shows that specialization and integration models of teaching CIE can co-exist. In the end, Crossley notes that, because the three trends described above are largely defining current CIE research, comparativists must critically address them in their teaching.

In the next chapter, Erwin H. Epstein argues that the Comparative and International Education Society (CIES) must clarify to its students and scholars that CIE is not one unitary field but rather 'two different though related fields'. Epstein believes that there has been a lack of clarity in understanding that CIE is two fields, as opposed to one, among many seasoned and novice comparativists alike. This lack of clarity on the part of many scholars and students, as perceived by Epstein, is identified as 'a problem' in need of a solution. For Epstein, the solution is dependent on agreement on the definitions of 'comparative education' and 'international education', which vary due to the differing epistemologies and perspectives held by comparativists themselves. After putting forth a separate definition for each field, Epstein asserts that degree programs, coursework and textbooks are, in his words, to 'conform to this convention'. While names, and the meanings they hold, are important considerations, Epstein does not disclose his own positionality as a former long-standing CIES historian. As such, his definition for comparative education privileges intellectual tools of history and the social sciences, while neglecting, for instance, the role of philosophy in comparative education. In essence, Epstein argues that there is a clear demarcation between comparative education and international education, that such demarcation matters, and that people should be aware of it. Epstein's concern also stems from a 2004 study he conducted with colleagues which found that at least a third of the CIES membership had not taken an introductory course in comparative education and that less than one third hold their highest degree in comparative education. While Epstein does well to acknowledge that students taking CIE courses come from a host of different programs with different emphases in their titles – sociocultural, multicultural, global, international and/or international development – what is of greater importance to us, as editors of this book, is that the scholars and the students they teach see the value of CIE, whether or not they are aware of, or concerned by, the fact that CIE is two separate but related fields.

In the last chapter of Part 1 of the book, Patricia K. Kubow and Allison H. Blosser argue that multicultural education is not enough to develop globally aware teachers. The authors make the case that comparative education is as relevant, if not more, to teacher education than multicultural education. Drawing upon Patricia Kubow and Paul Fossum's (2003, 2007) definition of comparative education as awareness and understanding of the theoretical and philosophical assumptions underlying educational issues and reforms in various nations to inform educational practice in one's own context, Kubow and Blosser note that it is rare to find a comparative education course taught at the undergraduate level in the United States. Graduates of CIE programs therefore find themselves teaching multicultural-oriented courses as opposed to comparative education courses in teacher education programs. And, while many comparativists (ourselves included) eschew the practical/utilitarian direction of teacher education in the United States and elsewhere, comparative education's academic orientation is both its strength and its biggest limitation in the present teacher education climate. Although both comparative education and multicultural education often challenge the master narrative in teacher education that equates teacher quality with student achievement, multicultural education, unlike comparative education, has positioned itself as vital to teacher education. Multicultural education is part of an ideological project to equip preservice teachers with the cultural competencies and pedagogies to reach non-dominant cultures (i.e. minority students) in classrooms and to thereby close the achievement gap between dominant-culture (i.e. majority) students and those from minority groups. Comparative education, in contrast, does not prescribe how inequality should be addressed, and, in that sense, has yielded less political sway in teacher education. However, the Council for the Accreditation of Educator Preparation (CAEP) now expects teachers to think globally. Comparative educators should draw upon these new CAEP standards for accreditation of preservice education programs to advance comparative education's position in teacher education, which will help future teachers to connect concepts and diverse perspectives through critical thinking and problem solving on authentic local and global issues. In this way, Kubow and Blosser believe comparative education can be made essential to, and required in, undergraduate teacher education.

In the book's second section focused on the aims and purposes of comparative and international education, Karen L. Biraimah discusses how she has sought to infuse CIE through study abroad in teacher education, thereby challenging academic instructors to move from a position of parochialism to one of globalism. Biraimah begins her chapter by making a case for more globally proficient pre-service teachers and the inclusion of study-abroad opportunities within teacher preparation programs. Study-abroad opportunities, she claims, are a means of incorporating CIE perspectives into teacher education when there is often little or no room to require a CIE course as part of a teacher licensure program. Biraimah bases her claim on data she collected as part of an empirical study of four study-abroad programs for current and preservice teachers (to Botswana and Southeast Asia, respectively). As part of the study-abroad programs, students were required to enroll in a course that included information about the host country's educational system and sought to fulfill the following CIE objectives: 'a) understanding how the national system of education evolved within particular historical and cultural contexts; b) exploring how education impacts national development; and c) acquiring and using skills necessary to critically analyze key issues within the host country's educational system (such as the impact of mother tongue on educational access)'.

To measure the impact of the course/experience, Biraimah used two instruments – a survey and open-ended questions – that were administered both prior to the trips and at their conclusion, to analyze participants' experiences. Biraimah found that the experiences and course content impacted students in many ways. Foremost, the programs increased students' knowledge of the languages and regions to which they were exposed. But there were also many affective outcomes of the programs, including, but not limited to: an increased awareness of the impact of social factors (e.g. poverty, language, ethnicity and the like) on educational outcomes; a deepened understanding of the 'global village'; and a heightened recognition of the need for culturally relevant curricula. Biraimah ultimately demonstrates that CIE perspectives can be successfully integrated into study-abroad courses in teacher education programs. Likewise, study-abroad programs can deepen students' understanding of important CIE perspectives. Finally, Biriamah contends that the inclusion of study abroad in teacher preparation may 'be the means by which comparativists gain and maintain critical positions within teacher education programs'.

In the next chapter, Irving Epstein affirms liberal inquiry as an alternative to the professional teacher education model by asserting the benefits of comparative education at the undergraduate level. He contends that the lack of attention to improving undergraduate learning at research-intensive universities has contributed to public dissatisfaction with higher education. Comparative education, situated within higher education, is charged with making itself relevant as well. The often uni-dimensionality of educational critique only reinforces the importance of the values and skills that liberal inquiry provides. Toward that end, Epstein asserts that comparative education offers unique advantages in pursuit of the goals of liberal inquiry. It is incumbent upon comparative educators therefore to make their courses relevant in the present environment of public critique of higher education. Epstein argues that comparative education reinforces liberal inquiry as students examine the relations between different forms of knowledge and consider how various ways of knowing contribute to more sophisticated understandings of larger principles and concepts. He explores the pedagogical challenges and opportunities of translating the benefits of comparative education into undergraduate courses of study, as comparative education study expects students to have some degree of methodological, language and intercultural expertise and a broader understanding of the roles of and relationships between schooling and social and political theory. These expectations indicate both the 'conceptual messiness and creativity' involved in constructing an undergraduate comparative education course of study. Irving Epstein contrasts the current standards-based teacher preparation model with the comparative advantage that comparative education affords preservice teachers – namely, the ability to use inquiry as a mode of learning to instill confidence in learners and to encourage them to question conventional wisdom in the process. For Epstein, such questions are grounded in the role of teachers who assume 'an ethical calling' that is realized not only through reason, but through curiosity, empathy and reflection, which is the modus operandi in the field of comparative education.

Maria Manzon in her chapter poses the question, 'Comparative education*s* to what ends?', as she examines the diverse aims and purposes of comparative education. By referring to comparative education*s* in the plural, Manzon draws upon Robert Cowen's (1982) work to reinforce the various conceptual distinctions and intentions that comparative education seeks to develop and thereby inform – namely, the academic (theoretical), the professional (teacher training) and the interventionist (policy advice). Comparative education, as Manzon argues, is as much differentiated by its intellectual bases as it is by its institutional locations. In addressing 'the aims of academic and professional forms of comparative education', she then offers a hybrid case of an educational institution where Cowen's tripartite aims of comparative education (academic, professional and interventionist) diverge and converge. The intersection of education and comparative inquiry is first explored from a philosophical vantage point, as Manzon considers the aims of education in general as a way to frame and evaluate the aims of comparative education in particular. Manzon examines fields of comparative inquiry to ascertain the purposes defining them and how they resonate with comparative education. Second, she applies an empirical case approach to argue that comparative education in Singapore is more a mode of educational governance than a form of historical and social scientific inquiry. Third, Manzon questions what it is that count as worthwhile purposes for comparative education at present and in the future, and reinforces the centrality of the moral purpose to the field. Confessing that her inquiry has perhaps yielded more questions than answers, she suggests that the real value of comparative education lies in its transcendent educational aims of authentic education (similar to Aquinas' view of that which is valuable – truth, goodness, beauty and unity), as opposed to a comparative education that leans toward marketability and employability.

In the third section of the book, which focuses on sociopolitical trends and issues influencing the practice of comparative and international education, Noah W. Sobe argues that the changing sociopolitical landscape should inform teaching practice and influence the units of analysis examined by students in CIE courses. Because globalization traverses borders and debates, Sobe asserts that greater attention should be given to having students wrestle with how schools are situated in, and in relation to, global processes and social phenomena. This can be accomplished, he surmises, by teaching 'with and against' the nation-state and by problematizing how the 'national' and the 'global' have been treated in the field over time. In teaching comparative and international education, the goal is to encourage students to put to question structures and concepts that have been taken as given and that have circumscribed analytical terrains. For Sobe, 'the nation-state' and 'the globalized world' are not uncontested realities, but rather social constructions and creations or, as Benedict Anderson (1983, 1991, 2006) contends, 'imagined communities'. While Sobe does not wish comparativists to abandon teaching about the nation-state, he argues that relations, phenomena and processes span national borders, giving rise to the need for 'imagining locals and globals'. Likewise, teaching against the nation-state is deemed necessary by Sobe so as to unsettle 'the politics of scale' that often frame inquiry in CIE. In addition, political elites in various locales around the world often share more in common with each other as a result of similar 'cosmopolitan convictions and commitments' than they do with people living in close proximity or elsewhere in their respective countries. In the end, Sobe surmises that 'learning how to teach with/against the nation-state holds promise for making known structures better known'. This, he says, will require that teachers develop students' understandings about heterogeneity, mobility and mutability.

Carlos Alberto Torres in his chapter considers the dialectics of the global and the local in teaching comparative education. Specifically, Torres focuses on the increasing importance of global citizenship education as emphasized in the UN's 2012 Global Education First Initiative. This emphasis offers CIE the opportunity to embrace a new narrative of education. For Torres, like many others in this volume, the first step toward embracing a new narrative involves calling into question the dominant methodological and ideological regimes in the field, like causal analysis, cognitive learning and achievement test scores. Global citizenship education, he further contends, is intimately connected to human rights, so CIE instructors have a duty to ensure that their students become more knowledgeable about the foundations of education and various theories that are inherently concerned with human rights (e.g. Critical Theory, subaltern theories, postcolonialism and so on). Likewise, students need to 'delve into the new domains of political sociology of education, educational anthropology, political science and political philosophy', as well as experiment with methodologies (e.g. qualitative methods, mixed methods and the like). Torres also notes how education can play a huge role in the sustainable development of our planet, so CIE instructors must begin teaching planetary citizenship. Ultimately, these practices are part and parcel of a relational analysis in education, wherein one analyzes the intricate connections between various dimensions and domains in education. To ground his argument, Torres describes his personal philosophy of education, which is based on Critical Theory, and the ways in which his co-authored textbook, *Comparative Education: the dialectic of the global and the local*, engages global citizenship.

In the final chapter of the book's third section, Marcelo Parreira do Amaral and Sabine Hornberg assert that comparative and international education is especially needed in university education to bridge society's demands for students' practical, performance-based competencies with the critical reflectivity that comparative education affords. Parreira do Amaral and Hornberg begin their chapter with an overview of the historical and contemporary trends shaping CIE in Germany. Current trends shaping the teaching, research and practice of CIE include an increase in scholarship on the state of the field in Germany (e.g. books, book series, journals and so on), the fragmentation of CIE into three primary areas (namely, education for sustainable development, intercultural education, and comparative and international education), and an increasing interest in and impact of international comparative tests (e.g. PISA). The influence of international test scores, Parreira do Amaral and Hornberg maintain, poses the greatest challenge for CIE practitioners in Germany because the popular assumption is that CIE's primary interest and purpose is conducting causal analyses of test scores. Moreover, international tests have contributed to the primacy of quantitative, empirical research, so much so that teacher education and education studies programs in Germany now require coursework in it, further diminishing the role of social foundations courses in teacher preparation. To illustrate how CIE in Germany can still maintain its academic and largely philosophical orientation despite the field's current association with large-scale international tests, the authors offer a detailed description of the aims, concepts and practices of two CIE courses offered at Technical University Dortmund and the University of Münster. Even though these two courses are ultimately part of highly prescriptive, practice-oriented programs, they offer students much-needed opportunities for critical reflection on the socio-cultural and normative aspects of education, as well as on the very melioristic trends that are shaping education in Germany.

The book concludes with an afterword by David Phillips, who comments on the value of the new book, *Teaching Comparative Education: trends and issues informing practice*, to the field and who reflects on comparative education through his personal story.

There are still lingering questions the book raises: what theories and methods should CIE students learn, both at the undergraduate and graduate levels? What does the current climate in teacher education mean for CIE as a field, and toward what goals and ends does CIE need to head? Given the changing career trajectories of graduates of CIE programs, how should (assuming they should) CIE professors prepare students for careers outside the academy? As we turn critical attention to trends in education (such as the 'big data' movement, accountability, marketization and the like), what will comparativists do with their critiques to improve policy and practice? How are we preparing future comparativists to exercise their agency and to become advocates for change, even as we teach them the skills they need to find jobs within the current educational milieu? Finally, what kinds of creative partnerships and avenues could comparativists forge with social science, liberal arts and other educational foundations professors to save critical academic inquiry and the foundations from oblivion in teacher education?

This brings us back to the question with which we began: what does, and should, the teaching of CIE look like going forward? We, in agreement with Bereday (1964), believe that the ultimate purpose of comparative education is not only to learn about other peoples, cultures and countries, but, through such inquiry, to better know ourselves. Thus, comparative education is needed to help both preservice and inservice teachers to build a comprehensive and in-depth knowledge of the epistemological and practical aims influencing education, and that education, in turn, can shape and influence. In this introductory chapter, we have argued for comparativists to exercise the critical agency that is often touted in their scholarship so that CIE can have a secure place in undergraduate and graduate teacher education programs. In framing the teaching comparative education terrain, we have come to the conclusion that there is a need for agentic practice on the part of comparative educators to mirror CIE's agentic theoretical perspectives, positions and aspirations. What is certain is the need for those in the field to engage deeply in reflection and dialogue about the threats, challenges and opportunities for CIE and its practice, now and in the future, and then to act on their convictions.

References

Anderson, B. (1983, 1991, 2006) *Imagined Communities: reflections on the origin and spread of nationalism*. London: Verso Books.

Bandura, A. (2001) Social Cognitive Theory: an agentic perspective, *Annual Review of Psychology*, 52, 1-26. http://dx.doi.org/10.1146/annurev.psych.52.1.1

Bereday, G.Z.F. (1964) *Comparative Method in Education*. New York: Holt, Rinehart and Winston.

Cowen, R. (1982) The Place of Comparative Education in the Educational Sciences, in I. Cavicchi-Broquet & P. Furter (Eds) *Les Sciences de l'éducation: Perspectives et Bilans Européens. Actes de la Xe Conférence de l'Association d'éducation Comparée Pour l'Europe*, pp. 107-126. Geneva: Section des Sciences de l'éducation, Faculté de Psychologie et de Sciences de l'Éducation, Université de Genève.

Kubow, P.K. & Fossum, P.R. (2003, 2007) *Comparative Education: exploring issues in international context*, 2nd edn. Upper Saddle River, NJ: Pearson, Merrill Prentice Hall.

CHAPTER 1

The Roles of the Social Sciences and Philosophy in Teaching Comparative Education

ROBERT F. ARNOVE & BARRY L. BULL

Arnove (2013) has identified the three principal dimensions of comparative education as: scientific/theoretical; pragmatic/ameliorative; and global/international understanding and peace. These three dimensions demonstrate how the field of comparative education can, and does, contribute to an enhanced understanding of the relations of education to society, to more equitable, effective and efficient education systems, and, ultimately, to a more peaceful world based on greater understanding of common interests across diverse cultures and societies.

On its face, the separation of the field into these three dimensions might seem to suggest that the first two, concerning how education systems operate and how they may be changed, are independent of the third dimension's concern with the moral ideals by which such operations and changes are to be evaluated. However, this putative conclusion is based on the assumption that empirical issues in comparative education can be neatly separated from normative issues, an assumption that is insupportable. For, first, one's choice of what specific factors to include in one's description from the large number present in any situation discloses the describer's implicit judgments about what matters are important, which in turn implies that normative judgments are already implicated in our descriptions. That is, in studying education systems we do not usually attend to their effects on something that has no moral value, but we do attend to their effects on, say, children's academic performance, which implies that academic performance is of normatively legitimate concern. Second, our normative ideals for education systems include empirical assumptions about what it is reasonable to expect a system to accomplish. That is, we do not expect the systems to improve the incomes of parents, not because we do not think that such improvement is not normatively valuable, but because we do not believe that it is likely that the education of children has an effect on the marketable skills of parents.

For this reason, we propose an approach to the teaching of comparative education that emphasizes simultaneously the descriptive and normative aspects of education. This approach includes teaching undergraduate and graduate students about how to understand and develop empirical case studies and how to use appropriate philosophical frameworks to inform and make judgments about the cases under consideration.

While employing philosophical frameworks for studying and teaching about the workings and outcomes of education systems can help to analyze and clarify the normative meanings and consequences of these decisions, doing so transnationally requires a different approach from ones often used with national policies and practices. In examining national policies, one frequent approach is to develop normative principles that are claimed to apply universally and comprehensively and then to apply those principles to specific cases. For example, the utilitarian principle of maximizing human satisfaction or happiness might imply that school systems should train students for the workforce because doing so maximizes economic productivity, which in turn maximizes the satisfaction experienced by the consumers of those products. In other words, the more goods produced the greater the satisfaction experienced by their consumers.

Another frequent approach is to identify principles that derive from local values and to apply them to cases that arise in that locality. For example, a local culture might restrict the roles of women in order to protect their safety and purity. Such a culture would restrict girls' opportunities for formal education and employment.

Neither of these approaches is appropriate for examining basic issues that are confronting education systems internationally. The first fails to acknowledge the relevance of local factors to judgments about normative issues. The second fails to acknowledge the relevance of universal factors to such judgments.

Instead of these traditional approaches, we propose introducing students to the philosophical frameworks that philosophers have developed recently that are universal but not comprehensive. These frameworks argue that certain core values are valid universally – for example, freedom and dignity. The values that fall outside this core are, then, appropriately determined by local and cultural considerations, and, even with such universal values, localities can seek to achieve them in ways that are true to their transnational meaning but are locally appropriate. Of course, no single version of this philosophical approach has emerged as most reasonable or perhaps ever will. Thus, students need to be introduced to the most plausible versions of the universal, non-comprehensive approach and to be given the opportunity to apply these versions to specific cases and to consider whether they are useful to determining a reasonable normative response to the cases.

In the next section, we will explain briefly several of the philosophical frameworks that seem to be useful for reaching judgments about educational practices, systems and policies in the international context. Then we will consider how to teach students to understand and develop case studies to which these frameworks can apply. Finally, we will construct an exemplary case to demonstrate how teachers and students can combine the empirical and normative to reach judgments about particular cases.

Philosophical Frameworks

The tradition in moral philosophy, particularly in the West, has been to propose and to attempt to justify ethical systems that are both universal and comprehensive. Universal ethical systems, such as those proposed by Immanuel Kant and John Stuart Mill, to take two prominent examples, claim that their values are legitimate for all people, in all places, and at all times. Comprehensive ethical systems claim that their values apply to all human activities. As noted in the introduction, such systems have no place for the contrary ethical judgments reached by either individuals or cultures. Social scientists noted correctly that these systems did not respect individual agency or especially cultural traditions (Benedict, 1934). As a result, these social scientists proposed that ethics was entirely relative to local culture. Such ethical relativism holds that there are no universal values, but that individual and social activities are to be judged exclusively according to local values. However, ethical relativism was widely rejected by philosophers because it is inconsistent with the universal respect for cultures that motivated the social scientists who proposed it (Honderich, 2005). That is, if a particular culture happens not to value other cultures, it is, according to relativism, justified in doing so because that is what local values dictate.

Even if ethical relativism does not solve the problem of disrespecting cultures, this disrespect is still an ethical concern with regard to traditional universal and comprehensive moral systems. In the last decades of the twentieth century, some philosophers, such as those we will discuss in subsequent paragraphs, began to propose ethical systems that attempted to resolve this problem of disrespect for individual and cultural judgment. Relativism had rejected the universalistic character of traditional philosophical ethics, but these more recent philosophers called into question the comprehensive character of those systems. They proposed instead that only certain values are universal but that in other arenas individual or local judgments of value should be respected. Thus, these proposals are only partially universal. Moreover, the philosophers we will discuss below are working explicitly in an international context, trying to develop ethical systems that are understood to apply to multiple cultures and nations. We propose that these systems are particularly appropriate for reaching normative judgments in comparative education because they simultaneously recognize that certain values apply universally and that others are properly a

21

matter of local determination and judgment. Below, we introduce briefly the work of these philosophers to provide an indication of the content that might be included in teaching comparative education.

Undoubtedly, the most well known of these recent philosophers is John Rawls. In his *Theory of Justice*, Rawls (1971) proposed a limited set of socially enforced values for societies in the liberal tradition – liberty, equality of opportunity, and the fair distribution of wealth and income. This theory has two important features. First, in liberal societies the value of personal and political liberty implies that individuals in those societies should have the right to determine for themselves what values to accept and live by beyond the specific commitments required by justice. Second, non-liberal societies are not bound by the account of justice proposed in *A Theory of Justice*. In *The Law of Peoples*, Rawls (1999, p. 37) argues that all peoples have a moral obligation to follow eight limited principles in relation to their own populations and to other peoples:

1. Peoples are free and independent, and their freedom and independence are to be respected by other peoples.
2. Peoples are to observe treaties and undertakings.
3. Peoples are equal and are parties to the agreements that bind them.
4. Peoples are to observe a duty of non-intervention.
5. Peoples have the right to self-defense but no right to instigate war for reasons other than self-defense.
6. Peoples are to honor human rights.
7. Peoples are to observe certain specified restrictions in the conduct of war.
8. Peoples have a duty to assist other peoples living under unfavorable conditions that prevent their having a just or decent political and social regime.

These principles recognize the moral legitimacy of both liberal and non-liberal societies that follow the principles. Rawls also recognizes limited grounds for intervening in other societies. First, peoples have a moral right to protect themselves and other peoples against the actions of outlaw societies that do not abide by the eight principles. Second, peoples have an obligation to assist burdened societies that accept the eight principles but do not have the material and organizational resources necessary to govern themselves according to their own values. However, neither type of intervention may aim to change the value commitments of other peoples beyond what is necessary for them to abide by the eight principles. Essentially all that is required of peoples is that they do not inappropriately interfere in the affairs of other peoples and that they provide other peoples with the limited assistance needed to make them self-governing.

Admittedly, the universal content of Rawls's proposal is extremely limited because it implies few obligations to assist other societies, and as a result other philosophers have been dissatisfied with his ideas. Amartya Sen

(1999, 2009), in response, has proposed a more robust but still non-comprehensive moral theory. On the one hand, he identifies the basic universal value of social institutions and arrangements as the enhancement of a particular kind of freedom – namely, that which comes from peoples possessing the '"capabilities" ... to lead the kind of lives they value – and have reason to value' (Sen, 1999, p. 18). On the other hand, he identifies some likely sources of injustice that, he believes, all members of all societies can readily recognize as patent restrictions of this universally valued sort of freedom – for example, 'such deprivations as starvation, undernourishment, escapable morbidity and premature mortality, as well as the freedoms that are associated with being literate and numerate, enjoying political participation and uncensored speech and so on' (Sen, 1999, p. 36). Importantly, these injustices do not derive from a philosophical account of value but only from people's common-sense recognition of what is morally problematic. Moreover, the list of injustices is not intended to be complete or definitive. That is, people can discern injustices that are not on any previously developed list, and people can find that any item on such a list is not necessarily unjust in particular circumstances. As a result, Sen's test for injustice is not whether the practice, policy or outcome falls on a list he provides but whether it is a deprivation of capability that people generally recognize in particular circumstances to restrict their freedom to lead lives that they have reason to value. According to Sen, it is universally valuable to avoid or correct the deprivations that satisfy this understanding. Thus, some of the moral obligations that exist in the international context are to assist and enable societies to avoid the manifold circumstances that are universally and intuitively recognized as unjust. And these obligations go far beyond what Rawls has in mind – namely, the right to self-defense and the ability of self-government.

While there are for Sen specific *injustices* that we all can recognize as imposing universal moral obligations to prevent and correct, Sen (2009) does not believe that any particular conception of *justice* can be justified as universally valuable. Therefore, the specific aims of a society beyond the avoidance of patent injustices are to be determined by the members of that society, and those aims may vary considerably from one society to another. This determination is to be made by a particular form of democracy, which he conceives as decision making by public debate and discussion. This democracy can be instantiated by a great variety of political arrangements, not only by the institutions of elections, representation and legislation as practiced in western democracies. Thus, there is also a universal moral obligation to enable societies to develop and realize forms of democratic governance that are consistent with the cultural values and practices of those societies.

Sen's unwillingness to be specific about the positive content of international justice has led Martha Nussbaum (2000, 2006) to argue for the universal obligation to provide all people with particular kinds of capabilities

– what she calls the central human capabilities. These capabilities are: life; bodily health; bodily integrity; senses, imagination and thought; emotions; practical reason; affiliation; other species; play; and control over one's environment, both political and material (Nussbaum, 2006). Nussbaum developed this list in conversation with women in India and with women in a wide variety of international non-governmental organizations about what capabilities are necessary for a life of dignity. As a result, the list can be modified by further discussion, but despite these potential modifications the list is to be understood as ultimately specifying the moral entitlements of all human beings in all societies. It is, thus, universal. However, there are human capabilities not on the list that some individuals or societies may value. Therefore, the list is not comprehensive, and Nussbaum's approach makes room for personal and cultural agency in a way that traditional moral theories do not.

These examples of recent universal but non-comprehensive moral theories that take the international context seriously are the most well known of such frameworks, but they are not the only ones. Other notable frameworks include those of Amy Gutmann (1999), Kwame Anthony Appiah (2006) and Philip Pettit (2014). At any rate, we recommend that students read, come to understand, and apply various frameworks to the empirical material that they study in comparative education courses. The best sources are the works of these philosophers themselves, but some responsible summaries are available, such as that of Harry Brighouse (2004). In addition, because these frameworks often reach different conclusions on particular cases, it is important to discuss with students the criticisms that may be made of each and whether a particular framework is especially appropriate for the normative analysis of specific cases or issues.

Problems immediately arise with regard to competing views of what the moral enterprise of education is. The cited philosophical frameworks can provide useful perspectives on this moral question, but some important normatively informed comparative educationists also provide helpful alternatives and raise questions specific to education. Therefore, we recommend that the study of these philosophical frameworks be supplemented by some of the normative works of comparative educators. For example, Arnove and Graff (1987) provide a useful examination of the values that have motivated large-scale campaigns to teach largely illiterate populations to read and write, often involving the propagation of particular religions or political ideologies. Historically, campaigns have aimed to forge a larger and more cohesive community based on certain doctrines, texts, symbols and leaders. Questions then arise as to which individuals are included or excluded by the language and content of the campaign from the emergent community.

Alternatively, the process of learning to read, as articulated in the philosophy and pedagogy of twentieth-century educator Paulo Freire (2000), also could be seen as empowering individuals and their communities to read the world and change it for the better. Freire's problem-positing strategy builds on learners' knowledge and the existential problems they face in order to raise a critical consciousness. His pedagogy of education for human freedom is based on a dialogue between educators and learners that is open ended. This conceptual and ethical framework does not restrict individuals to predetermined roles but fosters a broad expanse of possibilities for individuals to shape their own destinies.

These central notions of Freire fit with the philosophical concerns articulated in this chapter on how to teach comparative education. They are a concern for education policies and practices that respect the everyday realities of learners while promoting human freedom and competencies. Furthermore, the case-studies approach to teaching comparative education involves providing students with a set of normative questions to explore within a particular context.

That these philosophical frameworks and the theoretical work of comparative scholars are only partially universal makes it clear why case studies are particularly appropriate to the approach to teaching comparative education that we recommend. One could, for example, teach large-scale causal theories about how education systems function, such as those of James Coleman or Christopher Jencks, and then teach the empirical research that investigates the variables that those theories determine to be relevant for explaining education systems and their effects. There is potential value of such an approach, especially in identifying the effective factors for changing such systems. However, such causal approaches do not encompass all the information necessary to reach normative judgments about particular education systems. First, some of the concerns of both universal and local values with regard to education include matters not captured by a concern with the empirical effects of education systems. For example, it might be universally true that children have a right to a safe and healthy education environment no matter whether that environment produces results for the academic performance or future employability of children. A study of causal models is not likely to produce information about the features of education systems that are not causally efficacious even though those features are normatively relevant. Second, the study of causal models may not produce normatively adequate accounts of education systems because they emphasize features of such systems that are causally efficacious but not necessarily of universal or local normative concern. For example, a causal model of schooling may determine that local cultural practices have a negative effect on children's learning, although neither universal nor local values are affected by those practices. As a result of these two issues, an exclusively large-scale and causal focus in teaching may emphasize some factors that are not of normative interest and neglect others that are. The neglect of normative factors not of causal import is particularly problematic for the emerging philosophical frameworks that we have discussed above. For such frameworks will sometimes leave normative judgment in certain regards entirely to local values because such judgment does not implicate universal values. The causal approach to teaching comparative education ignores factors that do not have causal significance and thus may fail to document whether such systems are legitimate according to local values.

Social Science Frameworks

Briefly, the various social sciences include the following perspectives and insights that contribute to an understanding of the contexts in which normative judgments are made with regard to education policies and practices. Anthropologists provide the detailed descriptions of the ways people go about making meaning of the world, the values that guide individuals and their communities, the material objects to which they attach significance, and the ways in which their languages shape cognition and perceptions. Anthropologists and sociologists call attention to the major role education systems play in cultural transmission throughout history in preparing the young for adulthood. As culture is enacted in various societal roles, sociologists contribute to an understanding of the actions of individuals and their communities in their daily routines within social structures that have specific functions. Schooling, for example, is one such structure with its own norms regarding how students (of whatever age) should behave. Education systems not only prepare individuals for different societal roles, they are the major means by which nation-states select and credential individuals for the economy and polity. Political scientists contribute an understanding of the power differentials that influence what knowledge is most valuable, how it is attained, and how it is evaluated. Political sociology and political economy provide the concepts with which to examine who pays and who benefits from public policy, with education often being the largest item in a national budget and the occupational sector that employs the most individuals considered to be professionals or semi-professionals.

Given this very basic description of several of the social sciences, it is possible to see the desirability of linking the perspectives of the social sciences and philosophy when we examine an education system. In the process we would want to know, for example, what values an education system is transmitting through its curricula, and in whose languages with what consequences for what social groups. Are education systems passing on local values or more cosmopolitan ones that come from centers of power within and across national borders? What roles are individuals being prepared for in a society? Who enters and completes different levels of an education system with what outcomes related to occupation, income, social status, and influence in the political sphere?

As a result of these considerations, case studies that are attentive to local cultures and understandings of education, and that also speak to what philosophical frameworks tell us are universally valuable features of education systems, are particularly appropriate for teaching comparative education in a way that is relevant to normative concerns.

Case Studies

In this section, we address how students can use, understand and develop normatively appropriate case studies.

Why Cases in Comparative Education?

As noted above, case studies that are sensitive to both local and universal values seem necessary for the application of the philosophical frameworks that we have described. Comparative education researchers have a long tradition of developing such case studies. Research in this field may take the form of: (a) large-scale quantitative studies using a variety of survey research methods and pre-existing data sets; or (b) qualitative case studies, taking the form of more participatory, long-term, in-depth ethnographies (see e.g. Crossley & Vulliamy, 1997; Heath et al, 2008). Whereas quantitative research often involves viewing education systems using predetermined variables, qualitative research tends to involve open-ended 'thick description' of a particular sociocultural context in all its complexity (Geertz, 1973). Theory building in comparative education depends on attempts to generalize from individual case studies and to contextualize large-scale cross-national studies.

Case studies are likely to continue to be the most commonly used approach to studying education–society relations. Given the limited resources of most researchers in the academy, the tendency is to study areas that are familiar and readily accessible to researchers. Beyond their convenience, Charles Ragin (1987) argues that the comparative method is essentially a case-oriented strategy of comparative research, in which 'outcomes are analyzed in terms of intersections of conditions, and it is usually assumed that any of several combinations might produce a certain outcome' (p. 16). For further elaboration of the case-study method, see Yin (2009).

While Ragin's orientation is toward macro-level comparative studies and causal analysis, others, such as York Bradshaw and Michael Wallace (1991), view the value of case studies as residing in their contributions to the refinement and modifications of extant theory, and ultimately to the creation of new theory when existing explanatory frameworks are not applicable because they have been formulated in a few countries of the Global North (e.g. Becker, 2014).

Using Cases in Teaching Comparative Education

The first questions for teachers to consider in selecting a case are: how does this particular case speak to a significant problem in theory, policy or practice? Why have I selected this problem, and what are the appropriate units and levels of analysis? Does the case take place in particular types of sociocultural or political/economic contexts? [1] Usually the case will speak to salient issues in the discourse surrounding education within the teacher's own country, as well as in many others. For students who are asked to select or develop a case for a course assignment, the reasons for the choice may reflect a longstanding personal interest related to students' past experiences and career plans or a research requirement for an undergraduate or graduate degree.

The questions that are likely to be studied with regard to current issues in comparative education theory-building include: how do education and background factors – such as gender, race, ethnicity and social class – intersect and affect who enters and succeeds in an education system and with what outcomes related to subsequent occupational attainment, income, social status and political power (Farrell, 2013)? Who formulates educational policy and what combination of variables determines what happens to educational policy in the implementation process? Who benefits from current education reforms, such as school choice, decentralization and the privatization of education systems? How have these various reform initiatives impacted teaching as a profession and the work that teachers do? What criteria and measurements are used, and how valid are they for evaluating the workings and outcomes of an education system? Can education systems override existing socioeconomic disadvantages and contribute to social mobility? And if so, what particular policies and practices contribute to significant social change? Do certain types of political economies – namely, socialist or capitalist or some mix of them (such as market socialism on the Chinese Mainland) – lead to better results as measured by student learning and educational attainment and less variation across schools (Weber, 1964)?

In referring to certain ideal types of political economies, such as capitalism or socialism, it is important to point out that they are not static. Especially in a period of rapid change characterizing the current age of globalization, it is more useful to look at transitions, disjunctures, transformations and new combinations of different models of development (Larsen, 2010). In comparative education courses, relevant frameworks for using a case would involve the transitions from colonialism to post-colonialism, from racialist to post-racialist political regimes and societies (notably pre- and post-apartheid South Africa), or from capitalism to socialism (Carnoy et al, 1990), or from socialism to capitalism or some mix thereof (Silova, 2010).

In his case study on Nicaragua, Arnove (1994), for example, documented how in a span of fifteen years the country had undergone dramatic changes from a backward dependent capitalist state, ruled by a dynastic family and a praetorian guard, to a country embarked on the path to a socialized economy and non-aligned foreign policy, to a country, after 1990, trying to reintegrate itself into the global capitalist economy. How did these political changes play out in the education system? As the study illustrated, 'Education was used by a revolution regime to bring about a new social order and then by the conservative government that replaced it to restore elements of the previous status quo' (Arnove, 1994, p. 1).

For the Nicaraguan case study, Arnove advocated looking at international factors shaping the economy and political context of an education system – namely, the opportunities, constraints and contradictions facing education policy makers and practitioners in a society undergoing radical change. While a nation-state can be the major unit of analysis, many subunits of a country also require attention, as suggested by Mark Bray and Murray Thomas (1995). The authors provide a heuristic in the form of a cube to illustrate multilevel analysis along three dimensions: geographic/local, non-locational demographic groups, and aspects of education and society. They note that comparative education typically has focused on countries as the locational unit of analysis, but that the units may range from that of the world/regions/continents to that of schools/classrooms/individuals. The non-locational demographic groups may range from ethnic/age/religious/gender groups to entire populations. The aspects of education typically studied are curriculum, teaching methods, educational finance, management structures, as well as others.[2] Bray and Thomas (1995) argue that comparativists can make their contribution to improved theory and policy by attempting to introduce as many levels of analysis as possible and the interplay among them. Similarly, these factors are much in line with what Fran Vavrus and Lesley Bartlett (2008) have called 'vertical' case studies involving the description and analysis of how education policy and practice is embedded in different levels of influence from the global to the local and their dialectical relations. As noted by Bartlett (2014), 'The local cannot be divorced from national and transnational forces but neither can it be conceptualized as determined by these forces' (p. 30).

Case studies that are comprehensive in scope, as well as specific in detail, are excellent tools for teaching comparative education courses at the undergraduate and graduate levels. Studies that illustrate for students how case research introduces different levels of analysis and human agency include those by Peter Demerath (1999), Sandra Stacki (1999), Rachel Christina (2003), Katheryn Anderson-Levitt (2004) and Björn Nordtveit (2010). At their best, cases introduce students to the multiple factors and the key actors (individuals and institutions) shaping the sources, workings and outcomes of current issues in one or more countries. In using case studies, teachers can draw upon a great variety of primary and secondary sources of data, literary genres, visual and audio media, as well as knowledgeable persons on or off campus (via interactive technologies) to explore with students a significant education issue in greater depth.

The rich data provided by case studies, furthermore, have the potential to stimulate and enhance student empathy, or what Robert Hanvey (1975) has called a 'perspective consciousness'. This perspective, according to

Chadwick Alger and James Harf (1986), represents a value dimension of an international education; it teaches that people across the globe have different ways of viewing the world, ways that are equally valid and reflective of their life circumstances. At the same time, Hanvey (1975) advocates a global education that seeks out and builds upon what interests people have in common.

Case studies provide teachers with excellent opportunities to balance sensitivity to the different ways individuals and their cultures view the world with international trends promoting universal norms.

Case studies, however, have their limitations and pitfalls. Ragin (1987), Bradshaw and Wallace (1991) and others are well aware there is a danger in attempting to generalize from one case to other instances that are not appropriate and to view the world only from the lens of that which is most familiar. Major funding agencies for international research also tend to favor quicker quantitative studies that meet the exigencies of immediate decision-making and present the façade of being more scientific (Crossley & Bennett, 1997). Whether or not a case involves the employment of large-scale quantitative data sets, while adhering to the most rigorous standards of scientific research, there always will be ethical questions concerning the appropriateness of what is being studied, how it is being studied, and what conclusions are reached.

In the following section, we will develop one case study – that of South Africa – to suggest how the social sciences and philosophy can be employed to teach about empirical and normative issues that are common to most societies today. Our intention is merely to illustrate how a case can be constructed and analyzed using one of the philosophical frameworks identified above. We have chosen South Africa because Ubuntu, which originated in that country, has become an important if controversial moral concept and was the organizing theme of the 2015 Comparative and International Education Society's annual meeting.

South Africa as an Illustrative Case Study

This final section illustrates how a particular case can be developed and analyzed using philosophical frameworks. Such cases can be used by instructors as examples to students of how to develop and analyze the empirical and normative content of comparative education. Using such instructor-developed cases, students can be asked in class or in individual assignments to apply the philosophical frameworks as a way of enabling them to understand those frameworks in detail. Students can also be assigned to develop such cases on their own in order to solidify their understanding of the social science methods and the philosophical reasoning relevant to the academic study of comparative education.

The Context

South Africa merits our attention for various reasons. It represents a national context where major public efforts are under way to overcome the injustices of a highly inequitable and oppressive sociopolitical and education system. The country is a salient example of the challenges facing countries that have transitioned from colonialism to postcolonialism and, in the case of South Africa, from a racialist apartheid regime (1948 to 2004) – where people's education and life circumstances were determined by the color of their skin and kept apart (the meaning of the word 'apartheid') – to an inclusive, multicultural, democratic society. As compared with classical forms of colonialism and its modern manifestation of domination by countries of the metropolitan centers of Europe and North America over large areas of Africa, Asia, Latina America and Oceania, South Africa represents what may be called 'internal colonialism', in which a dominant minority rules over a numerically larger but significantly powerless majority population, most frequently of rural and of non-European descent. Other examples of a national urban minority dominating majority populations include the historically subordinate position of majority or plurality Indigenous populations in Peru, Bolivia and Guatemala. The forced isolation and oppression of Native Americans in the United States and Canada, although they are numerical minorities, is another example of internal colonialism (see Altbach & Kelly, 1978, for various types of colonialism).

In South Africa, socioeconomic data document the inequitable distribution and the poor quality of education provided to the non-White peoples defined by the apartheid racial system as Black (African), Coloured (mixed descent) and Indian. In addition to lack of adequate financing, high-quality material resources and qualified teachers for the non-White populations, language policy, as of 1974, mandated that at least half of high school courses were to be taught in the language of the oppressor, Afrikaans (Byrnes, 1996).

Education statistics show that at the height of the apartheid regime in the 1970s, the teacher–pupil ratio for Black students was 1:60 and for White students 1:22; while the annual expenditure on education per pupil was $45 for Black students, it was $696 for White students (Nova Scotia Department of Education, 1978). Less than 60 percent of the population was literate. The apartheid system was designed to keep the races segregated, with the Black majority schooled for menial jobs serving the White privileged minority.

Despite major efforts of the post-apartheid elected government of the African National Congress (ANC) to overcome past inequities in education, major problems continue to plague the country's school system. These include, according to Leteska Moeketsitaki (2013), significant differentiation of schooling along socioeconomic lines: 'Schools that serve the majority of poor and previously disadvantaged blacks suffer from systemic inefficiency and dysfunction, while the schools that serve the rich and affluent classes – black and white – are stable and efficient in their delivery of solid education'

31

(p. 74). Evidence of differences in the quality of education is found in the pass rates on Grade 12 exit exams. As documented by Moeketsitaki, 'About 20% of private and semiprivate schools in former white, suburban areas account for over 80% of the students who pass the Grade 12 exit exams. These schools serve privileged black and white children from upper-middle-income to rich families who can afford private school fees' (Moeketsitaki, 2013, p. 74; see also Carnoy et al, 2015).

There are serious problems with regard to what is actually learned in school. According to Pratish Mistry (2011), a 'national literacy and numeracy assessment in primary school revealed a disturbing truth. The majority of Grade 3 and Grade 6 students in the country cannot read and count. In Gauteng, almost 70% of the province's Grade 3 pupils were found to be illiterate.' Mistry asks the question: 'What has the government been doing since 1997?'[3] Lower-income Black students who do pass the exams and continue on to higher education face numerous challenges not experienced by the more affluent. Efforts to desegregate historically White universities in the post-apartheid period are documented in Kimberly King's case study of the University of the Witwatersrand (King, 1998) and Jonathan Jansen's case study of the University of Pretoria (Jansen, 2009). They provide rich data illustrating how affirmative action policies still do not adequately compensate for lack of home resources and study spaces, poverty, and inadequate campus support services, let alone a campus ethos that leads many to feel marginalized (see also Mabokela & King, 2001).

Access to an equitable and high-quality education is considered a human right in various international conventions (see e.g. Tomasevski, 2005; United Nations, 2009). For Zehlia Babaci-White (2014), in addition to rights to access to education, students have an equally important set of rights in education. Among them are the right to learn in a maternal or a regional language the student understands (Brock-Utne, 2000). To this end, the 1997 Constitution accords official status to eleven languages in South Africa. Another basic right involves being free from all forms of physical violence, ranging from corporal punishment to sexual assault and rape.

Corporal punishment of children is common in schools, even though it violates Section 28 of the Bill of Rights of the 1997 Constitution that pertains to individuals under the age of 18.[4] Among the protections provided for children is the right 'to be protected from maltreatment, neglect, abuse or degradation'. Harsh discipline, however, is not universally condemned because it accords with prevalent child-rearing norms (Hofmann, 2015). School authorities and teachers also frequently resort to physical punishment, believing that it is necessary for maintaining order in overcrowded and unruly schools in the post-1994 period (Hofmann, 2015). With the end of the hostilities over apartheid, young combatants returned to school, but adjusting to school routines was difficult for many.

Corporal punishment, throughout history and across societies, is not unique to South Africa; neither are the sexual harassment, assault and rape of female students. South Africa, however, is a notable case because it ranks near the top in the extensiveness of incidents of reported rape and the national attention given to it as a significant social and educational issue. According to Human Rights Watch (2001), 'In schools across South Africa, thousands of girls of every race and economic group are encountering sexual violence and harassment that impede their access and interrupt their education or leave school altogether because they feel vulnerable to sexual assault.'

Social Science Perspectives in Teaching about South Africa

General questions to be explored in a comparative education course from social science perspectives would involve to what extent race, social class, and gender, as well as geographic provenance (urban/rural), are taken into account in any existing affirmative action or positive discrimination policies favoring formerly disadvantaged groups. What issues arise, for example, if students' race or some other ascriptive status like class or caste (as in India) is given priority consideration in school admission and financial aid policies? In doing so, will other groups be discriminated against, and how will they react? A broader question arising from the South African case, for example, would involve what countries like the USA, with a history of racial segregation, can learn from efforts by South African universities to desegregate and to develop a more inclusive campus ethos for Black students. Also, what challenges do historically Black colleges in the USA and South Africa face in a context of systemic desegregation?

With regard to language policy, questions pertain to the match between what values are taught in school and how they accord or clash with home values. Also, is it possible to achieve a core curriculum that takes into account the major ethnic and linguistic differences in the country while preparing all students for success as adults?

Similarly important is the match between what languages are emphasized in school curricula and what languages are spoken at home. Also, what home education resources are available? For example, as schools turn to the use of information technologies to provide information, the issue arises that most information and communications technology (ICT) software in South Africa tends to be in English or Afrikaans. Which students are likely to be advantaged as schools assign more computer-based work to students?

The South Africa case further raises issues involving how to maintain orderly classrooms without resorting to corporal punishment, a very common form of discipline used by teachers around the world. It also raises questions about how to curtail sexual harassment and rape of females at all levels of education (both within and outside the formal setting of schools), an issue that is finally gaining attention at the highest levels of governments from North to South and East to West.

Social science research can provide both quantitative and qualitative data on the patterning of who gets what types of education, where and when, and with what consequences, as well as the sources of education policy. Also studies of policy need to take into account whether or not it is ever implemented and whether it ever becomes everyday meaningful practice for teachers and students as well as administrators and other constituents of an education system (Sutton & Levinson, 2001), and whether or not policy becomes actual practice. The social sciences can provide insights into why and how different sets of individuals respond to education initiatives based on the ways they affect their individual and collective identities (e.g. as teachers), the satisfactions they receive from the roles they play, and the values they hold dear. What social sciences generally do not provide is a set of ethical guidelines for determining the justice of the patterns that are described.

Philosophical Perspectives in Teaching about South Africa

As suggested, social science can help clarify the nature and distribution of educational processes and outcomes. Philosophy can help determine whether those practices meet universal and local normative standards. When there is a normative reason that the practices should be changed, social science can suggest what alternatives might be effective in satisfying normative standards, and philosophy can suggest how decisions about the alternatives should be made. It is not our intention here to provide the sort of detailed analysis that any philosophical perspective would require. Rather, we will illustrate in broad strokes how the three philosophers briefly described above would approach the case of South Africa's educational system.

Rawls tells us first that we must determine whether to regard post-apartheid South Africa as a plausibly liberal society, one that emphasizes the liberty of individuals to identify and pursue their own goods rather than a specific common good that all are to pursue. Because of the cultural, racial and ethnic diversity of South Africa, it is plausible to regard it as a liberal society, and thus equality of basic liberties, equality of economic and educational opportunities, and a distribution of income and wealth are the appropriate normative standards for judging South African society and its educational system. The disparities of treatment and outcomes according to ethnicity, race, economic status and gender in general and in the education system in particular are serious injustices that, for Rawls, need to be corrected.

Sen, by contrast, would focus, first, on whether segments of post-apartheid South Africa's population have been subject to the sorts of severe deprivations that are recognizably universal injustices – deprivations of, for example, nutrition and basic education. Although there is clear evidence of unequal treatment of some populations (e.g. in rural areas) in South Africa's educational system, it is uncertain whether such inequalities produce deprivations of the severity to be considered radically and obviously unjust that were typical of the apartheid era. Thus, the focus of Sen's attention is likely to fall on whether the education policies in South Africa plausibly result from democratic decision-making processes. Although we do not have details about how the education policies and practices have been determined, it is plausible to conclude that the extent of the economic and gender discrimination is such as to call the society's governance procedures into question. As a result, Sen's likely approach to correcting South Africa's normative shortcomings is to emphasize the adequacy of the society's governance system and the way in which the education system can contribute to its democratization.

Nussbaum would focus on whether the education system of post-apartheid South Africa has deprived some citizens of an opportunity to develop any of the ten central capabilities (life; bodily health; bodily integrity; senses, imagination and thought; emotions; practical reason; affiliation; other species; play; and control over one's environment, both political and material). Although the empirical record is not detailed enough to provide clear evidence about each of the ten capabilities, what we do know about economic and gender discrimination in South Africa suggests that girls and the poor are probably deprived of the chance to develop the central human capabilities up to a reasonable threshold level. More detailed empirical investigation would be needed to determine precisely what deprivations are occurring and how to correct them.[5]

This case and the analysis are, as noted, an example of what the instructor might include in a course or assign to students to develop on their own in regard to South Africa or any other country or set of countries.[6] One important issue that instructors may wish to address or to ask students to consider is which of the various philosophical perspectives is most reasonable and why.

Concluding Remarks

In this chapter, we have argued for the importance of combining philosophical and social science perspectives and analyses for studying education systems comparatively. We suggested that case studies have tended to be the most commonly used methodology for examining the sources, workings and outcomes of education systems in all their complexity and are particularly appropriate for making moral judgments about education–society phenomena. We selected the case of South Africa to illustrate how philosophy and the social sciences can be used to capture the dynamic interplay of some of the factors that shape the ways in which individuals and their communities interact with an education system, as well as to show what lessons might be learned about who pays for and who benefits from the education decisions a society makes.

Notes

[1] On examining cases as instances of the patterning of relationships in different types of historical, sociocultural and institutional configurations, see Weber (1964).

[2] Also see the edited volume by Bray et al (2007), in which the various contributing authors write chapters on these units of comparison: places; systems; times; race, class and gender; cultures; values; policies; curricula; pedagogical innovations; ways of learning; and educational achievements.

[3] Among the reasons listed by Mistry (2011) for the poor results on literacy and numeracy tests are the following:
1. Teachers struggle to maintain their motivation levels;
2. Student discipline and attendance is appalling;
3. Parental involvement is far from what it should be;
4. Principals and teachers are overwhelmed with departmental admin;
5. There is no concrete plan that is committed to by all stakeholders – the system is plagued by ad hoc requests and regular goal-post changes.

[4] Section 28 of South Africa's Bill of Rights in its Constitution (Constitution, 1996) specifically concerns individual citizens under the age of 18. It reads as follows:

Every child has the right
a) to a name and a nationality from birth;
b) to family care or parental care, or to appropriate alternative care when removed from the family environment;
c) to basic nutrition, shelter, basic health care services and social services;
d) to be protected from maltreatment, neglect, abuse or degradation;
e) to be protected from exploitative labour practices.
Quoted from UNICEF, 'Child Rights in South Africa'
(www.unicef.org/rightsite/sowc/pdfs/panels/Child rights in South Africa.pdf).

[5] It would be interesting to analyze this case using a fully developed conception of Ubuntu.

[6] For example, Kubow and Fossum (2007) compare the cases of South Africa and Brazil as 'developing countries' with remaining problems of educational access and opportunity. Students can select other countries that they consider appropriate for comparative purposes, perhaps along the dimensions of societies based on racial segregation or forms of internal colonialism.

References

Alger, C.F. & Harf, J.E. (1986) *Global Education: why? For Whom? About What?* Columbus: Ohio State University. ERIC Document EN 265107.

Altbach, P.G. & Kelly, G.P. (Eds) (1978) *Education and Colonialism.* New York: Longman.

Anderson-Levitt, K.M. (2004) Reading Lessons in Guinea, France, and the United States: local meanings of global culture?, *Comparative Education Review*, 48, 229-252. http://dx.doi.org/10.1086/421178

Appiah, K.A. (2006) *Cosmopolitanism: ethics in a world of strangers*. New York: W.W. Norton.

Arnove, R.F. (1994) *Education as Contested Terrain: Nicaragua, 1979-1938*. Boulder, CO: Westview Press.

Arnove, R.F. (2013) Introduction. Reframing Comparative Education: the dialectic of the global and the local, in R.F. Arnove, C.A. Torres & S. Franz (Eds) *Comparative Education: the dialectic of the global and the local*, pp. 1-25. Lanham, MD: Rowman & Littlefield.

Arnove, R.F. & Graff, H.J. (Eds) (1987) *National Literacy Campaigns: historical and comparative perspectives*. New York: Plenum. http://dx.doi.org/10.1007/978-1-4899-0505-5

Babaci-White. Z. (Ed.) (2014) *Giving Space to African Voices: rights in local languages and local curriculum*. Rotterdam: Sense Publishers.

Bartlett, L. (2014) Vertical Case Studies and Challenges of Culture, Context, and Comparison, *Current Issues in Comparative Education*, 16(2), 30-33.

Becker, H.S. (2014) *What about Mozart? What about Murder? Reasoning from Cases*. Chicago: University of Chicago Press. http://dx.doi.org/10.7208/chicago/9780226166520.001.0001

Benedict, R. (1934) *Patterns of Culture*. New York: Mentor Books.

Bradshaw, Y. & Wallace, M. (1991) Informing Generality and Explaining Uniqueness: the place of case studies in comparative research, *International Journal of Comparative Sociology*, 32 (January–April), 154-171.

Bray, M., Adamson, B. & Mason, M. (Eds) (2007) *Comparative Education Research: approaches and methods*, 2nd edn. Hong Kong: Comparative Education Centre, University of Hong Kong. http://dx.doi.org/10.1007/978-1-4020-6189-9

Bray, M. & Thomas, M.R. (1995) Levels of Comparison in Educational Studies: different insights from different literatures and the value of multilevel analysis, *Harvard Educational Review*, 65(3), 472-491. http://dx.doi.org/10.17763/haer.65.3.g3228437224v4877

Brighouse, H. (2004) *Justice*. Cambridge: Polity Press.

Brock-Utne, B. (2000) *Whose Education for All? The Recolonization of the African Mind*. New York: Falmer.

Byrnes, R.M. (Ed.) (1996) *South Africa: a country study*. Washington, DC: GPO for the Library of Congress.

Carnoy, M., Noward, M. & Oketch M. (2015) The Role of Classroom Resources and National Educational Context in Student Learning Gains: comparing Botswana, Kenya, and South Africa, *Comparative Education Review*, 59(2), 199-233. http://dx.doi.org/10.1086/680173

Carnoy, M. & Samoff. J., with Burris, M., Johnston, A. & Torres, C.A. (1990) *Education and Social Transition in the Third World*. Princeton, NJ: Princeton University Press.

Christina, R. (2003) *Tend the Olive, Water the Vine: negotiating Palestinian childhood development in the context of globalization.* Westport, CT: Praeger.

Constitution of the Republic of South Africa (1996) http://www.justice.gov.za/legislation/constitution/SAConstitution-web-eng.pdf

Crossley M. & Bennett, A.J. (1997) Planning for Case-study Evaluation in Belize, Central America, in M. Crossley & A.J. Bennett (Eds) *Qualitative Educational Research in Developing Countries*, pp. 221-243. New York: Garland.

Crossley, M. & Vulliamy, G. (Eds) (1997) *Qualitative Educational Research in Developing Countries.* New York: Garland.

Demerath, P. (1999) The Cultural Production of Educational Utility in Pere Village, Papua New Guinea, *Comparative Education Review*, 43, 162-192. http://dx.doi.org/10.1086/447553

Farrell, J.P. (2013) Equality of Education: six decades of comparative evidence seen from a new millennium, in R.F. Arnove, C.A. Torres & S. Franz (Eds) *Comparative Education: the dialectic of the global and the local*, pp. 149-174. Lanham, MD: Rowman & Littlefield.

Freire, P. (2000) *Pedagogy of the Oppressed*, 30th anniversary edn. New York: Continuum.

Geertz, C. (1973) *Thick Description: toward an interpretive theory of culture.* New York: Basic Books.

Gutmann, A. (1999) *Democratic Education*, rev. edn. Princeton, NJ: Princeton University Press. http://dx.doi.org/10.1515/9781400822911

Hanvey, R. (1975) *An Attainable Global Perspective.* Denver, CO: Denver University, Center for Teaching International Relations/New York Friends Groups Center for War/Peace Studies.

Heath, S.B., Street, B.K. & Mills, M. (2008) *On Ethnography: approaches to languages and literacy research.* New York: Teachers College Press.

Hofmann, E. (2015) La lute contre les violences de genre liées à la scolarisation: les méandres menan de l'injunction consensuella à des changements de pratiques banalisées. Paper presented at the International Conference on Education, *Governing Schools in the Global South: actors, politics, and practices*, University of Bordeaux, 5-7 February.

Honderich, T. (2005) *Oxford Companion to Philosophy*, 2nd edn. Oxford: Oxford University Press.

Human Rights Watch (2001) South Africa: sexual violence rampant in schools. https://www.hrw.org/news/2001/03/26/south-africa-sexual-violence-rampant-schools

Jansen. J. (2009) *Knowledge in the Blood: confronting race and the apartheid past.* Stanford, CA: Stanford University Press.

King, K.L. (1998) From Exclusion to Inclusion: a case study of Black South Africans at the University of the Witwatersrand. Unpublished doctoral dissertation, Indiana University, Bloomington.

Kubow, P.K. & Fossum, P.R. (2007) *Comparative Education: exploring issues in international context*, 2nd edn. Upper Saddle River, NJ: Pearson.

Larsen, M.A. (Ed.) (2010) *New Thinking in Comparative Education: honoring Robert Cowen.* Boston: Sense Publishers.

Mabokela, R.O. & King, L.K.L. (2001) *Apartheid No More: case studies of southern African universities in the process of transformation.* Westport, CT: Bergin & Garvey.

Mistry, P. (2011) Education and Illiteracy in South Africa. Wonkie News & Alternative Views: gamble online with your sanity! http://www.wonkie.com/2011/07/04/education-and-literacy-in-south-africa/

Moeketsitaki, L. (2013) South African Education has Promises to Keep and Miles to Go, *Phi Delta Kappan*, 94(6), 74-75. http://dx.doi.org/10.1177/003172171309400621

Nordtveit, B. (2010) Development as a Complex Process of Change: conception and analysis of projects and programs and policies, *International Journal of Educational Development*, 30(1), 110-117. http://dx.doi.org/10.1016/j.ijedudev.2009.06.004

Nova Scotia Department of Education (1978) Apartheid Statistics. rsbstaff.ednet.ns.ca/afergus/apartheid_statistics.htm

Nussbaum, M. (2000) *Women and Human Development: the capabilities approach.* Cambridge: Cambridge University Press. http://dx.doi.org/10.1017/CBO9780511841286

Nussbaum, M. (2006) *Frontiers of Justice: disability, nationality, species membership.* Cambridge, MA: Harvard University Press.

Pettit, P. (2014) *Just Freedom: a moral compass for a complex world.* New York: W.W. Norton & Company.

Ragin, C. (1987) *The Comparative Method: moving beyond qualitative and quantitative strategies.* Berkeley: University of California Press.

Rawls, J. (1971) *A Theory of Justice.* Cambridge, MA: Harvard University Press.

Rawls, J. (1999) *The Law of Peoples.* Cambridge, MA: Harvard University Press.

Sen, A. (1999) *Development as Freedom.* New York: Anchor Books.

Sen, A. (2009) *The Idea of Justice.* Cambridge, MA: Harvard University Press.

Silova, I. (2010) *Post-socialism is Not Dead: (re)reading the global in comparative education.* Bingley: Emerald Group. http://dx.doi.org/10.1108/S1479-3679(2010)14

Stacki, S. (1999) Rays of Hope for Women Teachers in India. Unpublished doctoral dissertation, Indiana University, Bloomington.

Sutton, M. & Levinson, B.A.U. (Eds) (2001) *Policy as Practice: toward a comparative sociocultural analysis of education policy.* Westport, CT: Greenwood.

Tomasevski, K. (2005) Globalizing What: education as a human right or as a traded service? *Indiana Journal of Global Legal Studies*, 12(2), 1-78. http://dx.doi.org/10.2979/GLS.2005.12.1.1

United Nations (2009) Rights of Children. http://unchildrights.blogspot.com/2009/03/summary-childrens-rights-convention.html

Vavrus, F. & Bartlett, L. (2008) Knowing, Comparatively, in F. Vavrus & L. Bartlett (Eds) *Critical Approaches to Comparative Education: vertical case studies from Africa,*

Europe, the Middle East, and the Americas, pp. 1-20. New York: Palgrave Macmillan.

Weber, M. (1964) The Fundamental Concepts of Sociology, in Talcott Parsons (Ed.) *Max Weber: the theory of social and economic organization*, pp. 87-157. New York: Free Press.

Yin, R.K. (2009) *Case Study Research: design and methods*, 4th edn. Thousand Oaks, CA: SAGE Publications.

CHAPTER 2

Reconceptualising the Teaching of Comparative and International Education

MICHAEL CROSSLEY

Introduction

This chapter builds upon previous work on the changing ideological and conceptual landscape of comparative and international education (Crossley & Watson, 2003, 2009), and draws upon related literature and extensive experience of teaching dedicated postgraduate courses in this field for the University of Bristol in the United Kingdom (UK) and in Hong Kong. Attention is given to the impact of intensified globalisation, the enduring place of studies of education policy transfer, the changing nature of the student base and the emergence of programmes designed to provide advanced research training. The growing need for mainstream educational researchers to learn from disciplined training in comparative education is also explored in the light of an analysis of the global impact of large-scale comparative surveys, notably those led by the Organisation for Economic Co-operation and Development (OECD) in the form of the Programme for International Student Assessment (PISA). In doing so, the chapter re-examines the development and place of key concepts, theories, ideologies and methodologies that have influenced the evolving nature of teaching in the field, and identifies major priorities for future teaching and research.

The Foundations of Comparative and International Education in the UK

There is a distinguished tradition of teaching in comparative and international education in the UK that initially drew upon familiar work that flourished in the post–World War II era. This included influential academic publications by writers such as Kandel (1959), Hans (1964) and Mallinson (1964) that emphasised history, disciplined scholarship and, for some such as

King (1965), the potential of the reformative element in comparative studies. Other influential figures, such as Holmes (1965), working at the University of London, Institute of Education, challenged this Sadlerian (Sadler, 1900 [1979]) tradition and advanced the scientific and quantitative approach to the field that characterised the origins of disciplined comparative education in the seminal work of Jullien de Paris (Jullien, 1817), and continues, through the work of bodies such as the OECD, to make a major impact today. At the same time, the post-war years saw the emergence of the international constituency of the field, underpinned by the growth of international development agencies and of international planning in low-income countries and the need for teaching in this arena.

The London Institute of Education was the first university department in the UK to focus upon the teaching of what we now know as comparative and international education. This was initially through the Colonial Department that was founded to meet the training needs of the British colonial administration. Over time, this was repeatedly rebranded, becoming, for example, the Department of Education in Developing Countries from the mid-1970s to the mid-1980s. Comparative education courses at the Institute of Education began in 1947 and were led by Joseph Lauwerys, although the history of these two related departments – the international and the comparative – reveals interesting intellectual tensions that inhibited close professional collaboration and that are still visible in the wider field today. We will return to such issues in later sections of this chapter.

For many, therefore, the 1960s and 1970s are seen as a time when the teaching of comparative and international education was enjoying a 'golden age' in terms of its popularity with students, particularly at the undergraduate and teacher-training levels, and its influence within the university sector. Other significant UK universities for the teaching of comparative and international education at this time included Oxford, Reading, Bristol, Birmingham, Cardiff, Edinburgh, Glasgow, Hull, Leeds, Manchester and Newcastle. Significantly, many UK colleges of education also ran pre-service training courses for prospective teachers, so, as Watson (1982) argues, this was, indeed, a heyday for specialist teaching in comparative and international education.

Challenges to the Field

Further details on teaching in the early years for the field can be found in previous work (Crossley & Watson, 2003, 2009), but here it is helpful to focus on the nature of the critique that emerged from the late 1970s. This critique was spurred on by the political changes that ushered in a new neoliberal rationale and a clear challenge to the role played by many of the then core disciplines in the preparation of teachers. These years also saw a fall in UK population growth and the financial crisis of 1977 – all of which led to reduced funds for higher education as a whole, and the tightening up of regulations for the training of teachers. In this new economic context, comparative education came to be regarded as an 'interesting luxury, a frill, but an unnecessary ingredient for a common core teacher education curriculum' (Watson, 1982, p. 194). As writers such as Schweisfurth (1999) and O'Sullivan (2008) argue, the neoliberal philosophies pressed teacher education providers to focus their programmes 'on the development of specific teaching competences ... that are related to actual performance in the classroom' (O'Sullivan, 2008, p. 139). This 'practical turn' in teacher education ushered in a major decline in the foundation courses for education, and this included those in comparative and international education.

From the late 1970s, criticism also increasingly came from within the field itself in the form of challenges to: the preoccupations of both teaching and research with the nation-state as the main unit of analysis; an over-emphasis upon policy; and activity that was perceived to have little impact upon improving the quality of teaching and learning in practice. Researchers such as Stenhouse (1979), for example, argued for more in-depth studies carried out within schools. This generated considerable innovation in the form of ethnography, practitioner research and case study – all designed to help inform successful change in practice. My own early work built upon this in developing qualitative approaches to research within the field of comparative and international education (Crossley & Vulliamy, 1984, 1997). By the 1990s, many were advocating multi-level analysis (Bray & Thomas, 1995), and by the end of the millennium the effect of globalisation increasingly prioritised macro-level analyses and studies of increasingly powerful international agencies and actors upon educational development worldwide (Dale, 2000).

But what did this mean for teaching within the field? To examine this, the chapter next reviews the collective response of the comparative and international constituency in the UK. This is followed by a more detailed account of related developments and teaching programmes within my own organisation – namely, the University of Bristol.

Reconceptualising Comparative and International Education: the influence of the British Association for International and Comparative Education (BAICE)

BAICE was created in 1997 when the former British Comparative and International Education Society (BCIES) was merged with the British Association for Teachers and Researchers in Overseas Education (BATROE). This merger built upon earlier efforts to bring the UK comparative education constituency closer to their colleagues engaged in teaching and research focused upon international education and development. In establishing the new society, an inaugural conference was held at the University of Reading in September 1998, with two keynote addresses adopting the theme of 'reconceptualising comparative and international education' (Watson, 2001). This theme encompassed both teaching and research although, to date, much of the existing literature has focused upon the research dimension. Here we, necessarily, draw upon this material, including my own keynote contribution to the reconceptualisation debate (Crossley, 1999), but it is to the implications of this for the reconceptualisation of teaching within the field in the UK that we now turn.

As already argued, the changing political economy of the UK posed significant challenges for the traditional form of Foundation Studies courses in education (Furlong & Lawn, 2009). For comparative and international education, this generated major cuts to programmes in the then teacher training colleges, and similar pressures were faced across the university sector. The creation of BAICE recognised this, and, in response, it is no surprise that the promotion and support of research was increasingly prioritised by the new society. This can be seen in the selected proceedings and keynote addresses of the annual BAICE conference that can be found in the association's journal *Compare: A Journal of Comparative and International Education*. In turn, a re-growth of innovative comparative and international research can also be seen within the university sector within the specialised comparative and international research centres that continued to maintain a strong profile. The significance of this heightened attention to externally funded research had, in itself, major implications for the teaching of comparative and international education, and it is this fundamental shift that is referred to here as a major reconceptualisation.

The field had responded rapidly to the critique of the orthodox teaching traditions: no longer was it dominated by courses for pre-service teacher training; the focus upon descriptive accounts and comparisons of education policy in nation-state systems had gone; and teaching in the research-led university sector had been fundamentally reconceptualised to support postgraduate programmes – and, most significantly, to contribute to research training. This was the reconceptualised field that the renewed national society re-shaped itself to support (Sutherland et al, 2007). In this model, efforts had been made to bring the comparative and international constituencies closer together, and teaching and research had become increasingly connected and mutually supportive. Replacing pre-service and undergraduate nation-state comparisons, postgraduate teaching in the field has increasingly focused upon the provision of research training and the in-depth analysis of key issues and challenges faced by contemporary educational policy and practice.

Within this, the detailed exploration of methodological and theoretical perspectives has been given increased attention – although this has also helped to refocus teaching upon the processes of educational policy borrowing and transfer, and upon the significance of context sensitivity in all educational development and research. Evidence for these trends can be seen in much of the recent literature where, for example, methodological texts and articles and a new wave of research on the processes of educational policy transfer have become increasingly influential (Crossley & Watson, 2003; Phillips & Ochs, 2003; Phillips & Schweisfurth, 2006; Auld & Morris, 2014). Auld and Morris, for example, identify what they call a 'new paradigm' of comparative education dominated by an 'influential intermediary network, which uses international data banks to compare education systems, and to identify and promote evidence of "what works"' (2014, p. 129). This lies largely outside the university sector and is supported by private consultancy groups that are closely aligned to a combination of neoliberal values and assumptions, and to the rationale underpinning large-scale quantitative surveys of student achievement such as the OECD's highly influential Programme for International Student Assessment (PISA). While research into such developments is now urgently called for (Crossley, 2014), their significance and impact upon ongoing education policy transfer worldwide, and upon the field of comparative and international education itself, is equally important as a focus for current and future postgraduate teaching. Indeed, this issue has as much potential for teaching within research training classes as it does for more generic courses. This also demonstrates the presence of ongoing tensions between the socio-cultural and more positivistic approaches to the field and to research that were identified in previous decades (as already discussed above).

A further dimension of the case for reconceptualisation that is central to my own work is the need for both research and teaching in the field to do more to bridge the worlds of theory, policy and practice (Crossley, 2000, 2008). To some extent, this contribution to the reconceptualisation thesis arose from understanding how the history of the field in the UK evidenced the prioritisation of theory and ideas in the comparative constituency, contrasted with an emphasis on matters of policy and practice in the international education community. As argued at length elsewhere (Crossley & Watson, 2003), there is much to be gained from a bridging between these two dimensions in ways that can strengthen theory and real-world impact in both research and teaching. This is not to argue for all things to be the same or for the loss of creative difference and specialised focus within different constituencies in the field (Crossley, 2008), but it does offer creative space for innovative and challenging teaching and for the strengthening of direct engagement with contemporary issues, challenges and priorities.

This aligns well with the call, now increasingly prominent, for researchers to demonstrate and document the tangible impact of their work on policy and practice in the real world. This lends further support for teaching that focuses upon current-day dilemmas and debates, such as the nature, place and implications of the so-called new paradigm that was identified above. How this has worked out in practice will be considered in the context of the University of Bristol in the next section.

Reconceptualising the Teaching of
Comparative and International Education in Practice

Reflecting the national picture and the history of comparative and international education as outlined above, prior to the creation of BAICE in 1997 teaching and research carried out at the University of Bristol, Graduate School of Education, was largely compartmentalised in ways that separated the comparative personnel from the international development group. In addition, the challenges faced by the foundation disciplines of education in the UK, as referred to above (Furlong & Lawn, 2009), had played a part in undermining institutional confidence in this dimension of teaching.

The provision of external funding in the education and international development arena by bodies such as the Department for International Development (DFID) meant that most teaching at that time had found a 'market' for students and a professional rationale in this dimension of the field. As might be expected, this teaching was at the postgraduate level (bachelor's and master's), attracted the majority of students from 'overseas', and was located within the ambit of the Centre for International Education. Recruitment was vibrant, and much teaching was closely related to the home contexts of the students and, to some extent, drew upon the related consultancy work of staff. Comparative research, and especially externally funded research, such as work by Broadfoot and colleagues on Europe (Broadfoot et al, 1993), at this point in time lay largely outside the Centre for International Education, leading to the two Bristol constituencies (the international and the comparative) having little in-depth interaction or collaboration. Given my own direct involvement in the foundation of the early years of BAICE, as vice chair and chair from 2000 to 2004, work on what I called the reconceptualisation of the society eventually came to influence similar developments within Bristol.

By the year 2000, the importance of strengthening the research profile of the Centre for International Education was seen as a key departmental priority. Similarly, ways of aligning this with related and innovative teaching programmes were being explored. Within this context for change, in 2001 the two constituencies were brought together under the new umbrella of the Research Centre for International and Comparative Studies (ICS). In many ways this reflected the parallel development of BAICE: comparative and international colleagues came together; teaching and research were more clearly aligned and mutually supportive; and teaching was focused upon the postgraduate level, and this combined master's-level courses in research training and thematic comparative and international analyses of contemporary issues. This was a very different model from previous eras in the UK, and it offered increased potential for a creative re-growth in both teaching and research. Beyond this, as argued at that time in an article published in the *Comparative Education Review* (Tikly & Crossley, 2001), the potential for specialists in comparative and international education to influence the content and cross-cultural sensitivities embedded within other teaching programmes across the Graduate School of Education was also enhanced.

With the intensification of globalisation at the turn of the millennium, the imperative for most postgraduate teaching to integrate cross-national material and perspectives was also becoming increasingly apparent. However, while the Tikly & Crossley (2001) article clearly recognised the importance of new ways of working and teaching, it also supported maintaining the place of specialised expertise in the field itself, given the dangers captured in the then all-too-popular phrase 'we are all comparativists now'. Further details of the three models for the teaching of comparative and international education that we identified can be found in the 2001 article, but in brief we demarcated the traditional specialisation model, separated from mainstream teaching; the integration model, where comparativists and comparative material would be built into broader educational studies programmes; and a transformation model advocating tutors working with 'frames of understanding derived not only as teachers and researchers within a specific field, but also as participants in diverse teaching and research activities within their institutions' (Tikly & Crossley, 2001, p. 574).

Reflections on these and other issues raised above are captured in the concluding extract from the earlier and directly related analysis that is reproduced below:

> Recent years have seen a major revitalisation of the field of comparative and international education. This has been inspired, in part, by changing geopolitical relations, the intensification of globalisation, and shifting intellectual perspectives and priorities. In the light of this, significant changes within the field itself are increasingly evident – and deserving of increased attention. In this article we have focussed upon the implications of contemporary developments for the nature and scope of the teaching of comparative and international education. This builds upon the broader international debate stimulated by the WCCES and complements parallel scholarship on the reconceptualisation of research within the field.
>
> In linking our work to the ongoing international debate, we have drawn upon our own international experience and a critical assessment of contemporary trends and developments within higher education in the UK. This underpins our formulation of a threefold theoretical framework that we hope will be helpful to others engaged in the documentation, analysis and reconceptualisation of the teaching of comparative and international education. In presenting these three models as a possible framework for analysis, we recognise that each has its own strengths and limitations; that others may wish to add to or challenge our portrayal; and that in the world of practice it is more likely that a combination of tendencies will be in operation

together. We, nevertheless, maintain that, in these times of rapid global change and reform in higher education, the analysis of the teaching of comparative and international education deserves concerted attention if such work is to more effectively meet the needs of future generations. We therefore hope that this largely conceptual analysis will help to clarify and discipline such thinking. We hope this may also stimulate more detailed, cross-cultural and empirically informed research relating to organisational learning, higher education and the teaching of comparative and international education worldwide. (Tikly & Crossley, 2001, pp. 579-580)

It is in this spirit that this present chapter is written, with a view to building upon this earlier work, and contributing to the continuation of innovative and creative debates about the future of teaching in the field. Further developments have, of course, emerged within the Graduate School of Education at Bristol, including the creation of specialised comparative teaching units at the Doctor of Education (EdD) level, the growth and rebranding of ICS, and the emergence of an important sister research centre with a focus upon research on globalisation. The latter deserves its own detailed account and attention, but it is not the intention to go into detail about such departmental developments here, although a number of related issues are pertinent.

With regard to the growth of doctoral-level teaching from the early 2000s, the EdD has grown to become one of the most successful programmes in the department, being taught in Bristol and in Hong Kong in association with the City University of Hong Kong. The overall theme of the programme currently relates to Learning, Leadership and Policy, enabling teaching to draw directly upon the research strengths and interests of the host department in Bristol. Both full-time and part-time enrolment is possible in Bristol, but the programme is targeted at part-time candidates in Hong Kong, enabling participation while continuing in employment. In Hong Kong this doctoral research programme will celebrate its twentieth anniversary in 2016, with a new cohort of approximately 25 students a year beginning their studies. This is, therefore, a significant departmental commitment in its own right. All teaching is carried out over intensive three-day blocks by visiting tutors who regularly travel to Hong Kong from Bristol. The teaching content and rationale closely mirror the teaching for the same programme in Bristol although, true to the spirit of comparative and international education, the specific issues, policies and practices dealt with are closely grounded in the Hong Kong context.

Within the Doctor of Education programme, and reflecting the specialised teaching model noted above, a dedicated unit titled 'Comparative Research' forms part of the suite of what now comprises six taught units. The content of the unit itself is built around the Bristol research centre's long-term research profile and focuses upon challenging uncritical international policy transfer in education. This applies comparative theories and models that deal with policy borrowing and transfer and is designed to engage students in exploring such implications in their own Confucian heritage cultures or other pertinent contexts. This is founded on work by writers such as Crossley and Watson (2003) and Phillips and Schweisfurth (2006) and actively engages with the many international comparativists and researchers who have more recently developed a new generation of challenging work in the education policy transfer arena. See, for example, the work by Auld and Morris (2014) and a review of other recent contributions provided in Crossley (2014). Close teaching relationships have also been developed over the years with colleagues at, and with the work of, the Comparative Education Research Centre (CERC) at the University of Hong Kong. This involves regular class input from CERC colleagues and publications and reciprocal forms of support from Bristol staff for CERC events and activities. Indeed, such is the strength of the relationships that have been built up over these two decades, that synergies between this teaching programme and the work of other Hong Kong universities are also increasingly strong, with many Bristol EdD graduates now working within the Hong Kong higher education sector and generating further forms of collaboration.

In addition, and capturing the spirit of the integration model, other taught units on the Doctor of Education programme relating, for example, to policy studies and leadership and management also purposefully incorporate comparative and international materials, theories, skills and perspectives. In this respect, work on globalisation and education and the political dimension of change is particularly prominent, as are approaches and theories of educational leadership and innovation that are respectful of cultural and contextual differences and the potential of distributed leadership models.

In terms of pedagogy, those undertaking the Doctor of Education programme as a whole are regarded as 'participants', reflecting their predominantly mid-career profiles and extensive professional experience – with the majority holding posts in the higher education sector, educational administration and the various school sectors throughout Hong Kong. Teaching emphasises seminar discussions, workshop activities and other forms of interactive work. This is designed to enable the participants to use their own professional experience in the form of discussion, analysis and written assignments. This is eventually focused more purposefully through a compulsory core of research methodology units that support each participant in planning, researching and writing an individual dissertation.

More than one teaching model is, therefore, built in to the teaching programmes at Bristol, and these are mutually supportive, allowing some specialisation in comparative and international education and some more generic study within which comparative perspectives are purposefully applied. Moreover, with specialised and integrated comparative and international teaching being available in a similar way at master's level, students can now progress from one level to the next with a significant specialisation in the field of comparative and international education. This is not without ongoing challenges relating to funding for students, evolving national and departmental priorities, and changing staff interests and profiles, but the programmes are popular, continuously evolving and in demand.

Perhaps somewhat inevitably, all research centres have been regularly reviewed since their formation, and in all cases this has resulted in name changes. The number of centres has been reduced but comparative and international remains a strong Bristol focus and priority. To strengthen coherence and identity, each centre title has common components relating to the style of wording. The most recent rebranding for ICS thus saw the new title approved in 2015 as the Centre for Comparative and International Research in Education (CIRE). The focus of all centres has also moved more directly to research, although CIRE has retained particularly strong links with related teaching programmes and students and maintains a vibrant collegial spirit in so doing.

It is in the light of the above that the final section of this chapter concludes by reflecting upon a number of key challenges and priorities facing the future of both teaching and research in comparative and international education.

Enduring Priorities and Emergent Challenges

The Bristol experience is unique in many ways, but it is also illustrative of the changing dynamics of teaching and learning in the field of comparative and international education in the UK context. In maintaining some traditional and enduring priorities, much of the teaching (and research) can be seen to be inspired and informed by a critical analysis of international education policy transfer. Advances in the socio-cultural approach to research are also prioritised in many funded projects and all teaching programmes, and staff research publications form the bedrock for much teaching. Illustrative of this is a new edited methodological collection, including work by numerous departmental doctoral students, on the theme of 'revisiting insider–outsider research in comparative and international education' (Crossley et al, 2016). This is designed to be a core text for the teaching of methodological courses within and beyond the comparative field. Also demonstrating the close synergies between teaching and research is a recent article with the title 'International Education Policy Transfer Borrowing Both Ways'. This is published in the BAICE journal *Compare*, is jointly authored by myself with EdD researcher Katherine Forestier, and is a development of work carried out for the Comparative Research taught unit in the Doctor of Education programme that is outlined above (Forestier & Crossley, 2015). The content of this article focuses upon the transfer of education policies from the United Kingdom to Hong Kong at the same time as research reveals how policy transfer can also be seen to be moving from Hong Kong to the United Kingdom. This article further demonstrates the nature of methodological training at the doctoral level and, as already noted, the centrality in much of the teaching of a collective challenge to uncritical policy transfer in education. To this must be added major contributions to the teaching and practical application of mixed methodologies, drawing upon the wider department's leading international profile in quantitative research. Access to this broad range of experience and expertise once again highlights the importance and potential of combinations between specialised and integrated models for teaching and learning for the advancement of this multidisciplinary field. The same experience also helps to identify a number of enduring priorities and emergent challenges for both teaching and research.

In conclusion, three key challenges are identified in the light of recent work published in the fiftieth-anniversary issue of the journal *Comparative Education* (Crossley, 2014). First, given the worldwide impact of cross-national surveys and related international league tables, such as the PISA studies (Mayer & Benavot, 2013), it is argued that the critical interrogation of this 'comparative' work is perhaps one of the most important contemporary teaching and research priorities for the field as a whole. This is argued at length in a *Compare* forum feature entitled 'The Power and Politics of International Comparisons' published in May 2015 (see Barrett & Crossley, 2015, and the six forum discussion contributors). From a teaching perspective this theme has major theoretical potential relating to international policy transfer in education; and, for teaching related to research training and methodology, the disciplined interrogation of the nature, use and impact of such globally influential studies is long overdue.

Second, a related priority that also has a combined teaching and research dimension concerns the emergence of what has become known as the 'big data' movement. To date, the existing literature is dominated by advocacy for the perceived benefits of the big data revolution (Mayer-Schönberger & Cukier, 2013), but the implications of this have been given little sustained critical attention. This, it is argued here, is especially important in the cross-cultural arena. There are real strengths in this work, and supporters clearly recognise how the contemporary economic discourse legitimates such technology, the potential for more detailed measurements, and what some believe is a search for certainty in our fast-paced world. However, the following can also be argued:

> While much can be gained from these developments the potential hegemony of statistical evidence in educational research and the social sciences – and in comparative and international education in particular – deserves ongoing critical attention. As Lawn (2013, 8) points out the 'rise of data in education systems' has a long history, but by the late twentieth century 'quantitative data had gained enormous influence in education systems through the work of the OECD, the European Commission and national system agencies'. The limitations of such forms of evidence, the place of

51

judgement and interpretation in their use, and the challenges
faced by all users and stakeholders in being able to realistically
evaluate and question the significance of decisions made on the
basis of big data will become increasingly important. (Crossley,
2014, p. 20)

Finally, a third emergent priority for attention, and one that illustrates the
importance of comparative teaching and research that spans low-income and
advanced economies, concerns the challenges that will need to be faced
relating to the uncritical international transfer of the expensive, large-scale
and big science modalities for educational and social research. As St. Clair
and Belzer (2007) point out, the current globalisation of such models and
modalities warrants more critical analysis if powerful and ideologically driven
models are not to 'be seen as an attempt to promote market managerialism in
educational research for political ends' (St Clair & Belzer, 2007, p. 471).
Highlighting the pertinence of such issues specifically for a comparative and
international education audience in a BAICE presidential address, Vulliamy
thus helps to return this discussion to some of the issues that opened the
chapter itself. He argues:

A concern for sensitivity to cultural context has been a key part of
the field of comparative education in England – all the way from
its pioneers ... to current exponents. Such concern for cultural
context also pervades sociological traditions underpinning the
development of qualitative research... The challenge for future
comparative and international researchers in education is to
harness the symbiosis of these two traditions to resist the
increasing hegemony of a positivist global discourse of educational
research and policy making. (2004, p. 277)

In conclusion, while Vulliamy highlights major implications for the future of
research in the field of comparative and international education, there are
further clear issues and priorities for teaching in the field. By addressing these
issues, disciplined teaching and related research training can do much to
strengthen capacity worldwide for the level of critical analysis that is now
urgently required. The three core priorities identified above, it is argued,
need the concerted and sustained attention of teachers and researchers within
this reconceptualised, reinvigorated and increasingly important specialist
field. In addition, active and informed support is essential for those working
with mainstream educationalists and for others who share these concerns in
other fields and disciplines across the social sciences. Finally, these are also
issues that demonstrate how teaching and research sit closely side by side in
the contemporary, ideological and conceptual landscape of the field of
comparative and international education.

References

Auld, E. & Morris, P. (2014) Comparative Education, the 'New Paradigm' and Policy Borrowing: constructing knowledge for educational reform, *Comparative Education*, 50(2), 129-155. http://dx.doi.org/10.1080/03050068.2013.826497

Barrett, A.M. & Crossley, M. (2015) The Power and Politics of International Comparisons, *Compare*, 45(3), 467-470. http://dx.doi.org/10.1080/03057925.2015.1027509

Bray, M. & Thomas. R. (1995) Levels of Comparison in Educational Studies: different insights from different literatures and the value of multilevel analyses, *Harvard Educational Review*, 65(3), 472-490.

Broadfoot, P., Osborn, M., Gilly, M. & Bucher, A. (1993) *Perceptions of Teaching: primary school teachers in England and France.* London: Cassell.

Crossley, M. (1999) Reconceptualising Comparative and International Education, *Compare*, 29(3), 249-267. http://dx.doi.org/10.1080/0305792990290305

Crossley, M. (2000) Bridging Cultures and Traditions in the Reconceptualisation of Comparative and International Education, *Comparative Education*, 36(3), 319-332. http://dx.doi.org/10.1080/713656615

Crossley, M. (2008) Bridging Cultures and Traditions for Educational and International Development: comparative research, dialogue and difference, *International Review of Education*, 51(3&4), 319-336. http://dx.doi.org/10.1007/s11159-008-9089-9

Crossley, M. (2014) Global League Tables, Big Data and the International Transfer of Educational Research Modalities, *Comparative Education*, 50(1), 15-26. http://dx.doi.org/10.1080/03050068.2013.871438

Crossley, M., Arthur, L. & McNess, E. (Eds) (2016) *Revisiting Insider–Outsider Research in Comparative and International Education.* Oxford: Symposium Books.

Crossley, M. & Vulliamy, G. (1984) Case Study Research Methods and Comparative Education, *Comparative Education*, 20(2), 193-207.

Crossley, M. & Vulliamy, G. (Eds) (1997) *Qualitative Educational Research in Developing Countries.* New York: Garland.

Crossley, M. & Watson, K. (2003) *Comparative and International Research in Education: globalisation, context and difference.* Abingdon: RoutledgeFalmer.

Crossley, M. & Watson, K. (2009) Comparative and International Education: policy transfer, context sensitivity and professional development, *Oxford Review of Education*, 35(5), 633-649. http://dx.doi.org/10.1080/03054980903216341

Dale, R. (2000) Globalisation: a new world order for comparative education, in J. Schriewer (Ed.) *Discourse Formation in Comparative Education.* Frankfurt am Maine: Peter Lang.

Forestier, K. & Crossley, M. (2015) International Education Policy Transfer Borrowing Both Ways: the Hong Kong and England experience, *Compare*, 45(5), 664-685. http://dx.doi.org/10.1080/03057925.2014.928508

Furlong, J. & Lawn, M. (Eds) (2009) The Disciplines of Education in the UK: confronting the crisis, *Oxford Review of Education*, 35(5), Special Issue.

Hans, N. (1964) *Comparative Education.* London: Routledge & Kegan Paul.

Holmes, B. (1965) *Problems in Education*. London: Routledge & Kegan Paul.

Jullien, M. (1817) *Esquisse d'un ouvrage sur L'education comparée*. Paris: De Fain. Reprinted by the Bureau International d'Éducation, Geneva, 1962.

Kandel, I.L. (1959) The Methodology of Comparative Education, *International Review of Education*, 5(3), 270-278. http://dx.doi.org/10.1007/BF01416895

King, E. J. (1965) The Purpose of Comparative Education, *Comparative Education*, 1(3), 147-159. http://dx.doi.org/10.1080/0305006650010302

Mallinson, V. (1964) *An Introduction to Comparative Education*, 2nd edn. Oxford: Heinemann.

Mayer, H.D. & Benavot, A. (Eds) (2013) *PISA, Power and Policy: the emergence of global educational governance*. Oxford: Symposium Books.

Mayer-Schönberger, V. & Cukier, K. (2013) *Big Data: a revolution that will transform how we live, work and think*. London: John Murray.

O'Sullivan, M. (2008) Comparative Education in Teacher Education in the UK and Ireland, in C. Wolhuter, N. Popov, M. Manzon & B. Leutwyler (Eds) *Comparative Education at Universities World Wide*, 2nd edn, pp. 136-142. Sofia: Bureau for Educational Services.

Phillips, D. & Ochs, K. (2003) Processes of Policy Borrowing in Education: some analytical and explanatory devices, *Comparative Education*, 39(4), 451-461. http://dx.doi.org/10.1080/0305006032000162020

Phillips, D. & Schweisfurth, M. (2006) *Comparative and International Education: an introduction to theory, method and practice*. London: Continuum Books.

Sadler, M. (1900 [1979]) How Far Can We Learn Anything of Practical Value from the Study of Foreign Systems of Education? In J.H. Higginson (Ed.) *Selections from Michael Sadler* (1979), pp. 48-50. Liverpool: Dejall & Meyorre.

Schweisfurth, M. (1999) Resilience, Resistance and Responsiveness: comparative and international education at UK universities, in R. Alexander, P. Broadfoot & D. Phillips (Eds) *Learning from Comparing: new directions in comparative educational research – contexts, classrooms and outcomes*. Oxford, Symposium Books.

St. Clair, R. & Belzer, A. (2007) In the Market for Ideas: how reforms in the political economy of educational research in the US and UK promote market managerialism, *Comparative Education*, 33(4), 471-488. http://dx.doi.org/10.1080/03050060701611870

Stenhouse, L. (1979) Case-study and Comparative Education: particularity and generalisation, *Comparative Education*, 15(1), 5-11. http://dx.doi.org/10.1080/0305006790150102

Sutherland, M.B., Watson, K. & Crossley, M. (2007) The British Association for International and Comparative Education, in V. Masemann, M. Bray & M. Manzon (Eds) *Common Interests, Uncommon Goals: histories of the World Council of Comparative Education Societies and its members*, pp. 155-169. Springer: University of Hong Kong.

Tikly, L. & Crossley, M. (2001) Teaching Comparative and International Education: a framework for analysis, *Comparative Education Review*, 45(4): 561-580. http://dx.doi.org/10.1086/447692

Vulliamy, Graham (2004) The Impact of Globalisation on Qualitative Research in Comparative and International Education, *Compare*, 34(3), 261-284. http://dx.doi.org/10.1080/0305792042000257112

Watson, K. (1982) Comparative Education in British Teacher Education, in R. Goodings, M. Byram & M. McPartland (Eds) *Changing Priorities in Teacher Education*. London: Croom Helm.

Watson, K. (Ed.) (2001) *Doing Comparative Education Research: issues and problems*. Oxford: Symposium Books.

CHAPTER 3

Why Comparative and International Education? Reflections on the Conflation of Names[1]

ERWIN H. EPSTEIN

Names have meaning, sometimes deep meaning. Names tell us a lot about who we are and what we hope to be. We name things differently to match how we and others think of them. We give children names that will resonate well as they grow up. My youngest grandchild's name is Geffen, which means 'vine' in Hebrew. His mother's name is Eynav, which means 'grape'. In Judaism, these names have special spiritual meaning. Yet, one would suppose that the child's name would be Eynav and the mother's name would be Geffen, since we think of the grape as the child coming from the mother as the vine. Think again. It is in fact the vine that grows first from the grape *seed*, making perfect sense to have the mother as the grape and the child as the vine.

Fields of study, and their respective associations, are named to convey collective and unique identities of the intellectual domains we pursue as students, teachers, scholars and practitioners. My first exposure to comparative education was to see a prominent sign posted outside a large office at the end of the third floor of the eponymous Judd Hall at the University of Chicago. That sign said 'Comparative Education Center'. I was a Master of Arts in Teaching student and passed that sign almost every day. My curiosity swelled with time and eventually drew me into the center's office and to its PhD program. My first course at the center was an introduction to comparative education. My first professional association was the Comparative Education Society. The major journal of my newly chosen field was the *Comparative Education Review*. That was in 1962.

How things have changed! Now a student in the 'field' could be in comparative education, to be sure, but more often than not in any number of disparately named programs. Today, for example, a comparative education graduate student could be in a Socio-Cultural and International Development Education Studies program (Florida State University); an International and Multicultural Education, Human Rights Education program (University of San Francisco); a Society, Culture and Literacies, Globalization and International Development program (University of Ottawa); an International and Comparative Education program (Indiana University); or a program containing words like 'global' (Drexel University, State University of New York-Buffalo, University of Wisconsin-Madison, University of British Columbia), 'development' (Boston University, Florida State University, University of Minnesota, University of Pennsylvania, St. Mary's University, University of Toronto-OISE), or 'cultural' or 'inter-cultural' or 'cross-cultural' or 'multi-cultural' (Bowling Green State University, Florida International University, University of California-Santa Barbara, McGill University). Notwithstanding the disparate names of these programs, students in them attend the same professional meetings and read essentially the same journals.

Indeed, at times it seems that programs in the field are competing for the longest names at the expense of simplicity and comprehension. For twenty years I taught sociology, a field with many more scholars than comparative education. Some universities have departments or programs named 'Sociology and Anthropology' or 'Sociology and Social Work', but never 'Sociology Anthropology' or 'Sociology Social Work'. Social (or cultural) anthropology is a major subset of anthropology, but one would never find a department of sociological anthropology. Even when sociology does not stand alone, there is rarely doubt about its place in a program that contains its name. What is the place of comparative education in a program named 'International Comparative Education' (Stanford University) or 'Comparative, International Development Education' (University of Toronto-OISE)? In such programs, does comparative education stand apart from international education or international development education or whatever?

First Impressions

Think about students from different universities meeting for the first time at a professional association conference. Graduate students in sociology at an American Sociological Association meeting do not assume students from programs at other universities are in any area but sociology. That is not the case with 'comparative education' students. In this regard, sociology is typical; whether it is political science, economics, physics or the great majority of academic disciplines, students know what field they are in. The dispersion of names for or associated with comparative education is not typical, not because it is a hybrid – all fields experience hybridization – but arguably because of the urge to stand out from the rest. The consequence of this dispersion is widespread misunderstanding.

When first learning a subject, students are outsiders trying to find their way in. Being new to a field, they know little and are in the class either because they are compelled to be there (a required course), because the class is recommended, because they see the benefits of taking it for their cultural or professional lives, or because they are intrigued by the course title and want to know something about the subject. The latter is often the main motive for taking comparative education and/or international education, especially among students who have traveled or worked abroad. They see an opportunity to connect their international travel experience with an interest in education. These students are at their most impressionable; having no working knowledge of the field(s), they are highly susceptible to lasting first impressions.

What is their very first impression? Surely, it would be gleaned from the very title of that first course and then from the titles of the materials they are assigned to read. For a glimpse of such impressions, Hilda Taba, writing more than fifty years ago, and disclaiming specialized knowledge of comparative education, tells us her initial impression of comparative education was one of blurred boundaries and asks, in bewilderment, 'Where ... does comparative education leave off and international education begin?' Even after that initial impression, she contends, 'Examination of recent articles in journals revealed that there is no clear line between the two' (Taba, 1963, p. 171).

One or Two Fields of Study?

Arguably, the most baffling attribute of the field is in regard to the term itself – comparative and international education – as if it refers to a singular field of study. The name of the first and largest professional association is the Comparative and International Education Society (CIES), and many of the field's associations similarly incorporate this title. Various scholars have tried to define what this term means, at times lumping together comparative education and international education as if they are one field, and at other times differentiating between them. The union of these education areas in the titles of many of the world's professional associations as well as in the titles of many courses and university programs contributes to the misunderstanding among many. Undoubtedly, the most extensive probe of this issue was done by David Wilson (1994), who asked whether comparative education and international education are 'fraternal' or 'Siamese' twins. He saw them as both, though his frequent allusion to comparative and international education, rather than to comparative education and international education separately, suggests that he favored 'Siamese'.

Unfortunately, the absence of a clear understanding of what comparative education and international education are gets little better after students' initial exposure. I, together with Bradley Cook and Steven Hite (Cook et al, 2004), showed serious deficiencies regarding knowledge of the history and development of comparative education among members of the Comparative and International Education Society. We attributed these deficiencies to the fact that more than one third of the Society's membership have never taken even an introductory course in comparative education and that less than one third have their highest degree in the field. Two recent prominent textbooks have attempted to address this deficiency by providing a solid foundation of knowledge about comparative education to those being exposed to it for the first time. As judged by the fact that these volumes have appeared in second editions, they are evidently widely read by individuals entering the field. These books are: Kubow & Fossum ([2003] 2007), *Comparative Education: exploring issues in international context*; and Phillips & Schweisfurth ([2007] 2014), *Comparative and International Education: an introduction to theory, method, and practice.*

The books by Kubow & Fossum ([2003] 2007) and Phillips & Schweisfurth ([2007] 2014) are both highly articulate and well organized, and display a remarkable depth for introductory volumes. Even more impressive is the vast ground they cover. Nevertheless, as with all introductory books, they are limited by how far they can probe; space to penetrate any particular segment of a field is perforce restricted in a textbook.

These books strive for comprehensiveness and clarity, and they largely succeed. Yet their limitations become evident especially in regard to explanations regarding theory and method, and, indeed, in their efforts to discern how the field has been defined. The books' titles hint at their differences in perspective. Kubow and Fossum ([2003] 2007) title theirs simply as *Comparative Education*, but insert *international context* into their subtitle. Phillips and Schweisfurth ([2007] 2014) use as their main title *Comparative and International Education*, following the lines taken by the first and largest professional organization in the field, the Comparative and International Education Society, as well as many other such associations. These are not token differences; they reflect a divergence in conceptualization, if not in the audience they are addressing. As such, they might appear to display a lack of unity about what constitutes the field(s) that can be confusing even to seasoned practitioners, let alone new readers.

As anticipated by their title, Phillips and Schweisfurth ([2007] 2014) take pains to define comparative and international education. Yet it is not at all clear whether they are defining one field – comparative and international education – or two fields – comparative education and international education. They seem to be doing both, not always certain whether it is one or two fields. It is not that they are oblivious to the confusion. As they acknowledge:

> In common usage ... 'comparative' studies are frequently (and in
> our view absurdly) associated with the western industrialized
> world, while 'international' education tends (for us wrongly) to

imply the study of education in all its forms in the developing world. These problems in usage have emerged largely as a result of the titles and focus of books and journals and from the nature of university courses. ([2007] 2014, pp. 7-8)

Phillips and Schweisfurth ([2007] 2014) immediately follow this show of disdain for how the two fields are commonly used by turning to my view (Epstein, 1994), differentiating one from the other but contending that they are complementary, with each building on the other. Phillips and Schweisfurth ([2007] 2014) then turn around and cite W.D. Halls (1973), who regards international education as one of a number of subsets of comparative education, and they follow this up with António Nóvoa's (1998) conflicting contention that comparative education is 'shot through by working practices which depend rather on a certain academic folklore than a systematic production of knowledge' but is nevertheless 'the quintessence of the educational sciences, since it is situated at ... "a higher epistemological level"' (p. 11). Phillips and Schweisfurth ([2007] 2014) then go on to describe a host of other views – by Maria Manzon (2011), Roland Paulston (Steiner-Khamsi, 2006), Patricia Broadfoot (1977) and George Bereday (1964) – which, when taken together, form a bewildering array of disparate perspectives, leaving open the question of whether we are delineating one authentic field or two muddled ones.

Nevertheless, Phillips and Schweisfurth ([2007] 2014) strive to make a distinction, however unclear, between the two areas, dwelling mostly on comparative education but devoting an entire chapter to international education. By contrast, Kubow and Fossum ([2003] 2007) totally ignore international education as a field and thus avoid the ambiguity of whether comparative and international education constitutes one or two fields by making it clear that comparative education looks at schooling as having an international context. For Kubow and Fossum, explicitly adding international to comparative education would be redundant.

Avoiding the terms '*international* education' or 'comparative and *international* education' and presenting the field as discrete and unitary under the simple term 'comparative education' may be a prudent way of avoiding the ambiguities described by Phillips and Schweisfurth ([2007] 2014). However, this remedy is not as simple as may appear at first blush. Like Phillips and Schweisfurth and all proper introductory textbooks, Kubow and Fossum ([2003] 2007) give a history of the field. Yet, shunning 'international' in terms describing the field perforce renders a distorted account of the field's development. That shunning extends even to avoiding mention of the Comparative and International Education Society (CIES). How can we understand the field's history without knowing about the role played by the field's first and largest professional association, as well as that of similarly titled organizations that followed CIES? Yet the absence of these associations in Kubow and Fossum's ([2003] 2007) account represents a real void. Kubow and Fossum's history is a kind of ontological and epistemological account, leaving out an important aspect of the field's *professional* development.

What, then, is the nature of understanding of the field conveyed to new students after reading one or the other of these two introductory textbooks? If it is from the book by Phillips and Schweisfurth ([2007] 2014), they will gain a comprehensive view but will have a sense of bewilderment, not knowing if they are being exposed to one, two or more fields. If, by contrast, exposure is to the one by Kubow and Fossum ([2003] 2007), students will gain a clearer understanding of *a* field, but it will be a limited and distorted one. I contend that the problem of an accurate and comprehensive exposure to comparative (and international) education lies not with these volumes but with the way the field has branded itself.

Why Include International Education?

This brings us to the question of why *international* is used at all as part of a title, especially if, indeed, comparative education implies in its very name the idea of international context. After all, the first widely recognized use of the term *comparative education* was by Marc-Antoine Jullien (Jullien, 1817), often considered the 'father' of the field, and he did not coin that term with *international* added on. One could argue, perhaps, that Jullien's research did not have an international context, inasmuch as it consisted of comparisons of Swiss cantons, and that is why he did not affix the additional word 'international'. Yet, Jullien's epistemology called for comparisons across nations; he focused on Swiss cantons only because he did not have the resources to move beyond Swiss boundaries. Still, Swiss cantons, being culturally and ethnically diverse, served his purpose even had he preferred cross-national comparisons. As a positivist, Jullien wanted to establish cross-cultural generalizations, which did not necessarily require moving across national borders.

Once the term *comparative education* came to be used, it took a long time before *international* was attached to titles. The titles of the field's first textbooks, in the first two thirds of the twentieth century, used exclusively *comparative education* or *comparative study of education* as the descriptor. *Comparative Study of National Education in Germany, France, Britain and the USA* by Yu Ji (1917) and *Comparative Education: studies of the educational systems of six modern nations*, edited by Peter Sandiford (1918), are generally recognized as the first textbooks. Undoubtedly, the most influential textbook during that period was Isaac Kandel's (1933) *Comparative Education*, and that was followed a quarter of a century later by another almost equally influential book by Nicholas Hans (1958) with the same title.

It was not until the Comparative Education Society (CES) modified its name in 1968 to include the word *International* that Comparative *and* International Education became widely used. After that, all sorts of modifiers were introduced in the names of programs and professional associations.

What caused the conflation of comparative education and international education? Louis Berends and Maria Trakas (2016) show that Joseph Katz, of the University of British Columbia and the leading founder of the World Council of Comparative Education Societies as well as a former president of the Comparative Education Society, initiated the motion before the Board of Directors to include international education in the society's name, and R. Freeman Butts, also a former president, moved to revise the CES Constitution to make the change. Katz first proposed the name change in the *CIES Newsletter* in January 1966, arguing that the addition of the word 'international' might better reflect the global character of the organization. Technically speaking, the first association to use the term 'Comparative and International Education' in its title was the Canadian Society, which was founded in 1967 with Katz as its president. Nevertheless, it was the change in name by the US-based Comparative Education Society in 1968, the first and largest such association, that had the most influence on the field.

Berends and Trakas (2016) report heated debate in the Comparative Education Society over changing its name. Those who favoured the change gave practical reasons. They emphasized the growing importance of cultural and student exchanges and potential ties to national and international government and non-governmental organizations, activities in line with the idea of *international* education. Those who opposed the change made their arguments based on theoretical and epistemological grounds.

Clearly, the arguments emphasizing the practicalities of cultural exchanges and ties to governmental and non-governmental organizations won out over epistemological arguments. The context for the debate is critical to understanding the outcome. From the time of its inception in the 1950s, the founders of the Comparative Education Society, mainly Gerald Read and William Brickman, had led periodic visits of North American educators to countries around the world. These visits were informally tied to the CES by virtue of their promotion by that organization and its founders. In other words, the CES was engaged in *international* education for more than a decade since its founding while its professional meetings and its journal, the *Comparative Education Review*, focused on academic and theoretical matters. In this regard, the CES was really a comparative education *and* international education society, though its name included only the comparative side.

The period of the debate, from Katz's proposal in 1966 to the adoption of the change in name in 1968, was propitious. Global events at this time were especially salient in influencing national governmental policy and did much to drive the arguments in favor of practicality. In particular, the International Education Act was approved by both houses of the US Congress in October 1966, raising expectations of a windfall of funding for international education activities. As described at the time by Gerald Read (1966):

The task force [appointed to propose legislation leading to the International Education Act] recognized the significant contribution to international education made over the years by universities and scholars on their own resources, and with aid from various philanthropic foundations. But the proposed acts reflect a carefully reconstructed view of our foreign relations and the role that education is to play in them. Their provisions represent a long-term commitment of the Administration to international education in the national interest. Higher education is now to receive a variety of incentive grants, supplementary assistance, and research encouragement. (p. 407)

Here was a rare opportunity to draw national resources for the CES and its members' programs and activities. Many in the CES viewed the name of the Comparative Education Society as an obstacle to what could be a highly advantaged position to draw on the act's provision of funding for international education if only the society would add 'International' to its name. The siren song of money was too strong to ignore.

Why Not to Include International Education?

The opponents of a change in name based their arguments on academic and epistemological grounds and criticized the arguments in favor of the change as 'opportunistic'. According to CES Minutes of 14 February 1968 (CES, 1968, quoted in Sherman Swing, 2007):

It has taken rather more than ten years to get this far in Comparative Education, and only now are we beginning to lay serious claim to being able to make any worthwhile comparisons, and to adopt methods which are presumed to underlie our studies. We have lacked good data, good methods, good training, and above all, as in so many aspects of education, we have lacked good theories. Now that these deficiencies are less obvious in Comparative Education, it might be preferable to capitalise on the skills we have acquired. In this respect International Education remains a more diffuse, more amorphous concept, and I cannot see many testable theories emerging in this area. (pp. 103-104)

I made a similar argument in a letter published that year in the *Comparative Education Review*, in which I noted the disparity between the proposed change in name to include 'International' and the society's journal, the *Comparative Education Review*, which did not concomitantly change its name (Epstein, 1968). I contended that the content of the field, as embodied in its most notable journal, should delineate its boundaries and give it substance. I wrote, 'the field is identified with the *Comparative Education Review*, because that journal displays the field's content. It is what is contained in the *Review*, therefore, rather than how the Society is composed, that should govern the nature of the field and suggest its name' (p. 377).

However many ways international education may be defined, its meaning was clear to those who in the 1960s debated the change in name of the Comparative Education Society. Elizabeth Sherman Swing's (2007) account is instructive:

> It was argued that responsibilities such as cultural exchanges, student exchanges, Peace Corps, UNESCO, United States Agency for International Development, the International Education Act, world colleges, and university-to-university programmes had transformed the academic discipline of comparative education as it was practised during the era of Michael Sadler and I.L. Kandel. Professionals in Administration, guidance and curriculum, it was asserted, were more likely to want affiliation with an international organization than with an exclusively academic organization. (p. 102)

While many of its members were clamouring for a change in the name of the society, it is revealing that there was no concomitant appeal to alter the contents of the society's journal to include international education activity. In other words, none of the individuals wishing to expand the organization's membership in order to bring in international educators pushed to have the *Comparative Education Review* adjust accordingly or to create a second journal to cover international education. For them, comparative education was to remain pure as an academic field, protected by the sanctity of the society's one and only journal.

Hence, the members of the society pushing for a change of name had a clear view of the differences between the two fields. They considered international education as a practical activity in the form of cultural exchanges, Peace Corps, educational aid and such, and comparative education as an academic field embodying humanistic and social scientific epistemologies. They judged that both, however distinct they might be, needed to be incorporated into the organization by virtue of their symbiotic relationship. In doing so, they solidified a debate that had been raging since the inception of the society, when, in William Brickman's words (Brickman, 1977, 1966, quoted in Sherman Swing, 2007), 'the first objective was to rescue the term 'comparative education' from association with 'junketlike' tours abroad and the resultant courses run by amateurs – to gain for the field 'recognition in the academic and professional world as a group of scholarly-minded, serious specialists with high standards of teaching, research, and publication' (Sherman Swing, 2007, p. 95). Here, Brickman was not opposing international education, but insisting that international education be placed in the hands of genuine comparativists – humanistic and social science scholars – whose life work focuses on international issues of education. Indeed, among its very first activities, and for several years, the

Comparative Education Society sponsored educational excursions to a large variety of countries.

Nevertheless, even at its inception, the society's most prominent scholars were divided over the incorporation of international education activities. Brickman believed that such activities should be an outcome of, and informed by, comparative education, so that participation in excursions abroad and other such engagements in international education would be conducted by true comparativist scholars. By contrast, arguably the field's most prominent scholar at that time, Isaac Kandel, resigned from the society's board of directors over the decision to sponsor such activities, arguing that such engagement debased the field. The rupture between those like Brickman, who believed that international education should be an integral activity of the society, and those like Kandel, who vigorously opposed the intrusion of such activity on the terrain of comparative education, represented a tension that endures. I hasten to add that these two great comparativists had strong scholarly interests in common and greatly admired each other (Epstein, 2013), however much they differed in their approach to the inclusion of content in their field.

The Comparative Education Society during the first decade of its existence was actively engaged in international education by virtue of the foreign excursions that it sponsored. For the first eight years, the society formally sponsored 'seminars and field study abroad' in Europe, 1956; South America, 1957; USSR, 1958; Japan and Korea, 1959; USSR, 1960; north-western Europe, 1961; Africa, 1962; and Latin America, 1963 (Bereday, 1963). Ironically, this kind of international education activity began to ebb about the time the society chose to incorporate 'international' into its name. From the mid-1960s on, the society no longer sponsored excursions, though Gerald Read continued to lead academic tours abroad under the banner of Phi Delta Kappa. Moreover, there is little evidence to suggest that CIES benefited directly from the largesse promised by the International Education Act of 1966.

Paradoxically, therefore, the society was less involved in the type of international education that inspired the change in name *after that change* took effect than it was before. Nevertheless, as Allison Blosser (2016) shows, graduate programs in the field frequently advertise career trajectories in governmental and non-governmental agencies, private consulting firms and international development organizations. In other words, the type of international education that gave rise to the society's name change may have diminished as other forms may have become more prominent.

The Opacity of Terms

Prior to the society's change of name in 1968, the demarcation between comparative education and international education was clear, although the term 'international education' was not prominently used in the debates over incorporation of international education activity. That demarcation was also clear in the debates over the change of name in the 1960s. Unfortunately, the leaders of the society in the 1960s, however clear they were regarding the line of demarcation between the two fields, neglected to make that demarcation clear to the membership at large. Hence, members had no unified grasp of what is meant by *comparative and international education*. Only by reading the minutes of the debates taking place at the time could one understand that those leaders referred to two different areas of activity – comparative education and international education – not to one field or discipline, as in comparative international (without the '*and*') education, or international comparative education, as the program at Stanford University would have it.

The consequence of this lack of clarity has given rise to a large-scale disuse, if not misuse, of the term 'comparative education' in the North American lexicon. Timothy Drake (2011), in his study of graduate programs in the United States, lists almost no universities having simply 'Comparative Education' as a stand-alone descriptor. By contrast, four universities have programs named 'International Education' as a stand-alone descriptor – George Washington University, New York University, University of Massachusetts-Amherst, and the University of Minnesota – and one, the program at Vanderbilt, is named 'International Education Policy Management'. If we take the names of these programs at face value, and employ the perspective of members responsible for the change in name of the society in 1968, the outside observer could only conclude that these programs are devoid of comparative education. Even my own university, Loyola University Chicago, upon my retirement as director of its program, plausibly the only one left in North America to have simply 'Comparative Education' as its name, presented me with a lovely crystal memento that redundantly reads, 'Recognizing Your Life's Work in Comparative *International* Education' (italics mine).

Prior to 1968, 'comparative education' predominated as a title for our field across the globe. Today, 'comparative education' almost never stands by itself, if, indeed, it stands at all as an institutional program, at least in North America. Some professional societies, most notably the British association, in similar fashion to the society founded in the United States, began with a name that included 'comparative' but not 'international'. Then, in the 1970s, it changed its name to the British Comparative and International Society, and eventually, in recognition of the primacy of international education, to the British Association for International and Comparative Education (Sutherland et al, 2007). By contrast, many professional societies across the world – especially those that were founded prior to 1968 – such as the Comparative Education Society in Europe, the Japan Comparative Education Society, the Korean Comparative Education Society and the Spanish Comparative Education Society – still carry 'comparative education' in their titles without any other descriptor. This raises the question of whether these societies declined to follow the lead of the US-based organization in changing names as a display of attachment to the boundary purity of comparative education, or whether they simply believed it was not worth the effort to make the change.

In a recent work, Mark Bray (2015) sheds light on this question and proposes various motives for not including 'international' in the name of some societies. For example, the Spanish society declined to include 'International' in its name, preferring instead to change its name from Sociedad Española de Pedagogía Comparada to Sociedad Española de Educación Comparada, and the Japanese Society declined to insert 'International' in its name to avoid confusion with another Japanese association that had 'International Education' in its name.

The proliferation of titles for coursework, programs and associations in our field is seemingly limitless. A student entering graduate study in comparative education, international education, multicultural education, or any of the other related subjects confronts a bewildering array of names that often stand for same field. In coursework, depending on the textbook they use, students are faced with either a comparative education in chaotic relationship with international education, as displayed in the Phillips and Schwiesfurth ([2007] 2014) volume, or a unitary field without formal association with kindred fields, as in the Kubow and Fossum ([2003] 2007) text. Either way, the result is likely to be an uneasy and insecure attachment to the student's chosen field.

I believe that the fault lies not with the textbooks but with the Comparative and International Education Society itself, beginning from the time it failed to clarify important meanings when it changed its name in 1968. Contrary to what I argued in my 1968 'Letter to the Editor' in the *Comparative Education Review*, I now believe that the society's reasons for incorporating international education were worthy, however unworthy was its indifference to the clarity of meanings.

Conclusion

It is not too late to remedy the current opacity in the conceptualization of these fields. The Comparative and International Education Society can do this by making clear that 'comparative and international education' is not a unitary field but two different though related fields: comparative education and international education, both of which have a place in the society. Achieving such clarity requires an agreement on definitions that encompasses a vast array of perspectives and epistemologies, from positivism to relativism (Epstein, 2008), from institutional theory (Wiseman et al, 2014) to filter-effect theory (Epstein, 2006), and from the acute anti-capitalist comparative education in Eastern European scholarship during the Soviet era (Sokolova et al, 1978) to southern 'turn theory' (Connell, 2007; Takayama, 2011).

As I have argued elsewhere (Epstein 2008), comparative education should be viewed as *the application of the intellectual tools of history and the social sciences to understanding international issues of education.* By contrast, international education should be seen as *the application of an understanding of international issues of education to enhance the administrative effectiveness of foreign aid, outreach and study programs.* Note well the functional linkage between the descriptors: enhancing the administrative effectiveness of programs – the international education side – is informed by understanding international issues – the comparative education side.

Agreement on these definitions will make evident the symbiotic relationship between these fields. The Comparative Education Society had its impetus in international education when William Brickman sought the creation of a group of comparativist scholars to ensure an intellectual foundation for a program of foreign visits. Thus, from our society's very beginning, comparative education was put in the service of international education. To define international education as the application of an understanding of international issues to enhance the effective administration of programs implies a reliance on comparative education to underpin the work of international education.

Examples of this reliance can be found in leading journals of our field. Two articles in the November 1992 issue of the *Comparative Education Review*, forming a special focus section on international students in the United States, are especially informative. The first study, by Wimberley et al (1992), examined factors that influence the success of Indonesian graduate students in US universities. The second study, by Xinshu Zhao and Yu Xie (1992), revealed the extent to which living in the West altered the ideological beliefs and political attitudes of Chinese graduate students in the United States. A decade later, the *Comparative Education Review* published an article by Nadine Dolby (2004) that focused on students' citizenship identity linked to their study abroad. Examples of the reliance of international education on comparative education in articles of other journals can be found in a fine study by Bernhard Streitwieser, Emily Le and Val Rust (Streitwieser et al, 2012). These articles, and studies like them, have theoretical import by extending the discourse in comparative education to the factors that influence student behavior in varying settings, and have practical value in international education by furnishing knowledge on how learning structures for international students can be most effectively shaped to produce intended outcomes. Founded on empirical and historical research, they form a natural basis for study abroad and foreign aid policy, the essence of international education.

On the other side of the symbiotic relationship, international education often serves as the catalyst for comparative education. When I was a graduate student in comparative education at the University of Chicago, most of my fellow students were returnees from the Peace Corps whose experience abroad ignited their interest in the field. Virtually all of my comparative education graduate students at Loyola University Chicago had study-abroad experience. I believe that more than anything else it is the familiarity with foreign cultures gained from international education programs that drives initial interest in comparative education and generates ideas for doing research in the field.

In brief, the founders of the Comparative Education Society in the 1950s were correct in seeing the need to have comparative education serve as a platform for international education. And the leaders of the society in the 1960s were also correct in changing the name of our organization to incorporate international education into the fold. Yet they were at fault for not clearly and explicitly demarcating the two fields and proclaiming their symbiosis.

What are the consequences of this lack of clarity regarding comparative education and international education and of the connection between them? For one thing, the lack of clear definitions can diminish the sense of identity comparativists and internationalists of education have with their fields. How can students and scholars have a strong identification with a field without having a stable common understanding of what that field represents? How can they sustain close scholarly associations if they vary in their understanding of the nature of the field with which they wish to identify? Indeed, how do instructors teach about a field, whether it be comparative education or international education, without being able to explain clearly what that field is? Or, if they 'explain' the field, how adequate can their explanation be when others 'explain' the field differently?

For another thing, a lack of clarity obscures the symbiosis of these two fields. Identifying this symbiosis is the key to understanding and appreciating why these fields are, and should be, linked by name in so many programs, courses and professional associations. The moniker 'comparative and international education' should not be an irrelevant label, but the emblem of a strong, worthy and evocative symbiotic partnership. Without a common recognition of that partnership, comparativists and internationalists of education will continue to misjudge the degree to which the two fields rely on each other.

It is time to remedy the problem and bring clarity to the students, scholars and practitioners of our profession. Current leaders of our field, in North America and elsewhere, can do this by incorporating unambiguously the meaning of these fields in formative documents such as their constitutions and websites, and by noting clearly in public venues how they differ and how they relate to the mission of their professional associations. Instructors can do this by explicitly identifying comparative education and international education as distinct fields, and by showing that, however diverse these fields may be, the relationship between them is symbiotic. I can only hope that institutional programs, coursework and textbooks will likewise conform to this convention – and that those new to comparative education and international education will pursue their studies with transparency and a secure sense of identity.

Notes

[1] Prepared as the George F. Kneller Memorial Lecture, Meeting of the Comparative and International Education Society, Vancouver, British Columbia, Canada, March 2016.

References

Bereday, George Z.F. (1963) Editorial, *Comparative Education Review*, 6(3), 169-170. http://dx.doi.org/10.1086/444930

Bereday, George Z.F. (1964) *Comparative Method in Education*. New York: Holt, Rinehart & Winston.

Berends, Louis & Maria Trakas (2016) Inserting International Education in the Comparative Education Society, In Erwin H. Epstein (Ed.) *Crafting a Global Field: six decades of the Comparative and International Education Society*. Hong Kong: Springer.

Blosser, Allison (2016) Program Development, in Erwin H. Epstein (Ed.) *Crafting a Global Field: six decades of the Comparative and International Education Society*. Hong Kong: Springer.

Bray, Mark (2015) International and Comparative Education: boundaries, ambiguities and synergies, in Mary Hayden, Jack Levy & Jeff Thompson (Eds) *The SAGE Handbook of Research in International Education*. London: SAGE.

Brickman, William W. (1966) Ten Years of the Comparative Education Society, *Comparative Education Review*, 10(1), 4-15. http://dx.doi.org/10.1086/445184

Brickman, William W. (1977) Comparative and International Education Society: an historical analysis, *Comparative Education Review*, 21(2/3), 396-404. http://dx.doi.org/10.1086/445950

Broadfoot, Patricia (1977) The Comparative Contribution: a research perspective, *Comparative Education*, 13(2), 133-137. http://dx.doi.org/10.1080/0305006770130109

Comparative Education Society (CES) (1968) Minutes, 14 February.

Connell, Raewyn (2007) *Southern Theory: the global dynamics of knowledge in social science*. Sydney: Allen & Unwin.

Cook, Bradley J., Hite, Steven J. & Epstein, Erwin H. (2004) Discerning Trends, Contours, and Boundaries in Comparative Education: a survey of comparativists and their literature, *Comparative Education Review*, 47(2) (May), 123-149.

Dolby, Nadine (2004) Encountering an American Self: study abroad and national identity, *Comparative Education Review*, 48(2) (May), 150-173.

Drake, Timothy A. (2011) US Comparative and International Graduate Programs: an overview of programmatic size, relevance, philosophy, and methodology, *Peabody Journal of Education*, 86(2), 189-210. http://dx.doi.org/10.1080/0161956X.2011.561187

Epstein, Erwin H. (1968) Letter to the Editor, *Comparative Education Review*, 12(3) (October), 376-378.

Epstein, Erwin H. (1994) Comparative and International Education: overview and historical development, in Torsten Husén & T. Neville Postlethwaite (Eds) *International Encyclopedia of Education*, 2nd edn, pp. 918-923. Oxford: Pergamon.

Epstein, Erwin H. (2006) Echoes from the Periphery: challenges to building a culture of peace through education in marginalized communities, in Y. Iram (Ed.) *Educating towards a Culture of Peace*. Charlotte, NC: Information Age Publishing.

Epstein, Erwin H. (2008) Setting the Normative Boundaries: crucial epistemological benchmarks in comparative education, *Comparative Education*, 44(4) (November), 373-386.

Epstein, Erwin H. (2013) Taught to be evil, *Hoover Digest*, 1 (Winter), 184-196.

Halls, W.D. (1973) Culture and Education: the culturalist approach to comparative studies, in Reginald Evans, Brian Holmes, & John Van de Graaf (Eds.) *Relevant Methods in Comparative Education*, pp. 119-135. Hamburg: UNESCO Institute for Education.

Hans, Nicholas (1958) *Comparative Education*. London: Routledge.

Jullien, Marc-Antoine (1817) *Esquisse d'un ouvrage sur l'éducation comparée* .[A plan for a work on comparative education]. Paris: L. Colas.

Kandel, Isaac (1933) *Comparative Education*. New York: Houghton Mifflin.

Kubow, Patricia K. & Fossum, Paul R. ([2003] 2007) *Comparative Education: exploring issues in international context*. Upper Saddle River, NJ: Pearson.

Manzon, Maria (2011) *Comparative Education: the construction of a field*. Hong Kong: Springer. http://dx.doi.org/10.1007/978-94-007-1930-9

Nóvoa, António (1998) *Histoire et comparaison (Essais sur l'Éducation)*. Lisbon: Educa.

Phillips, David & Schweisfurth, Michele ([2007] 2014) *Comparative and International Education: an introduction to theory, method, and practice*. London: Bloomsbury.

Read, Gerald (1966) The International Education Act of 1966, *The Phi Delta Kappan*, 47(8), 406-409.

Sandiford, Peter (Ed.) (1918) *Comparative Education: studies of the educational systems of six modern nations*. London: J.M. Dent & Sons.

Sherman Swing, Elizabeth (2007) The Comparative and International Education Society (CIES), in V. Masemann, M. Bray & M. Manzon (Eds) *Common Interests, Uncommon Goals: histories of the World Council of Comparative Education Societies and its members*, pp. 94-115. Hong Kong: Comparative Education Research Centre.

Sokolova, M.A., Kuzmina, E.H. & Radionov, M.L. (1978) *Comparative Pedagogy*, trans. from Russian. Moscow: Editorial Prosveschenie.

Steiner-Khamsi, Gita (Ed.) (2006) Interview of Roland Paulston, in *Comparatively Speaking*, DVD of interviews, Comparative and International Education Society.

Streitwieser, Bernhard T., Le, Emily & Rust, Val (2012) Research on Study Abroad, Mobility, and Student Exchange in Comparative Education Scholarship, *Research in Comparative and International Education*, 7(1), 5-19. http://dx.doi.org/10.2304/rcie.2012.7.1.5

Sutherland, Margaret B., Watson, Keith & Crossley, Michael (2007) The British Society for International and Comparative Education (BAICE), in

V. Masemann, M. Bray & M. Manzon (Eds) *Common Interests, Uncommon Goals: histories of the World Council of Comparative Education Societies and its members*, pp. 155-169. Hong Kong: Comparative Education Research Centre.

Taba, Hilda (1963) Cultural Orientation in Comparative Education, *Comparative Education Review*, 6(3) (February), 171-176.

Takayama, K. (2011) A Comparativist's Predicament of Writing About 'Other' Education, *Comparative Education*, 47, 449-470. http://dx.doi.org/10.1080/03050068.2011.561542

Wilson, David N. (1994) Comparative and International Education: fraternal or Siamese twins? A Preliminary Genealogy of Our Twin Fields, *Comparative Education Review*, 38(4), 449-486. http://dx.doi.org/10.1086/447271

Wimberley, Dale W., McCloud, Donald G. & Flinn, William L. (1992) Predicting Success of Indonesian Graduate Students in the United States, *Comparative Education Review*, 36(4) (November), 487-508.

Wiseman, Alexander W., Astiz, M. Fernanda & Baker, David P. (2014) Comparative Education Research Framed by Neo-institutional Theory: a review of diverse approaches and conflicting assumptions, *Compare*, 44(5), 688-709. http://dx.doi.org/10.1080/03057925.2013.800783

Yu, Ji (1917) *Comparative Study of National Education in Germany, France, Britain and the USA*. Shanghai: China Book Company.

Zhao, Xinshu & Xie, Yu (1992) Western Influence on (People's Republic of China) Chinese Students in the United States, *Comparative Education Review*, 36(4) (November), 509-529.

CHAPTER 4

Multicultural Education is Not Enough: the case for comparative education in preservice teacher education

PATRICIA K. KUBOW & ALLISON H. BLOSSER

Introduction

In the United States, comparative education (CE) has and continues to be taught primarily at the graduate level. Though the field has experienced various periods of popularity and expansion – namely, between the 1950s and 1970s (Wolhuter et al, 2008) – it has not secured its place in undergraduate teacher education despite the many benefits it offers preservice teachers. In a previous work, we argued that it is imperative for comparativists to assess the viability of the field through focused attention on the teaching of CE (Kubow & Blosser, 2014). It is in that spirit that we make a case for CE's place in teacher education. We make our case by comparing CE with multicultural education (ME), a field that has positioned itself as vital to teacher education. We chose ME as a point of comparison because both ME and CE share many social aims, as well as ideological and epistemological concerns. We ultimately argue that CE is as relevant to teacher education as ME, if not more so. The theoretical lens of -*scape*, which captures the fluidity and irregularity of the American educational landscape, is used to argue that comparative education should be made a required course in undergraduate teacher preparation, recognizing that the United States is only one of many countries experiencing a changing economic and demographic scene.

We specifically draw upon Appadurai's (1996) notion of *ethno-* and *ideoscape* to advance the position that CE is needed in preservice teacher education to help future teachers to understand and work effectively with the racial, ethnic, linguistic, cultural and ideological influences shaping formal schooling in the twenty-first century (Kubow, 2011). While we frame this

75

chapter largely from a US perspective, the utilitarian direction of teacher education is a global concern and certainly applies to other countries as well. Planel (2008) describes this trend in England, for example, and the numerous contributors to this present book discuss the technicist or utilitarian impulse toward the development of teacher competencies and student outcomes, leaving much less curricular attention on the social foundations – the philosophical, sociological and historical aspects of schooling.

Teacher Education in the United States[1]

Several economic and demographic indicators reveal that the ethnoscape of the United States is rapidly changing, posing increasing challenges for schools and teachers. *The State of America's Children 2014* report by the Children's Defense Fund reveals that child poverty in the United States has reached record levels, with children of color disproportionately poor. According to the report, one in five children (16.1 million) are poor, and one in 10 children (7.1 million) are extremely poor. The report also asserts that in 2012, for the first time in the United States, the majority of children under the age of two were children of color, as were the majority of children in 10 states (i.e. Arizona, California, Florida, Georgia, Hawaii, Maryland, Mississippi, Nevada, New Mexico and Texas, as well as the District of Columbia). By 2019, according to *The State of America's Children 2014*, it is expected that children of color will be the majority of children nationwide. In relation to the United States' racial and ethnic diversity, the report found that Black children, American Indian/Native Alaskan children and Hispanic children are among the poorest. The 2014 report by the Children's Defense Fund also cited that the achievement gap between American students and those in top-performing countries, such as Finland and Korea, cost the United States approximately $1.3-2.3 trillion in 2008, equivalent to 9-16% of gross domestic product (GDP). Comparing Black child well-being in the United States with that of other nations, UNICEF concluded that 72 nations have lower infant mortality rates, including Sri Lanka, Cuba and Romania; and 132 nations have lower incidence of low birth weight, including the Congo, Cambodia and Guatemala (Children's Defense Fund, 2014). Referring to the soon-to-be-released report of the Center for Immigration Studies, Stephen Dinan (2014), writing for *The Washington Times*, stated that one fifth of the people in the United States speak a foreign language at home, with Arabic and Urdu among the fast-growing languages.

These trends create a significant challenge for the four million teachers who work in America's public and private schools. Almost 86% of US teachers are employed at public elementary and secondary schools and assigned the difficult task of meeting the needs of 47 million students (US Department of Education, 2010). In addition, the US teacher workforce is an aging one, with approximately one fifth of teachers in 2008 over 55 years old and more than a third having taught for more than 15 years (Ludwig et al, 2010). The teaching force is also predominately female. At the elementary level, 84% of teachers in public schools and 87% in private schools are female, while at the secondary level, 59% of public and 53% of private school teachers are female (US Department of Education, 2010). A major challenge facing US schooling is the unequal distribution of high-quality teachers (Darling-Hammond et al, 2005; Murnane & Steele, 2007). In what has been termed 'apartheid schools' that serve more than 90% students of color, the majority of teachers are inexperienced and uncertified (Darling-Hammond, 2010). Figures for 2007-2008 reveal that more than 80% of US public school teachers are White, and Black and Hispanic teachers comprise only 7% of the teaching force and are concentrated in urban as opposed to suburban, town or rural schools (Ludwig et al, 2010).

Likewise, university teacher education faculty, and the preservice students they teach, are largely White. According to the US Department of Education (2010), the racial and ethnic profile of preservice education mirrors the current K-12 teaching force; White students comprise almost 78% of students enrolled in teacher preparation programs, and White teachers constitute almost 80% of the teaching workforce. It is unlikely that the diversity of the US teaching force will change dramatically in the near future (Ludwig et al, 2010). To bridge the cultural divide, the typical approach in US teacher education is to add a course on multicultural education, English as a Second Language, or urban education, while leaving the rest of the curriculum intact (Zeichner & Hoeft, 1996; Villegas & Lucas, 2004; Zeichner, 2009) and virtually devoid of a comparative and international-oriented education course. Increasingly, graduates of comparative and international education doctoral programs find themselves teaching multicultural education courses at universities and colleges that do not offer courses in CE.

In US schools and teacher preparation programs, emphasis on the knowledge economy has become the prominent ideoscape. As Carnoy and Rhoten (2002) explain, 'global economics and ideology are increasingly intertwined ... [and] promulgate particular strategies for educational change' (p. 2). To illustrate, in 1991, US Secretary of Labor Robert Reich asserted that the growing inequalities between individuals and nations were the result of differences in children's knowledge and skills (as cited in Spring, 2008). In 2001, No Child Left Behind (NCLB) legislation demanded 'highly qualified' teachers in every US classroom. The education reform agenda for schools, as defined by the nation-state's plan of human capital development, focuses on raising students' achievement levels. In preservice teacher preparation programs, attention has been given to skill formation in the form of cultural competencies, scientific and technological literacies, and adaptation to rapid change (Stewart, 2009).

Part of the ideological project in teacher education has been to require preservice educators to take a multicultural education course. The goal of the course is to equip future teachers with skill sets so as to teach toward students' varied learning styles. Globalization discourses tied to national development and the knowledge economy view cognitive and technical skills as strong predictors of educational attainment. Causality therefore is envisioned between individual competencies (of both teachers and students) and economic growth. The skill level achieved – or not achieved – by students is considered by the American public and its policymakers to be directly related to the quality of teacher instruction. We turn now to how this larger ideological project affects teacher education.

Over the past two decades, a master narrative has emerged in teacher education that equates teacher quality with student achievement. As such, education scholars and policymakers have scrambled to consider the kinds of policies and practices that might lead to a high-quality education. Toward that end, an important component of teacher program accreditation is that of diversity training whereby preservice teachers take an ME course (often only one) to learn how to make a difference in the lives of students from diverse socioeconomic and cultural backgrounds. An ME course usually incorporates concepts such as 'cultural competence' and 'culturally relevant pedagogy' (Ladson-Billings, 1995) – concepts that sound akin to CE but that often do not encourage preservice teachers to wrestle with the complex intersections of modernity, globalization and hegemony within the United States, much less across countries.

Kubow (2011) found at least five aspects informing this master narrative for teacher education in the United States and elsewhere. One aspect upon which the master narrative is spun is the acceptance of the knowledge economy paradigm and its role in directing teacher education reform. The following statements from US teacher educator Linda Darling-Hammond illustrate this particular ideoscape and the responsibility imposed upon teacher education:

> In the knowledge-based economy we now inhabit, the future of our country rests on our ability, as individuals and as a nation, to learn much more powerfully on a wide scale. This outcome rests in turn on our ability to teach much more effectively, especially those students who have been least well supported in our society and our schools. (Darling-Hammond, 2010, p. 35)

> The notion that we can remain a world-class economy while undereducating large portions of our population – in particular, students of color and new immigrants, who are fast becoming a majority in our public schools – is untenable. Mostly because of these underinvestments, the United States continues to rank far behind other industrialized nations in educational achievement: 28th out of 40 nations in mathematics in 2003, for example, right behind Latvia. Meanwhile, leaders of countries like Finland that experienced a meteoric rise to the top of the international rankings

have attributed their success to their massive investments in
teacher education. (Darling-Hammond, 2007, p. 42)

A second aspect undergirding the master narrative is the belief that variations
in student learning, as measured by high-stakes achievement tests, are linked
to the quality of classroom teaching (Kubow, 2011). Low student
achievement is associated with low-performing teachers and the negative
impacts they have upon students. For example, the National Council on
Teacher Quality (NCTQ, 2008) asserted that a teacher's literacy level – as
measured by vocabulary and standardized tests – affects student achievement
more than any other teacher characteristic. A third aspect of the master
narrative in teacher education is a belief that high-performing schools attract
the right people to the teaching career (Kubow, 2011). In the United States,
however, a concern is that teachers are recruited from the bottom third of
college-bound high school students (National Center on Education and the
Economy, 2007).

The fourth aspect is that teacher education must give greater attention
to developing teachers' skills sets. Studies of teacher preparation in the
United States have found that teacher effectiveness improves significantly
after the third year of teaching and that attention to classroom effectiveness
in the initial years can reduce teacher attrition (Clotfelter et al, 2007; Boyd et
al, 2008; Darling-Hammond, 2010). The fifth aspect underlying the master
narrative in teacher education is that purposeful policies are needed to
support high-quality teaching (Kubow, 2011). For example, while teachers in
Finland meet weekly to plan lessons and share materials, teachers in the
United States have only three to five hours for lesson planning, and such
planning is most often conducted in isolation from their colleagues (National
Commission on Teaching and America's Future, 1996).

Teacher educators and educational policymakers in the United States
continue to seek common features or characteristics of teacher education that
might account for student achievement in top-performing educational
systems worldwide so as to apply them back home. This has led to an
increased emphasis on science and math, high-stakes tests, and adapting
teaching delivery modes to help students meet educational standards (Carnoy
& Rhoten, 2002). Toward that end, multicultural education has been seen as
the answer to equipping preservice teachers with cultural competencies and
sensitivity to diversity without necessarily challenging the knowledge
economy ideoscape. The field that does challenge this formulation of
modernity is comparative education, though it is rarely included in teacher
preparation programs. Because a complex intersection of historical,
sociopolitical, economic, philosophical and cultural factors influences
teaching and learning in the United States and elsewhere, it is this complexity
that must be studied by preservice teachers.

Challenging the Master Narrative in Teacher Education: points of convergence and divergence between comparative education and multicultural education

The inspiration for this chapter emerged from the authors' recognition that scholars trained in CE sometimes find themselves teaching ME courses. Likewise, ME courses sometimes seek to integrate central concepts from CE. We asked why. Specifically, we wanted to understand why the two fields are often lumped together in education curricula and academic conversations. Further, we wondered just how akin the two fields are. And why is ME often the parent course that integrates CE as opposed to the other way around? Why did ME secure a place in teacher education programs, while CE did not? Finally, we asked what CE could offer future teachers that ME cannot. What might be gained or lost as a result of focusing on one over the other, or on both? These are the questions addressed here.

ME is defined as a 'field of study and an emerging discipline whose major aim is to create equal educational opportunities for students from diverse racial, ethnic, social class, and cultural groups' (Banks & Banks, 1995, p. xi). For Banks (2010), multicultural education is 'an idea or concept, an educational reform movement, and a process' (p. 3). As an idea or *concept*, 'all students – regardless of their gender, social class, and ethnic, racial, or cultural characteristics – should have an equal opportunity to learn in school' (Banks, 2010, p. 3). As an education reform movement, multicultural education seeks to change educational institutions through curriculum and school environment so that all students have opportunities to learn. As a process, ME is ongoing (Banks, 2010). From Banks' (2010) perspective, ME's ideals (e.g. freedom, liberty and justice) represent important aims toward which humans strive, even though they are never wholly achieved.

CE, in contrast, is defined as 'a field of study that applies historical, philosophical, and social science theories and methods to international problems in education' (Epstein, 1994, p. 918). It involves 'an engagement in making explicit comparisons in education as a cultural phenomenon in two or more national educational systems' (Planel, 2008, p. 386) and works from the premise that 'awareness and understanding of the theoretical and philosophical assumptions underlying educational issues and educational reform in various nations are necessary for thoughtful, informed educational practice in each nation' (Kubow & Fossum, 2003, 2007, p. 5). For Kubow and Fossum (2003, 2007), the benefit of comparative education is that it asks teachers and students to examine the complexity and tensions influencing education and to consider how cultural, social, political and economic values coalesce, shaping educational issues and their interpretation in different settings.

While distinct in definition, CE and ME converge at many points. Foremost, they share a central goal: to eliminate educational inequality. But the two fields share other goals as well: to increase understanding of one's own educational system; to improve educational practice; to build cultural knowledge; and to develop awareness of the impact of global forces and trends on different groups of people. Further, they share ideological interest in historically marginalized populations and epistemological interest in the ways dominant cultures shape education for non-dominant cultures. The fields' shared epistemological and ideological concerns mean that the two fields sometimes rely upon the same scholars and theoretical perspectives (e.g. Freire/critical theory and Bourdieu/social reproduction). Finally, comparison is an inherent method of both fields. Given these points of convergence, one must wonder how and why ME has positioned itself as an essential component of teacher education, while CE has not.

Unlike CE, ME has held a secure place in teacher education programs in the United States for over 25 years. In 1979, the National Council for Accreditation of Teacher Education (NCATE) began requiring that teacher education programs 'show evidence of planning for multicultural education in their curricula' (AACTE, 1978). Indeed, through its links to various social justice movements (e.g. the civil rights movement, the women's rights movement, the ethnic studies movement) (Banks, 1993; Gorski, 1999) and the active efforts of several influential scholars (i.e. Baker, Banks, Gay and Grant) (Banks, 1993), ME gained a political foothold in teacher education. The field also asserted its contemporary relevance and emphasized its practical purposes through offering tools for educators. Many of the practices advocated by ME scholars can be taken up by education practitioners and, more importantly, *observed* in schools.

James Banks (1993), a prominent leader in the ME movement, has outlined five dimensions of ME that are prevalent in its scholarship: content integration; knowledge construction; prejudice reduction; equity pedagogy; and empowering school culture. Each of these dimensions is concerned with a set of practices that educators and schools can employ to achieve educational equality. For example, equity pedagogy offers teachers 'techniques and methods that facilitate the academic achievement of students from diverse racial, ethnic, and social class groups' (Banks, 1993, p. 3). Likewise, content integration is a dimension that encourages educators to incorporate texts and information from various cultures into their curricula (Banks, 1993). In our current educational milieu with its emphasis on skill sets, it is no wonder that a field that offers tangible reforms has secured a place in teacher education.

CE approaches its aim of educational equality differently from ME, and it is likely that CE's approach has kept it from becoming a required component of teacher preparation in the United States. First, those outside the field often misunderstand CE because the field is largely 'synthetic', meaning that it draws upon the methods and theoretical perspectives of many related disciplines (Paulston, 2006; as cited in Phillips & Schweisfurth, 2008, p. 11). But second and more significantly, 'comparative education is not normative: it does not prescribe rules for the good conduct of schools and teaching ... It tries instead to understand what is done and why' (Lauwerys, 1969, as cited in Phillips & Schweisfurth, 2008, p. 14). Essentially, CE does not sell itself as a toolkit; rather, it affords scholars and practitioners particular lenses for examining education policies and practices. CE develops in its students the ability to critically evaluate the theoretical, philosophical and ethical assumptions underlying educational issues and reforms in locales throughout the world. Comparativists generally maintain that such abilities can (and should) be used in the service of reducing educational inequalities and improving educational practice. But it is exactly CE's concern with the theoretical and philosophical, as opposed to a more practical orientation, which has rendered it superfluous to most teacher education programs. Indeed, CE has been criticized for being 'too abstract' and 'lacking empirical evidence as well as applicability in educational practice' (Mitter, 1997, p. 404). Some scholars have also claimed that CE 'has not been concerned enough with pedagogy and curriculum' (Planel, 2008, p. 389). And many comparativists (the authors included) eschew the practical/utilitarian direction that teacher preparation in the United States has taken. Ultimately, CE's academic orientation is both its strength and its biggest limitation in the realm of teacher education.

Yet, ME is not without its own limitations. In addition to its largely practical orientation, ME has also suffered from the reputation that its practice is only for the benefit of students of color (Wills, 1996; Lucas, 2010). Wills (1996) attributes this reputation to the prevalence of scholarly attention concerning the ways in which a multicultural curriculum benefits students of color. A belief that ME is only for students of color reduces teacher buy-in of it, especially for teachers who are currently teaching in, or who plan to teach in, predominantly white schools. White Euro-Americans' perceptions toward ME courses in teacher preparation in the United States tend toward a superficial receptive attitude toward such education classes (Sleeter, 2001). Moreover, although the intent of ME is to help preservice educators deconstruct educational structures and to question socioeconomic and political relationships of power and knowledge in education, such courses are often an isolated part of the teacher education curriculum and reinforce the attitudes that preservice teachers bring to the course (Locke, 2005). Finally, ME has been a point of political contention in the United States (Wills, 1996). As Wills (1996) writes, 'Critics have attacked multicultural educators as radicals out of touch with mainstream American society, have argued that the emphasis on race and ethnicity in the curriculum is divisive, and have attacked multicultural curricula as intellectually weak and victim to political correctness' (p. 365). CE, however, does not experience these drawbacks.

Currently, there are two primary approaches to the teaching of CE – namely, specialization and integration (Tikly & Crossley, 2001). Drawing upon the work of Tikly and Crossley (2001), Manzon (2011) states that specialization advocates view CE as 'a distinct specialty or separate subfield of education studies, with its distinctive attributes, perspectives, and literatures', while integration 'promotes the infusion or integration of comparative perspectives into other courses or programs of education studies' (p. 40). It is our opinion that integration does not offer students enough exposure to the field of CE and poses risks to the field itself – namely, the field runs the risk of losing its theoretical and philosophical emphasis when integrated into more practical-oriented courses like ME. Specialization, however, has its drawbacks as well. For example, Tikly and Crossley (2001) explain how specialization 'does not always maximize the kind of cross-fertilization with other disciplines and subfields that is necessary if the comparative and international canon is to advance creatively' (p. 20). Such drawbacks are why Tikly and Crossley (2001) advocate an alternative approach for teaching CE: transformation. A transformative approach to teaching CE seeks to free the field from education departments alone by offering advanced CE courses across departments and disciplines as part of continuing teacher professional development (Manzon, 2011). While in this chapter we are immediately advocating for the inclusion of CE alongside ME in teacher education programs, we ultimately agree with Tikly and Crossley (2001) about the need for a transformative approach to CE, if the field is to survive.

The Relevance of Comparative Education to Teacher Education

We argue that CE is as relevant to teacher education programs today as ME, if not more so. As Aydarova and Marquardt (forthcoming) point out, the Council for the Accreditation of Educator Preparation (CAEP) now expects teachers to think globally. CAEP's 2013 accreditation standards claim that they want to ensure 'that educators enter the classroom ready to have a positive impact on the learning of all students and prepare them to compete in today's global economy' (CAEP, 2013, p. 5; Aydarova & Marquardt, forthcoming). CAEP also wants teachers who understand 'how to connect concepts and use differing perspectives to engage learners in critical thinking, creativity, and collaborative problem solving related to authentic local and global issues' (CAEP, 2013, p. 12; Aydarova & Marquardt, forthcoming). CE can fulfill these aims. While Aydarova and Marquardt (forthcoming) critique the language of these statements (and rightly so), such standards offer an opening for comparativists to demonstrate the relevance and utility of CE for teacher education. This is not to say that we advocate the utilitarian direction teacher education has taken; rather, it is to acknowledge that reality and offer comparative educators a way to advocate for the field by both challenging the master narrative and working within it. Put another way, while we do not go as far as Aydarova and Marquardt to claim that CE needs a 'pragmatic reorientation' in order to secure its place within teacher education curricula, we do believe that CE needs to better market its pragmatic qualities and emphasize how it can help teacher education programs and preservice teachers to meet CAEP's expectations.

In this section, we discuss why CE courses, in particular, could develop in teachers both the competencies CAEP expects of them as well as other abilities that we deem are necessary for educators today. Research conducted by Zhao et al (2007) reveals that undergraduate students enrolled in a large teacher education program in the United States demonstrated 'a high degree of inattention, insularity, and lack of awareness' about the world (p. 142). To address such concerns, Kubow and Fossum (2003, 2007), in their book *Comparative Education: exploring issues in international context,* have argued for *comparative perspective taking* to be made an essential part of teacher professional development. They argue that, by looking outward to other nations and cultures, teachers are able to view education anew in their local contexts. The aim, therefore, is for teachers to use comparative knowledge – a combination of global and local perspectives – to inform educational decision-making. Through CE, students can learn about shared dilemmas that transcend national boundaries (Sutton & Hutton, 2001; Kubow & Fossum, 2003, 2007), develop critical perspectives to clarify their own viewpoints (Hanvey, 1982), and consider the complex interplay of environmental, economic and humanitarian developments (Gutek, 1993). Unfortunately, it is extremely rare to find a CE course taught at the undergraduate level in the United States. Even for educators seeking advanced degrees, a CE course is seldom required in their US teacher education programs. This must change.

Helping teachers gain what Hanvey (1982) describes as 'perspective consciousness' will enable educators to recognize that their own beliefs and experiences about the world are not necessarily universally shared and that other ways of living are also valid (Cushner, 2007). Along those lines, Planel (2008) argues that comparative pedagogy – an area of study in CE wherein a comparative approach is applied to the 'theory and practice of teaching' (p. 368) – can build teachers' 'intercultural competence' 'in order to meet the needs of pupils whose experience of education, or whose parents' experience of education, is of a different national system of education' (p. 390). In addition, comparative pedagogy can help teachers to more deeply understand and reflect upon the teaching and learning processes in general (Planel, 2008). In many ways, CE exposes teachers to an economic and political awareness that can help them as professionals to understand the complex *ethnoscapes* and *ideoscapes* shaping education and societies in the twenty-first century.

Further, while ME seeks to develop in teachers the abilities to meet the needs of all of their students and to strive to create more equitable schooling experiences for students, a focus on ME in teacher education often does not equip preservice teachers with 'the skills to systematically explore the key issues affecting educational policies, practices, and reforms at home and abroad' (Kubow & Fossum, 2003, 2007, p. iii). Moreover, CE reaches beyond national borders at a time when the nation-state is becoming less important as a unit of analysis (Sobe, 2016), whereas ME, in contrast, often focuses on educational inequalities within national boundaries (Lucas, 2010). While scores on international tests drive education reform globally, it is essential that teachers have the know-how to decipher these test scores, conduct comparative research to elucidate reasons for those scores, critique the educational policies and practices that emerge in response to them, and evaluate the motivations of policy-making entities, governmental and nongovernmental alike. We ultimately agree with Aydarova and Marquardt (forthcoming) that CE is the best-positioned field to teach such skills. The next step, then, is to require preservice teachers to complete a course in CE, in addition to the more US-based multicultural course to which they are currently exposed.

The Future of Comparative Education in Teacher Education

It is easy for those of us in the field to recognize the value of CE for current and burgeoning educators, but the bigger question is what are we going to do about our convictions? Given the current state of teacher education, replete with its over-packed curriculum and competencies-based models, it will take serious efforts to secure CE's place in teacher education. Without such efforts, however, the future of CE in US universities and departments of education is uncertain at best and bleak at worse. Foremost, to secure CE's place in teacher education, it is time that we move away from decades-old internal debates within the field (e.g. positivism/relativism, comparative education/international education), as they only weaken the perception of the field by those outside it. If we do not abandon such debates, there will be no field about which to debate.

Another task for comparativists is to view education as informed by individual and collective experiences. While the nation-state may continue to be an important unit of analysis, there is need to also analyze education from the standpoint of individuals within a larger transnational community or world. Further, there are creative ways to expose preservice teachers to CE and to promote the field. In the spirit of Tikly and Crossley's (2001) transformative model of CE (discussed above), Blosser, for example, has worked outside the mandated teacher education curriculum at her university to create an undergraduate CE course called *Education in the Age of Globalization* that fulfills students' global studies course requirement as part of their university core curriculum. While teacher-licensure candidates are not currently required to take this course to fulfill their university global studies requirement, School of Education advisors strongly encourage them to do so since the course is housed in the School of Education and is relevant to their major. While many preservice teachers do enroll, the course is also open to students from across the university, which means that students from a wide variety of majors are exposed to CE. Further, as part of the course, international faculty from across the university are invited to present on the educational systems and issues of their home countries, which not only enriches students' cultural knowledge and understanding, but emphasizes the field's import to faculty members from other disciplines. Such practice also opens doors to interdepartmental faculty collaborations. Blosser has also worked to make the course a required one for students in the non-licensure education minor and major, again helping to secure the field's place in her university's School of Education.

In conclusion, we have argued in this chapter that multicultural education is not enough for preservice teachers; rather, comparative education has a central role to play in developing both global and local perspectives to aid education policy and practice. Harnessing the theoretical and philosophical – as well as the practical skills that comparative inquiry offers (e.g. cross-cultural sensitivity, global awareness, engagement from differing vantage points, and the like) – will contribute to international understanding and informed educational decision-making. The ultimate purpose of comparative education is not only to learn about other peoples and cultures, but to help one know oneself (Bereday, 1964). Comparative education can not only help preservice teachers recognize the social 'scapes' at home and abroad, it can also enable them to identify and build a comprehensive and in-depth knowledge of the epistemological and practical aims that influence education, and that education, in turn, can shape.

Notes

[1] This section draws upon Kubow (2011).

References

American Association of Colleges for Teacher Education (AACTE) (1978) *Multicultural Education in Teacher Education: the state of the scene.* Washington, DC: ACCTE.

Appadurai, A. (1996) *Modernity at Large: cultural dimensions of globalization.* Minneapolis: University of Minnesota Press.

Aydarova, O. & Marquardt, S.K. (forthcoming) The Global Imperative for Teacher Education: opportunities for comparative and international education, *Forum for International Research in Education.*

Banks, J.A. (1993) Multicultural Education: historical development, dimensions, and practice, *Review of Research in Education,* 19, 3-49.

Banks, J.A. (2010) Multicultural Education: characteristics and goals, in J.A. Banks & C.A. McGee Banks (Eds) *Multicultural Education: issues and perspectives,* 7th edn, pp. 3-30. Hoboken, NJ: John Wiley & Sons.

Banks, J.A. & Banks, C.A.M. (Eds) (1995) *Handbook of Research on Multicultural Education*. New York: Macmillan.

Bereday, G.Z.F. (1964) *Comparative Method in Education*. New York: Holt, Rinehart & Winston.

Boyd, D., Grossman, P., Lankford, H., Loeb, S. & Wyckoff, J. (2008) Teacher Preparation and Student Achievement. Working Paper 14314, September. Cambridge, MA: National Bureau of Economic Research.

Carnoy, M. & Rhoten, D. (2002) What Does Globalization Mean for Educational Change? A Comparative Approach, *Comparative Education Review*, 46(1), 1-9. http://dx.doi.org/10.1086/324053

Children's Defense Fund (2014) *The State of America's Children 2014*. Washington, DC: Children's Defense Fund.

Clotfelter, C., Ladd, H. & Vigdor, J. (2007) How and Why Do Teacher Credentials Matter for Student Achievement? NBER Working Paper 12828. Cambridge, MA: National Bureau of Economic Research.

Council for the Accreditation of Educator Preparation (CAEP) (2013) CAEP Accreditation Standards and Evidence: aspirations for educator preparation. https://www.google.com/url?sa=t&rct=j&q=&esrc=s&source=web&cd=1&ved=0 CB4QFjAAahUKEwinyr-niLvIAhWLzIAKHbJHBdw&url=http%3A%2F%2Fedsource.org%2Fwp-content%2Fuploads%2Fcommrpt.pdf&usg=AFQjCNEAH2gSFeXWAcIzTIc8K hETglV-pA&sig2=FVYeWIM__7d5vSCNioViIg&cad=rja

Cushner, K. (2007) The Role of Experience in the Making of Internationally-minded Teachers, *Teacher Education Quarterly*, 34(1) (Winter), 27-39.

Darling-Hammond, L. (2007) A Marshall Plan for Teaching. *Social Policy*, 37(3/4) (Spring/Summer), 41-44.

Darling-Hammond, L. (2010) Teacher Education and the American Future, *Journal of Teacher Education*, 61(1-2), 35-47.

Darling-Hammond, L., Holtzman, D.J., Gatlin, S.J. & Heilig, J.V. (2005) Does Teacher Preparation Matter? Evidence about Teacher Certification, Teach for America, and Teacher Effectiveness, *Education Policy Analysis Archives*, 13(42). http://dx.doi.org/10.14507/epaa.v13n42.2005

Dinan, S. (2014) An eye-popping 20% of U.S. residents abandon English at home: Cultural changes prompt surge in foreign languages, *The Washington Times*, 6 October. http://www.washingtontimes.com/news/2014/oct/6/one-in-five-in-us-dont-speak-english-at-home-repor/?page=all (accessed 10 October 2015).

Epstein, E.H. (1994) Comparative and International Education: overview and historical development, in T. Husen & T.N. Postlethwaite (Eds) *The International Encyclopedia of Education*, 2nd edn, pp. 918-923. Oxford: Pergamon Press.

Gorski, P.C. (1999) A Brief History of Multicultural Education, *EdChange*, November. http://www.edchange.org/multicultural/papers/edchange_history.html

Gutek, G.L. (1993) *American Education in a Global Society: internationalizing teacher education*. White Plains, NY: Longman.

Hanvey, R.G. (1982) An Attainable Global Perspective, *Theory Into Practice*, 21(3), 162-167. http://dx.doi.org/10.1080/00405848209543001

Kubow, P.K. (2011) Teacher Education Worldwide and the United States Case, in P. Anastasiades, P. Calogiannakis, K. Karras, & C.C. Wolhuter (Eds) *Teacher Education in the Modern Era: trends and issues*, pp. 73-92. Crete, Greece: University of Crete, Department of Primary Education, Teachers In-Service Training Division 'Maria Amariotou', and Ministry of Education, Lifelong Learning and Religious Affairs, Pedagogical Institute.

Kubow, P.K. & Blosser, A.H. (2014) Trends and Issues in the Teaching of Comparative Education, in A.W. Wiseman & E. Anderson (Eds) *Annual Review of Comparative and International Education 2014*, pp. 15-22. Bingley: Emerald Group Publishing.

Kubow, P.K. & Fossum, P.R. (2003, 2007) *Comparative Education: exploring issues in international context*, 2nd edn. Upper Saddle River, NJ: Pearson, Merrill Prentice Hall.

Ladson-Billings, G. (1995) Toward a Theory of Culturally Relevant Pedagogy, *American Educational Research Journal*, 32(3) (Autumn), 465-491.

Lauwerys, J.A. (1969) Comparative Education, in E. Blishen (Ed.) *Blond's Encyclopaedia of Education*, pp. 152-155. London: Blond Educational.

Locke, S. (2005) Institutional Social and Cultural Influences on the Multicultural Perspectives of Preservice Teachers, *Multicultural Perspectives*, 7(2), 20-28. http://dx.doi.org/10.1207/s15327892mcp0702_4

Lucas, A.G. (2010) Distinguishing between Multicultural and Global Education: the challenge of conceptualizing and addressing the two fields, *The Clearing House*, 83, 211-216. http://dx.doi.org/10.1080/00098650903505373

Ludwig, M., Kirshstein, R., Sidana, A., Ardila-Rey, A. & Bae, Y. (2010) An Emerging Picture of the Teacher Preparation Pipeline: a report by the American Association of Colleges for Teacher Education and the American Institutes for Research. Washington, DC: AACTE.

Manzon, M. (2011) *Comparative Education: the construction of a field*. London: Springer. http://dx.doi.org/10.1007/978-94-007-1930-9

Mitter, W. (1997) Challenges to Comparative Education: between retrospect and expectation, *International Review of Education*, 43(5/6), 401-412. http://dx.doi.org/10.1023/A:1003084402042

Murnane, R.J. & Steele, J.L. (2007) What is the Problem? The Challenge of Providing Effective Teachers for All Children, *Future of Children*, 17(1) (Spring), 15-43.

National Center on Education and the Economy (US) New Commission on the Skills of the American Workforce (2007) *Tough Choices or Tough Times: the report of the New Commission on the skills of the American workforce*. San Francisco: John Wiley & Sons.

National Commission on Teaching and America's Future (1996) *What Matters Most: teaching for America's future*. New York: National Commission on Teaching and America's Future.

National Council on Teacher Quality (NCTQ) (2008) *Increasing the Odds: how good policies can yield better teachers*. Washington, DC: NCTQ.

Paulston, R. (2006) Recorded Interview, in G. Steiner-Khamsi (Ed.) *Comparatively Speaking*, DVD of interviews. Comparative and International Education Society.

Phillips, D. & Schweisfurth, M. (2008) *Comparative and International Education: an introduction to theory, method, and practice*. London: Continuum International Publishing Group.

Planel, C. (2008) The Rise and Fall of Comparative Education in Teacher Training: should it rise again as comparative pedagogy? *Compare*, 38(4), 385-399. http://dx.doi.org/10.1080/03057920701467867

Reich, R. (1991) *The Work of Nations: a blueprint for the future*. New York: Vintage.

Sleeter, C.E. (2001) Preparing Teachers for Culturally Diverse Schools, *Journal of Teacher Education*, 52, 94-106. http://dx.doi.org/10.1177/0022487101052002002

Sobe, N. (2016) Comparative Education, Globalization and Teaching with/against the Nation-state, in. P.K. Kubow & A.H. Blosser (Eds) *Teaching Comparative Education: trends and issues informing practice*. Oxford: Symposium Books.

Spring, J. (2008) Research on Globalization and Education, *Review of Educational Research*, 78(2) (June), 330-363.

Stewart, V. (2009) Benchmarking for Success: an international perspective. Presentation to Governors and Education Policy Advisors. Asia Society, Partnership for Global Learning, 7 June.

Sutton, M. & Hutton, D. (Eds) (2001) *Concepts and Trends in Global Education*. Bloomington: Indiana University, ERIC Clearinghouse for the Social Studies. ERIC ED 460 930.

Tikly, L. & Crossley, M. (2001) Teaching Comparative and International Education: a framework for analysis, *Comparative Education Review*, 45(4) (November), 561-580.

US Department of Education (2010) The Condition of Education 2010. Indicator 27: characteristics of full-time teachers. Washington, DC: Institute of Education Sciences, National Center for Education Statistics, United States Department of Education.

Villegas, A.M. & Lucas, T. (2004) Diversifying the Teacher Workforce: a retrospective and prospective analysis, in M. Smylie & D. Miretzky (Eds) *Developing the Teacher Workforce*, pp. 70-104. Chicago: University of Chicago Press.

Wills, J.S. (1996) Who Needs Multicultural Education? White Students, US History, and the Construction of a Usable Past, *Anthropology & Education Quarterly*, 27(3), 365-389. http://dx.doi.org/10.1525/aeq.1996.27.3.04x0354p

Wolhuter, C., Popov, N., Manzon, M. & Leutwyler, B. (2008) Mosaic of Comparative Education at Universities: conceptual nuances, global trends, and critical reflections, in C. Wolhuter, N. Popov, M. Manzon & B. Leutwyler (Eds) *Comparative Education at Universities World Wide*, 2nd expanded edn, pp. 319-342. Sofia: Bureau for Educational Services.

Zeichner, K.M. (2009) *Teacher Education and the Struggle for Social Justice*. New York: Routledge.

Zeichner, K. & Hoeft, K. (1996) Teacher Socialization for Cultural Diversity, in J. Sikula (Ed.) *Handbook of Research on Teacher Education*, 2nd edn, pp. 176-198. New York: Macmillan.

Zhao, Y., Lin, L. & Hoge, J.D. (2007) Establishing the Need for Cross-cultural and Global Issues Research, *International Education Journal*, 8(1), 139-150.

CHAPTER 5

From Parochialism to Globalism: infusing comparative and international education through study abroad in teacher education programs

KAREN L. BIRAIMAH

Introduction

As Engstrom and Jones (2007) have observed, globalization demands that educators initiate programs that promote understanding of global issues and country-specific interventions to address transnational problems. To this end, calls for schools to adequately prepare students to live in the 'global village' have become commonplace (Merryfield, 1995; Phillion et al, 2009; Alfaro & Quezada, 2010), and point to the need for more effective teacher preparation programs. These include the need to prepare educators who can provide: (1) inclusive pedagogical practices; (2) cultural and contextual knowledge; (3) instruction that meets the needs and challenges of a culturally and linguistically diverse student community; (4) approaches to address stereotypes and prejudices; and (5) conceptualizations to effectively address issues of global interconnectedness and cultural sensitivity.

Moreover, advocates have underscored the importance of incorporating a global perspective into education so that students might better understand and benefit from an increasingly interdependent network of world cultures, economies and political systems. For example, the current National Council for the Social Studies position paper uploaded to the NCSS website on *Preparing Citizens for a Global Community* states that 'an effective social studies program must include global and international education ... [as it is] imperative for students to develop the skills, knowledge and attitudes needed for responsible participation ... in a global community' (NCSS, 2011, p. 1).

Clearly, twenty-first-century schools have the responsibility to prepare students for a new, globalized community, and research has suggested that one of the most effective means of doing so is for future educators to immerse themselves in other cultures and countries (Hadis, 2005; Stachowski & Sparks, 2007). Not only do these future teachers gain first-hand knowledge that allows them to integrate an international perspective throughout the curriculum, but their international multicultural experiences and challenges also make them more responsive to cultural diversity within the classroom.

Unfortunately, up until now, students in teacher education programs were often among the least prepared with regard to international content and exposure to diverse cultural settings. In a recent study on the development of pre-service teachers' multicultural competencies, for example, Sharma et al (2011), whose research has built upon that of Sleeter (2008a), suggest that most pre-service teachers in the United States are White, middle class and monolingual English speakers, with relatively little or no experience within cultures other than their own. They also suggest that the bulk of current pre-service teacher candidates not only have little contact with diverse cultural settings, but are also underrepresented in conventional study-abroad programs. Thankfully, this deficiency was recently noted and acted upon by a US Department of State (2012) request for proposals entitled 'Capacity Building Program for US Undergraduate Study Abroad', which strongly encouraged projects that focused on non-traditional fields for study abroad, including undergraduate pre-service teacher preparation programs. US Fulbright-Hays Group Projects Abroad also focus on improving curricular content while providing teachers with meaningful international experiences.

Unfortunately, until now, the degree to which these programs could longitudinally impact the quality of teaching and school classrooms has remained unclear. For example, in 2006, Millar asked if the positive effects of programs such as Fulbright-Hays could be retained once teachers return to their classrooms (Millar, 2006), while Jarlais and Stein (2005) asked if there was any lasting impact on US tribal college faculty members' traditional ways of knowing after participants return from their study-abroad programs. Moreover, most literature on university study-abroad programs have focused on a collection of lesson plans emanating from their experiences (Johnson, 1997; Bloom, 1998; Walter, 2002), an analysis of participants' perceptions of their host countries (McClam & Woodside, 2000), or rather brief and simplistic program descriptions (Johnson, 1997). Unfortunately, few studies have focused on the longitudinal impact of study-abroad programs on participants' dispositions, knowledge and teaching methodologies (see Biraimah, 2001; Kruger et al, 2009).

Clearly there is a need for more research on the benefits of study-abroad programs. Moreover, this research should include an analysis of their potential for providing a controlled environment where educators might also experience being a minority in another's culture, thus providing teachers with the opportunity to develop the necessary skills and empathy to meet the needs of their future students, while helping to defuse stereotypical notions. Such exposure for US preservice teachers is essential as it prepares them to cope successfully with challenging intercultural and transnational societal issues.

While traditional comparative and international education (CIE) courses might cover similar critical perspectives on the role of education in national development, as well as the impact of globalization on pedagogy and educational outputs, many teacher preparation programs have little room to include such courses. Fortunately, by merging carefully designed study-abroad programs with select aims and objectives of CIE, teacher education programs have the opportunity to provide future teachers with a transformational international experience embedded with essential CIE perspectives, theories and applications. Though most of these study-abroad opportunities are usually limited to short-term programs during summer vacations, or longer one-term internships overseas, when carefully designed they can still provide future teachers with life-changing and career-enriching experiences grounded in key CIE perspectives.

For example, certain CIE content and objectives appear uniquely positioned to enhance traditional study-abroad programs, and thus provide future teachers not only with invaluable cross-cultural experiences, but also with the theoretical foundation necessary for them to better understand these experiences and to apply them successfully within their classrooms. In particular, the following CIE objectives seem well suited to preparing future teachers for twenty-first-century classrooms: (a) understanding how national systems of education have evolved within particular historical and cultural contexts; (b) exploring how education is intrinsically linked to national development; and (c) obtaining the skills that are necessary to critically analyze educational issues within a global context, with particular emphasis on the role of race/ethnicity, class, gender and language on equitable access to quality education.

However, while study-abroad programs might appear to be a panacea for preparing highly qualified teachers for the twenty-first-century globalized classroom, they remain fraught with multiple impediments, including state-mandated certification guidelines and overloaded programs with few or no electives. To overcome these challenges, this chapter argues that study-abroad programs for teacher education students can successfully prepare educators for a globalized world by infusing critical CIE concepts and content within their overseas experiences and coursework. The chapter will first highlight current impediments to the inclusion of CIE courses within initial teacher education programs, and then provide solutions through the development of study-abroad programs enhanced with critical CIE content and objectives.

Challenges to the Inclusion of CIE Courses in Initial Teacher Education Programs

Inherent challenges to infusing CIE content, concepts, aims and purposes within initial teacher certification courses include: (1) compression created by university/community college transfer programs; (2) directives from licensing boards and state departments of education; (3) lack of 'stand-alone' CIE courses within certification programs; (4) lack of faculty qualified to teach CIE in traditional colleges of education; and (5) the narrow perspectives of current teacher certification programs focused on skills, competencies and accountability to the detriment of problem-solving and critical thinking.

Unfortunately, for many institutions in the United States and elsewhere, undergraduate teacher education programs are so overloaded with state licensure requirements that little or no time is available for more theoretically based education courses, such as those offered through CIE programs. Moreover, when working within institutions that support a '2+2' program (where undergraduates complete their first two years at a community college, and then transfer to a 4+-year institution for the last two years of study, concentrating only on their major coursework), there is literally no available time left for electives or other courses not mandated by state departments of education. Unfortunately, few state-approved teacher education programs offer and/or require any CIE courses such as 'Comparative Education'. Moreover, many of these initial teacher education programs are so mired in accomplishing a strict set of skills and knowledge components that they have little, if any, time left to focus on critical thinking and problem-solving. For example, the Florida Department of Education (2013) requires every state-approved initial teacher preparation program to include multiple accomplished practices, such as the ability to 'align instruction with state-adopted standards at the appropriate level of rigor' (p. 1).

Though the intention may not be to deskill or disempower teachers, the outcome may be just as debilitating – namely, future educators taught to follow a predetermined set of objectives and methodologies rather than to question and reflect upon the impact of their actions in the classroom (see Wong, 2006, Pennington et al, 2013, and Gur, 2014, for extended teacher-deskilling discussions). Clearly, the teacher education curriculum is very long on learning to follow prescribed methodologies, but very short on preparing teachers to think critically. For example, teacher education courses usually focus on effective pedagogy for students living in poverty, but not on why these students are in this situation or on education's responsibility to promote positive change. Within this type of 'training' program, it is hard to imagine the inclusion of challenging and thought-provoking CIE content which focuses on the impact of factors such as race, class and gender on educational access and outcomes.

Moreover, this obsession with inundating future teachers with rubrics, assessment skills and wholesale adoption of commercial 'cures' for inadequate teaching, such as the Marzano Plan adopted by multiple school districts in Florida and elsewhere (Marzano & Heflebower, 2012), has left virtually no space for courses designed to infuse critical thinking or culturally responsive instruction (Gay, 2010). Few initial teacher certification programs, for example, have the time or inclination to focus on comprehensive inclusive and culturally responsive pedagogy which includes: (1) culturally responsive caring in the classroom; (2) early childhood care and education; (3) mother-tongue instruction to achieve effective and equitable education; (4) culturally diverse curriculum content; (5) provision within the classroom for students with disabilities; (6) effective pedagogy for teaching students living in poverty; and (7) instructional strategies that promote equitable, quality education for all students. While some of these pedagogical practices might be included within various classrooms, they are often overshadowed by the current emphasis on standardization and high-stakes accountability programs.

Of course, it is possible to find CIE courses offered to undergraduate teacher education students in select institutions such as Colgate University (*308: Comparative Education*), though it is more likely to find them ensconced within programs found outside the United States. For example, courses in CIE for teacher education students are frequently found in African and Asian universities, such as: Kenyatta University in Nairobi, Kenya, where the Bachelor of Education degree includes *EFN 402: Comparative Education*; North-West University, Potchefstroom Campus in South Africa, that has *VGLO 624: Education Systems: Structure and Function-CE*); and the University of Hong Kong's *MEDD 7013: Comparative Education – Methods, Issues and Lessons*.

Unfortunately, even if multiple teacher education programs were to transform their curriculum to include one or more CIE courses, the issue of qualified academic staff would remain. The majority of faculty employed by colleges of education in the United States, for example, are well qualified in topics such as educational psychology or elementary mathematics methodologies, though few have the qualifications to teach extensive CIE courses or programs. However, with additional mentoring and the inclusion of faculty from disciplines including sociology, anthropology or world studies, for example, it would be possible to provide faculty qualified to lead study-abroad programs enhanced with select CIE perspectives.

Methodology and Data Sources

To assess the ability of study-abroad courses to infuse significant aspects of CIE into teacher preparation courses, a systematic review of pertinent literature was conducted, along with an analysis of participant experiences within a 1995 Fulbright-Hays Group Projects Abroad in Singapore and Malaysia (11 participants), a 2011 Fulbright-Hays Group Projects Abroad in Botswana (11 participants), and two study-abroad programs in Botswana during 2013 and 2014 (10 participants in each program), that were part of a US Department of State grant, *Capacity Building Program for U.S. Undergraduate Study Abroad*, awarded to the University of Central Florida (UCF) and the University of Botswana in August 2012.

The overarching objective of all four study-abroad programs was to focus on participant internalization of the notion that culture is a major variable in society and schooling, and as such must be valued by educators as a means to promote educational equity and equality among all students. To this end, participants enrolled in UCF's *EDG 4954: International Education Field Experiences*, a course which included an examination of historical and current critical issues within the host's national school system from both academic and experiential perspectives, as well as an appreciation of the challenges faced by local educators (such as the effects of poverty, exceptionality, race, ethnicity, language and gender on access to quality education). The course was also designed to allow students to gain insights into select CIE objectives, including: (a) understanding how the national system of education evolved within particular historical and cultural contexts; (b) exploring how education impacts national development; and (c) acquiring and using skills necessary to critically analyze key issues within the host country's educational system (such as the impact of mother tongue on educational access).

To assess the impact of study-abroad programs on participants' knowledge base and dispositions, factors including perceived challenges and rewards, perspectives on cultural issues, and the expected impact on their future teaching careers were examined. To this end, all participants completed mandatory written assignments, assessments, reflections and questionnaires. For example, students were required, both before and after the completion of their overseas study program, to respond to questions such as, 'How might religion and/or religious affiliation affect the educational and life chances of children in your host country?' Students were also required to develop a research project that focused on 'one challenge, such as poverty, that impacted the quality of life and educational opportunities within the host country, and how this challenge was dealt with.'

In addition, two research instruments were used to: (1) measure participants' knowledge of the local area (e.g., geography, history, culture and education), the national language, and perspectives on cultural issues prior to orientation and at the conclusion of their program; and (2) obtain pre-and post-program reflections through open-ended questions such as, 'Compare your initial expectations of your host country with the impressions you have now. How do they compare? Has there been much change? Why or why not?' and 'What were your most rewarding and most challenging experiences during the study abroad program?' Results were analyzed, with open-ended responses grouped within overarching categories derived from the participants' responses. For example, responses to 'most rewarding' and 'most challenging' experiences were grouped under: *Schools/Education* (e.g.

classroom observations, student discipline and teacher conversations); *Cross-Cultural Exchanges* (e.g. language issues); *Geographic and Historical* Sites (e.g. visits to tropical rainforests or caves); *Personal Relations* (e.g. making new friends and irritating habits of participants); *Physical Environment* (e.g. weather issues); and *Lectures and Schedules* (e.g. length/number of lectures and packed schedules).

Data were tested using univariate statistics such as frequency distributions and percentages – statistical procedures deemed appropriate for managing descriptive assumptions (one variable). In addition to these quantitative procedures, a qualitative analysis of participant responses, highlighted by participant journal excerpts, was included to provide a clearer understanding of a program's unique challenges and rewards.

Findings

This discussion begins with a focus on the relationship between international experiences and participants' knowledge base and perspectives regarding the rewards and challenges of their study-abroad experiences.

Basic Knowledge Acquisition

Whether from assigned coursework, group orientation sessions, and/or in-country activities while in Southeast (SE) Asia or Botswana, results indicated an increase in participants' knowledge base after participation in the project. For example, participants in the 1995 SE Asia program ($N = 11$) doubled their factual knowledge of SE Asia and the Bahasa-Malaysia language. More specifically, the average knowledge base of the area and of the Bahasa Malaysia language increased from 37% to 65% (area knowledge and language scores were not separated). Similar gains were obtained from all three programs in Botswana, where participants also doubled their basic knowledge of Botswana and southern Africa. For example, in the case of the 2014 Botswana program ($N = 10$), general knowledge of Botswana and southern Africa increased from 49% to 94%, while the average level of knowledge of the Setswana language increased from 31% to 79%. Clearly, if the success of study-abroad experiences was only measured by cognitive growth, then all the time and energy contributed to these study-abroad programs would have been wise investments.

Perspectives on the Quality of Participant Experiences

While obtaining a knowledge baseline is always important, it's quite possible that participants might have been able to acquire this knowledge online or during a few weekends in the library. Perhaps more important, though more difficult to measure, however, were the affective outcomes of study-abroad programs. Gilson and Martin (2010), for example, suggest that while many outcomes and insights might have been obtained without leaving the United States, they reconfirm their belief that study-abroad programs also provide a culturally rich and extended lived experience. Sleeter (2008b) reinforces this perspective when she suggests that these 'extended immersion experiences have potential to promote the deepest learning, mainly because they compel a person to deal with discomfort and confusion, and to learn from other people in the host cultural context' (p. 9).

This study of study-abroad programs in SE Asia and Botswana focused on participants' perceptions of program quality in order to assess the propensity of these programs to provide transformational experiences. Through an open-ended journaling format, participants were asked to identify and reflect upon their most rewarding and challenging experiences. They were asked to complete this exercise both before their first orientation session and after the completion of their study-abroad program.

Participants' Most Rewarding Experiences

Results reflecting participants' most rewarding experiences were not surprising, though there were some variations over time. At the conclusion of all three programs in Botswana participants indicated that *Educators and Schools* (such as interactions with students or teachers) provided the most rewarding experiences (73%, $n = 8$, in 2011; 80%, $n = 8$, in both 2013 and 2014) – most likely due to their program's emphasis on school activities. However, as the program in SE Asia emphasized the development of area studies/curricular content, as opposed to school service-learning projects, *Cross-Cultural Experiences* (such as participating in local family functions) remained the most rewarding experience for all pre-departure participants (100%, $n = 11$), as compared with 64% ($n = 7$) of the participants at the close of the project.

The following journaling excerpts help illustrate these perspectives. For example, at the completion of the 2013 program in Botswana, one participant reiterated the importance of experiences in schools when she mentioned: 'The most rewarding experience for me was meeting incredible students who are full of life and eager to learn. Their resilience is inspiring' (Participant #1, Post-Project Reflection, 2013). For the participants in SE Asia, however, *Cross-Cultural Experiences* remained more important, both before and after the program, as reflected in the following statement: 'Getting to know some of the people, and the exchange of ideas and curriculum will undoubtedly be a highlight. Interaction with the people is really the best way to gain an understanding of their culture' (Participant D, Pre-departure, 1995).

The categories of *Geographic and Historical Sites* (such as visiting a rainforest) and *Personal Relations* (such as developing friendships within the group) received minimal mention, particularly at the conclusion of the study-abroad programs. For example, after completing their overseas experience, only 0% to 27% of participants from all four programs mentioned *Geographic and Historical Sites* as their most rewarding experience, and only 0% to 18% mentioned *Personal Relations* as their most rewarding experience.

These results support expectations regarding how study-abroad experiences help to enrich the lives of the participants, and suggest that these participants now view their academic and intercultural worlds from far more complex perspectives – perspectives that are also key outcomes of multiple CIE courses. For example, participants were now more aware of factors which impacted student access to quality education, as well as of the impact of social class and mother tongue on school outcomes.

Participants' Most Challenging Experiences

Research (Merryfield, 1995; Phillion et al, 2009; Alfaro & Quezada, 2010) frequently touts the positive outcomes of study-abroad programs, as mentioned above. However, these programs can also impact participants in significant and unintended negative ways. One study conducted by Koskinen and Tossavainen (2003), which focused on this potentially negative impact, suggested that while some nursing students who participated in a study-abroad program in Finland demonstrated extensive intercultural competence, other students 'were unable to overcome the culture shock and the language barrier sufficiently to allow the intercultural learning process to be initiated' (p. 376). This phenomenon was corroborated by a study by Foronda and Belknap (2012) of a program in Ecuador. In this instance, the researchers found that

> the stress of language, culture, education, and housing inhibited
> students' ability to participate and learn... Participants
> experienced an emotional journey comprised of fear,
> shock/surprise, frustration, and sympathy as opposed to empathy.
> No participant demonstrated transformation or a desire to take
> social action in the future. (p. 158)

To determine if these negative outcomes also occurred in the SE Asia and Botswana programs, all participants ($n = 42$) were asked to identify and reflect upon their most challenging experience(s). As with their most rewarding experiences, participants were asked to anticipate their greatest challenge prior to arriving in the country, and to reflect upon what they considered to be the greatest challenges once the program concluded. The data indicate that pre-departure participants in all four programs expected that *Cross-Cultural Exchanges* would be the most challenging (ranging from a high of 90%, $n = 9$, in the 2014 Botswana program, to a low of 55%, $n = 6$, in the 1995 SE Asia program). For example, prior to departure for SE Asia, one participant noted: 'I expect that the most difficult experience for me will be adjusting to the language ... to be in an environment where I am totally immersed in this language will be a huge culture-shock for me' (Participant

K, Pre-Departure Reflection, 1995). Similarly, one pre-departure participant to Botswana in 2013 commented: 'I believe my most difficult experience will be learning and truly understanding the culture ... My concern is doing something that may not be correct according to their culture' (Participant #5, Pre-Departure Reflection, 2013).

After completing their program in SE Asia, 45% (*n* = 5) of the participants indicated that both *Personal Relations* and experiences linked to *Physical/Environmental Issues* remained their greatest challenges. For example, as one participant noted: 'The group dynamics of 12 independent Americans! Ha. That was an education in itself that I hadn't anticipated' (Participant J, Post-Project Reflection, 1995). However, with regard to the Botswana programs, results differed between the 2011 Fulbright-Hays program (which focused on the development of area study curriculum) and the 2013 and 2014 State Department programs, which focused on life in Botswana's rural and isolated Remote Area Dweller schools (RADs). In 2011, 64% (*n* = 7) of the pre-departure Fulbright-Hays participants expected *Cross-cultural Exchanges* to be the most challenging, while after program completion, 55% (*n* = 6) of the participants now indicated that *Personal Relations* had become the greatest challenge. However, while pre-departure participants in both the 2013 and 2014 Botswana programs also perceived *Cross-cultural Exchanges* to be the most challenging (80%, *n* = 8, and 90%, *n* = 9, respectively), like the Fulbright-Hays participants, their perceived challenges changed over time. After completing their study-abroad program in Botswana, 80% (*n* = 8) of the 2013 participants continued to perceive *Cross-cultural Exchanges* as being the most challenging, while 40% (*n* = 4) now viewed their experiences in the rural schools to be the greatest challenge. For example, an excerpt from one participant's journal in 2013 included the following statement on the challenges faced during their in-school immersion: 'The most difficult experience was witnessing the ... conditions that some students must cope with in their boarding schools' (Participant #1, Post-Project Reflection, 2013). This perception grew stronger in 2014 (perhaps with a more extended experience in Botswana's RADs), when 80% (*n* = 8) of the participants indicated that *Schools/Educators* were now their greatest challenge. For example, at the conclusion of the 2014 program, one participant stated:

> Having to witness the way the children ... were living and being treated had to be the most difficult for me. Students were at times denied access to a decent meal, clothing, and even a bed... In addition to these unfortunate living conditions, it had become apparent that students ... were denied equal, adequate access to education. It was observed that some teachers were neither interested nor committed to students' personal and educational growth... Most of the children seemed to be emotionally strained from these burdens ... and some even seemed confused by my

kindness and affection. (Participant #4, Post-Program Reflection, 2014)

Clearly, these experiences, coupled with participants' reflections, helped them to build competencies linked to CIE objectives, such as appreciating the linkages between education and national development and the effect of ethnicity, class and mother tongue on students' educational opportunities. Moreover, while not directly linked to CIE curriculum (though clearly related to future classroom interactions), it was of interest to note how group dynamics affected the quality of experiences within two of the programs. As previously mentioned, *Personal Relations*, while not anticipated as a challenge for participants prior to their SE Asian experience, became a far more serious issue at the end of the program. In this particular instance, adult participants found it increasingly difficult to live and travel together over a six- week period due to cramped/shared accommodations, long bus trips and the lack of sufficient time for individual exploration. This led to increased group tension, often triggered by relatively minor issues such as lack of punctuality. Likewise, at the conclusion of the 2011 Botswana program, 55% ($n = 6$) of the participants indicated that *Personal Relations* had become more challenging; a situation which emanated from the growing tensions between one project leader and multiple participants, as reflected by this post-project journal excerpt: 'The most difficult experience has been working with one co-coordinator who refused to engage in group activities (bonding) during car rides, dinners or down time' (Participant #3, Post-Project Reflection, 2011).

However, while these challenges should not be ignored when developing future study-abroad programs, it also appears that positive outcomes, such as the enhancement of problem-solving skills, did emerge from some of the participants' most challenging experiences. For example, one SE Asian program participant observed:

> Despite my frustrations from group dynamics as well as from congested travelling schedules, I have learned significant problem-solving skills and as an individual I have truly developed personally and professionally. (Participant C, Post-Project Reflection, 1995)

The problem-solving skills alluded to often focused on the ability of participants to overcome the challenge of an exhausting itinerary by negotiating schedule changes with their program directors, or solving the problem of annoying individual participant behaviors through applied counseling techniques. Moreover, while many Botswana program participants felt that their immersion in the RADs was their greatest challenge (as RADs were usually populated by minority ethnic groups and situated in rural villages or cattle posts, often without amenities such as running water, electricity or reliable Internet service), this did not keep participants from learning and growing from their experiences. Unlike results reported by Koskinen and Tossavainen (2003) and Foronda and Belknap

(2012), the Botswana program participants' immersion in the project provided a wealth of knowledge and insights that helped inform their socio-cultural experiences, a key outcome of many CIE courses. For example, participants learned first-hand about the effects of poverty and mother tongue on a student's ability to access quality education in both Botswana and SE Asia – objectives central to CIE.

Clearly, the 2013 and 2014 participants faced multiple challenges, such as uncomfortable living conditions in rural areas, concerns over the equality of instruction in RADs, extended and cramped bus journeys, and lack of time to explore Botswana individually. Those challenges, however, also helped forge stronger individuals with a greater appreciation of the 'global village' and a desire to help every child succeed. The desire to build upon their experiences is reflected in the following student comment:

> My most rewarding experience was being able to spend time in the RAD schools. Meeting those children has changed my life and how I perceive things. It has showed me how I need to be appreciative of what I have. (Participant #4, Post-Project Reflection, 2013)

Impact on Future Teachers' Cultural Perceptions and Awareness

To assess the impact of the SE Asia and Botswana study-abroad programs on future teachers' perceived cultural awareness, participants were asked to respond to a series of statements regarding cultural attitudes and behaviors. For example, participants were asked to indicate their level of agreement or disagreement with the statement, 'I encourage a diversity of values, lifestyles and viewpoints.' Participants completed this instrument prior to orientation and again at the conclusion of their study-abroad program. And, while there are always limitations to self-reporting exercises, the data suggest that participants responded in a thoughtful manner, with some items reflecting positive growth over time, while other data suggest a decline, which may in some cases have simply reflected a more critical self-assessment of their cultural-adaptation skills.

As noted in Table I, the statement that received the strongest agreement from participants in all four programs was, 'I encourage a diversity of values, lifestyles and viewpoints', with 80% ($n = 8$) of the 2014 Botswana participants, 70% ($n = 7$) of the 2013 Botswana participants, and 64% ($n = 7$) of the 2011 Botswana participants in strong agreement after the program was completed. Likewise, 64% ($n = 7$) of participants in the 1995 SE Asia study-abroad program reported that they 'strongly agreed' with this perspective. A similar pattern of strong agreement emerged with regard to the statement, 'I prevent stereotypical thinking from influencing my expectations of students.' In all three Botswana programs, 64% ($n = 7$ in 2011) to 70% ($n = 7$ in 2013 and 2014) 'strongly agreed' with this statement at the conclusion of their program, and 55% ($n = 6$) of the SE Asia program participants 'strongly agreed' with this statement regarding stereotypical notions, both before and at the conclusion of their program.

Statement	SE Asia 1995 ($n = 11$)		Botswana 2011 ($n = 11$)		Botswana 2013 ($n = 10$)		Botswana 2014 ($n = 10$)	
	Pre	Post	Pre	Post	Pre	Post	Pre	Post
Strong Positive Response; and/or Increasingly Positive								
1. Encourage a diversity of values, lifestyles & viewpoints.	45% (5)	64% (7)	64% (7)	64% (7)	60% (6)	70% (7)	80% (8)	80% (8)
2. Prevent stereotypical thinking from influencing my expectations of students.	55% (6)	55% (6)	73% (8)	64% (7)	60% (6)	70% (7)	60% (6)	70% (7)
Weak Positive Response; and/or Increasing Weakness								
3. I'm informed about international events	27% (3)	27% (3)	46% (5)	46% (5)	60% (6)	30% (3)	20% (2)	30% (3)
4. Comfortable speaking in language other than English	27% (3)	36% (4)	18% (2)	18% (2)	20% (2)	20% (2)	10% (1)	0 (0)

Note: Pre-departure measures knowledge level prior to orientation; Post-Project measures knowledge level at the end of the study-abroad program. Percentages may reflect multiple responses.

Table I. Participants' assessment of their cultural awareness.

Conversely, it also appears that program participants questioned the strength of previously held cultural attitudes at the conclusion of their study-abroad program. For participants in all four programs, the item causing the greatest concern focused on their ability to comfortably speak in a language other than English. Though all groups experienced intensive, yet brief sessions on the Bahasa-Malaysia or Setswana language, their confidence did not increase significantly over time, with only 36% ($n = 4$) of the participants of the SE Asian program, and only 0% ($n = 0$ in 2014) to 20% ($n = 2$, 2013) of participants in the Botswana program 'strongly agreeing' that they were '[c]omfortable speaking in a language other than English' at the conclusion of their program.

Participants in all four programs ($n = 42$) also reported similar weaknesses with regard to being informed about international events. Only 27% ($n = 3$) 'strongly agreed' both before and after the conclusion of the program in SE Asia that they were well informed about international events, while only 30% ($n = 3$ in 2013 and 2014) to 46% ($n = 5$ in 2011) of participants at the conclusion of all three Botswana programs 'strongly agreed' that they were '[i]nformed about international events'. While these results will certainly impact future study-abroad program orientation content, they also suggest that study-abroad alumni may have a greater empathy toward their future English Language Learner students. Moreover, the results suggest that one benefit from participating in a study-abroad program was the realization that they may not have been as well connected, with regard to international events, as they had once assumed. Clearly, at the conclusion of their study-abroad programs participants seemed more aware of a significant void in their understanding of current international events, which also underscores select aims of CIE such as obtaining the necessary skills to critically analyze educational issues within a global context, with particular emphasis on the role of race/ethnicity, class, gender and language on equitable access to quality education.

Impact of Study-abroad Programs on K-12 Schools

To measure the impact of study-abroad programs on K-12 schools, this study examined the impact of these programs on teachers' professional development and assessment of curricular resources. As only the two Fulbright-Hays programs in SE Asia (1995) and Botswana (2011) included practicing teachers among their participants, results from the 2013 and 2014 Botswana programs will not be discussed in this section.

Teachers' Professional Development

To assess the perceived impact of study-abroad programs on schools, participants in the 1995 SE Asia and 2011 Botswana Fulbright-Hays programs were asked to reflect on how their experiences impacted their professional development, and how it affected their ability to critically analyze curricular materials. As the data in Table II indicate, prior to their departure, 82% ($n = 9$) of the participants in the SE Asia program and 100% ($n = 11$) of the participants in the Botswana program 'strongly agreed' that the greatest impact on their professional development would be improvement in their ability to 'Teach Effectively' (e.g. improved pedagogy, curricular decisions, and the like). For example, before departing for her SE Asian program, one participant commented:

> This experience will further expand my global perspective of education. It will give me great ground for sharing experiences with my students who believe that the world does not exist outside their front doors. It will also provide me with some ideas on how to re-structure the curriculum in my content area. (Participant #6, Pre-Departure, 2011)

However, after experiencing a five-week Fulbright-Hays program that focused on area studies curriculum development, only 25% ($n = 3$) of the participants of the SE Asian program and 18% (*n* = 2) of the participants in the Botswana program remained convinced that their increased ability to 'Teach Effectively' was the greatest positive impact on their professional careers.

Time period	Teach Effectively	Knowledge Enhancement	Infuse Authentic Experiences	More Culturally Sensitive	More Critical Perspectives
SE Asia (*n* = 11)					
Pre-	82%	36%	54%	18%	0%
Depart.	(9)	(4)	(6)	(2)	(0)
Post-	25%	52%	8%	33%	33%
Project	(3)	(5)	(1)	(4)	(4)
Botswana (*n* = 11)					
Pre-	100%	91%	0%	0%	0%
Depart.	(11)	(10)	(0)	(0)	(0)
Post-	18%	18%	18%	45%	45%
Project	(2)	(2)	(2)	(5)	(5)

Note: Botswana data collected in 2011. Southeast Asia data collected in 1995. Percentages reflect portion of participants selecting 'Strongly Agree'. Percentages may reflect multiple responses. Botswana Pre-Depart. = Prior to orientation; Post-Project = 4 months after return to USA. SE Asia Pre-Depart. = Prior to orientation; Post-Project = One year after return to USA.

Table II. Impact on Professional Development percentage and number of participants who 'strongly agreed'.

However, at the completion of their programs, 52% (*n* = 5) of the participants of the SE Asian program now believed that the program's greatest impact on their professional development was 'Knowledge Enhancement' (i.e. improved SE Asian area studies content), while 45% (*n* = 5) of the participants in the Botswana program 'strongly agreed' that both 'Cultural Sensitivity'(such as empathy for students' cultural differences) and 'A More Critical Perspective on US Education' (such as increased critical perspectives on content/curriculum and educational materials in US classrooms) reflected the greatest programmatic impact on them as professional educators. One participant at the conclusion of her program in Botswana, for example, mentioned how the project helped increase cultural sensitivity among her students:

> I can already see a positive impact on my educational profession.
> My students have been exposed to the culture of Botswana
> through a storybook I wrote, they have watched a video I created
> on my experiences abroad, and they have viewed a 'Classroom

> museum' of artifacts I brought home. Their knowledge on travel, culture, and diversity is growing because of my personal experiences. (Participant #3, Post-Project, 2011)

And another participant, reflecting on her experiences in Botswana, mentioned that it made her more critical of US education, stating: 'It made me more aware of ethnic groups that are not strongly represented in the curriculum' (Participant #4, Post-Project, 2011).

Impact on Teachers' Assessment of Curricular Resources

To assess the impact of the SE Asian and Botswana study-abroad programs on teachers' ability to critically evaluate classroom materials, participants were asked to reflect on a series of statements regarding their ability to assess curricular resources, such as 'I know where to obtain bias free educational materials' and 'I regularly supplement curriculum with materials that are culturally appropriate.'

Comparing responses over time, the average percentage of participants in the Botswana program who 'strongly agreed' with all four statements was 34% (ranging between $n = 2$ and $n = 5$) before departure and 61% (ranging from $n = 4$ to $n = 8$) after returning home. From these data, it appears that experiences in Botswana were associated with a growth in confidence regarding participants' ability to obtain quality curricular resources and to exhibit appropriate professional practices. Moreover, Botswana participants reported the strongest positive growth in two areas over the course of their program. Thirty-six percent ($n = 4$) of the participants prior to the program and 73% ($n = 8$) of the participants after the Botswana program 'strongly agreed' that '[d]iversity/global materials are an integral part of my curriculum' and that they '[r]egularly supplemented curriculum with culturally appropriate materials'.

Overall, the Botswana study-abroad program had a positive impact on participants' awareness of the need for culturally appropriate and bias-free classroom materials. These findings also underscore the assertion that one of the advantages of study-abroad programs is that they help educators develop deeper consciousness about other cultures, as well as their own, thus ultimately helping participants to become more effective teachers in their own local environments.

In contrast, responses from participants in the SE Asia program indicate a negative pattern, wherein participants became less confident in the quality of curricular materials currently in their classrooms or of their ability to include these materials in their lessons after spending almost six weeks in Singapore/Malaysia. For example, as the data in Table III indicate, before departure, an average of 45% ($n = 5$) of the participants of the SE Asia program 'strongly agreed' with statements about the availability of curricular resources, but only an average of 20% (ranging from $n = 1$-8) did so after returning home. In particular, areas indicating the greatest decline and lowest level of support were: 'I know where to obtain bias-free educational materials' and 'I know how to evaluate instructional materials for fair treatment of cultural diversity.' In both instances, 45% (n = 5) of participants 'strongly agreed' before departure, but only 9% (n = 1) 'strongly agreed' at the completion of the study-abroad program.

Statement	Southeast Asia (n = 11)			Botswana (n = 11)		
	Pre	Post	Change	Pre	Post	Change
1. Know where to obtain 'bias free' educational materials	45% (5)	9% (1)	−36	18% (2)	36% (4)	+18
2. Evaluate instructional materials for fair treatment of cultural diversity	45% (5)	9% (1)	−36	46% (5)	64% (7)	+18
3. Diversity/global materials are an integral part of curriculum	45% (5)	36% (4)	−9	36% (4)	73% (8)	+37
4. Regularly supplement curriculum with materials that are culturally appropriate	45% (5)	25% (8)	−20	36% (4)	73% (8)	+37
Category average	*45%*	*20%*	*−25*	*34%*	*61%*	*+27 (3)*

Note: Botswana data collected in 2011. Southeast Asia data collected in 1995. Percentages reflect portion of participants selecting 'Strongly Agree'. Botswana 'Pre' = Prior to orientation; 'Post' = 4 months after return to USA. SE Asia 'Pre' = Prior to orientation; 'Post' = One year after return to USA.

Table III. Participants' assessment of Curricular Resources and Practices percentage and number of participants who 'strongly agreed'.

While at the outset these results may appear problematic, when we reflect upon the type of learning environments experienced in Botswana (a nation struggling to provide equitable education for all) and in SE Asia (nations with well-educated populations, high educational expectations and high-quality learning materials), these results are more understandable. It appears that participants in the SE Asia program realized that in comparison with Singapore and Malaysia, their own US classrooms contained a relatively poor quality of curricular materials, and that this caused program alumni to critically assess their classroom materials. This realization was coupled with participants' insistence that their school administrators acquire more appropriate materials, particularly those focusing on world history, geography and/or literature. In the case of the participants in the Botswana program, whose new knowledge of Botswana also allowed them to be more critical of curricular materials in their own classrooms, it was noted through journaling and post-program debriefings that these program alumni were now gaining more confidence in their ability to use appropriate materials in their classrooms. Moreover, the participants in the SE Asia project became far more critical of the American educational system, while Botswana program participants' appreciation of their own US system grew. Based on these data, we might conclude that while study-abroad programs have a positive impact on participants, they also have inherent challenges and complexities, especially with regard to curriculum integration, reform and the infusion of transformational strategies.

The Way Forward: concluding remarks

This chapter will close by returning to its initial focus on how study-abroad programs can provide an alternate means of infusing CIE content within initial teacher education programs. Based on this analysis of four study-abroad programs in Africa and SE Asia, the results suggest that this approach may be a viable means of including CIE perspectives and content within professional teacher education programs – programs which have little or no space (or perhaps inclination) to include CIE content within required course offerings. Moreover, this study has demonstrated how critical CIE content and objectives can be successfully included within study-abroad programs for education majors, and that these perspectives in turn provide participants with the means to more accurately interpret and learn from their international experiences. For example, through their experiences in SE Asia and Botswana, teacher education students were now better able to: (a) understand how national systems of education have evolved within particular historical and cultural contexts; (b) explore how education is intrinsically linked to national development; and (c) obtain the necessary skills to critically analyze educational issues within a global context, with particular emphasis on the role of race/ethnicity, class, gender and language on equitable access to quality education. A case in point is the effect of extended service learning in rural RAD schools, which provides participants with real examples of how ethnicity, language and poverty can effectively exclude students from quality education. When study-abroad courses provide students with the tools to 'make meaning' of their lived experiences through CIE theory and content, those participants not only gain more understanding of their particular international experience, they also gain the means to apply critical pedagogy to their future professional careers.

Finally, not only will the inclusion of CIE content within study-abroad programs enrich and transform the experience for participants and their future teaching careers, it will also provide a base for including more comparativists within traditional teacher education programs. Clearly, a study-abroad experience has often been the trigger that has drawn candidates into the field of CIE, and it may also be the means by which comparativists gain and maintain critical positions within teacher education programs. Granted, many comparativists are currently employed within institutions that do not necessarily have full-fledged CIE courses or programs, though they possess the knowledge to effectively teach education courses linked to sociology, anthropology or the like. However, if we build upon the concept that CIE has a valued place within study-abroad programs, not only will students and institutions prosper, but in addition, more scholars may perceive the field of CIE as a viable and rewarding career option.

References

Alfaro, C. & Quezada, R.L. (2010) International Teacher Professional Development: teacher reflections of authentic teaching and learning experiences, *Teaching Education*, 21(1), 47-59. http://dx.doi.org/10.1080/10476210903466943

Biraimah, K.L. (2001) Teacher Perceptions and Methodologies: a Fulbright-Hays experience in Southeast Asia, *World Studies in Education*, 2(1), 81-94. http://dx.doi.org/10.7459/wse/02.1.05

Bloom, J. (1998) Culture and Conflict in the Middle East: whose Jerusalem? A High School Curriculum. Fulbright-Hays Summer Seminars Abroad, 1998 (Israel and Jordan). Washington, DC: Center for International Education (ERIC ED437300).

Engstrom, D. & Jones, L. (2007) A Broadened Horizon: the value of international social work internships, *Social Work Education*, 26(2), 136-150. http://dx.doi.org/10.1080/02615470601042631

Florida Department of Education (2013) Florida Educator Accomplished Practices. Tallahassee: Florida Department of Education. http://www.fldoe.org (accessed 26 August 2015).

Foronda, C. & Belknap, R.A. (2012) Transformative Learning through Study Abroad in Low-income Countries, *Nurse Educator*, 37(4), 157-161. http://dx.doi.org/10.1097/NNE.0b013e31825a879d

Gay, G. (2010) *Culturally Responsive Teaching: theory, research, and practice*. New York: Teachers College.

Gilson, T.W. & Martin, L.C. (2010) Does Student Teaching Abroad Affect Teacher Competencies: perspectives from Iowa school administrators, *Action in Teacher Education*, 31(4), 3-13. http://dx.doi.org/10.1080/01626620.2010.10463531

Gur, B.S. (2014) Deskilling of Teachers: the case of Turkey, *Educational Sciences: Theory and Practice*, 14(3), 887-904.

Hadis, B.F. (2005) Why Are They Better Students When They Come Back? Determinants of Academic Focusing Gains in the Study Abroad Experience, *Interdisciplinary Journal of Study Abroad*, 11, 57-70.

Jarlais, D. & Stein, W. (2005) Southern Wisdom: tribal college faculty revaluation traditional ways of knowing, *Tribal College Journal*, 16(4), 10-14.

Johnson, C. (1997) India, '95. Fulbright-Hays Summer Seminar Abroad Project. Washington, DC: Center for International Education (ERIC ED414216).

Koskinen, L. & Tossavainen, K. (2003) Intercultural Nursing: benefits/problems of enhancing students' intercultural competence, *British Journal of Nursing*, 12(6), 369-377. http://dx.doi.org/10.12968/bjon.2003.12.6.11245

Kruger, D.P., Gandy, S.K., Bechard, A., Brown, R. & Williams, D. (2009) Writing a Successful Fulbright Group Projects Abroad Grant: voices from a journey to South Africa, *Journal of Geography*, 108, 155-162. http://dx.doi.org/10.1080/00221340903428772

Marzano, R.J. & Heflebower, T. (2012) *Teaching & Assessing 21st Century Skills: the classroom strategies series*. Bloomington, IN: Marzano Research Laboratory.

McClam, T. & Woodside, M. (2000) Human Services in India: a Fulbright-Hays experience, *International Education*, 29(2), 21-36.

Merryfield, M.M. (1995) Institutionalizing Cross-cultural Experiences and International Expertise in Teacher Education: the development and potential of a global education PDS network, *Journal of Teacher Education*, 46(1), 19-27. http://dx.doi.org/10.1177/0022487195046001005

Millar, K.J. (2006) Teacher Learning from Professional Development 'Abroad'. Paper presented at the International Studies Association 2006 Annual Meeting (Accession number: 27207075). San Diego, CA, March 22-25.

National Council for the Social Studies (NCSS) (2011) Position on *Preparing Citizens for a Global Community*. http://www.ncss.org (accessed 20 February 2012).

Pennington, J.L., Brock, C.H., Palmer, T. & Wolters, L. (2013) Opportunities to Teach: confronting the deskilling of teachers through the development of teacher knowledge of multiple literacies, *Teachers and Teaching*, 19(1), 63-77. http://dx.doi.org/10.1080/13540602.2013.744199

Phillion, J., Malewski, E.L., Sharma, S. & Wang, Y. (2009) Reimagining the Curriculum: future teachers and study abroad, *Interdisciplinary Journal of Study Abroad*, 18, 323-339.

Sharma, S., Phillion, J. & Malewski, E. (2011) Examining the Practice of Critical Reflection for Developing Pre-service Teachers' Multicultural Competencies: findings from a study abroad program in Honduras, *Issues in Teacher Education*, 10(2), 9-22.

Sleeter, C. (2008a) An Invitation to Support Diverse Students through Teacher Education, *Journal of Teacher Education*, 59(3), 212-219. http://dx.doi.org/10.1177/0022487108317019

Sleeter, C. (2008b) Preparing White Teachers for Diverse Students, in M. Cochran-Smith, S. Feiman-Nemser & D.J. McIntyre (Eds) *Handbook of Research on Teacher Education: enduring questions in changing contexts*, 3rd edn, pp. 559-582. New York: Routledge.

Stachowski, L.L. & Sparks, T. (2007) Thirty Years and 2,000 Student Teachers Later: an overseas student teaching project that is popular, successful, and replicable, *Teacher Education Quarterly*, 34(1), 115-132.

US Department of State, Bureau of Educational and Cultural Affairs (2012) Capacity Building Program for US Undergraduate Study Abroad, ECA/A/S-12-1. http://fundingopps.cos.com (accessed 5 March 2012).

Walter, K. (2002) Mexican Muralists: Rivera, Siqueiros, and Orozco. Curriculum Projects, Fulbright-Hays Summer Seminars Abroad Program. Washington, DC: Center for International Education (ERIC ED475821).

Wong, J.L.N. (2006) Control and Professional Development: are teachers being deskilled or reskilled within the context of decentralization? *Educational Studies*, 32(1), 17-37. http://dx.doi.org/10.1080/03055690500415910

CHAPTER 6

Comparative Education at the Undergraduate Level: affirming liberal inquiry as an alternative to the professional teacher education model

IRVING EPSTEIN

The Higher Education Landscape

I begin this chapter with the assumption that context is important, and that if one is to appreciate the role the study of comparative education plays and can play in the future within the academy, one must first acknowledge the landscape in which proponents of the field operate. Few of us involved in higher education in the United States would disagree with the contention that we are in trouble. Although the variety of post-secondary alternatives within the United States setting is certainly impressive, every institutional type, be it the research or the comprehensive university, the community college, the technical college, the undergraduate liberal arts college, or the for-profit school, has been subjected to extensive and sometimes scathing external scrutiny and critique. It is within such a climate that the need to engage students in ways that affirm the importance of inquiry based upon the values of the liberal arts becomes so important, and it is my contention that the study of comparative education presents unique advantages in pursuing this goal. Nonetheless, such a challenge is daunting given the climate in which comparative education academicians reside.

The rising costs associated with attending post-secondary schooling in the face of growing student indebtedness, larger concerns raised regarding the short- and long-term economic benefit of attending college or university, the difficulties in negotiating an appropriate match between educational attainment and career preparation, and the effects of insipid credentialism have all served to raise questions regarding the efficacy of making extended investments in, and commitments to, institutions that comprise the higher education sector. Research and comprehensive universities [1] confront fiscal realities that impose severe reductions in state funding, while federal grant monies have correspondingly dried up; smaller institutions whose revenues are predominantly tuition based confront unkind demographic trends characterized by fewer numbers of qualified applicants whose parents are able, or willing, to make the financial sacrifices that accompany university matriculation.

At the same time, higher education institutions are struggling to define their mission and sense of purpose according to terms that make sense given these pressures. Research universities have difficulty defending the public good derived from pure research that is increasingly specialized and is viewed by many as arcane and incomprehensible to the general public. Those engaged in applied research confront the issue as to why such work needs to be sponsored by the academy as opposed to government or private agencies and corporations (Cole, 2009). More generally, complex institutions tend to develop correspondingly ambiguous missions that rationalize the purpose of their multifaceted activities, but in ways that can be contradictory and unclear. What should the role of teaching be within institutions that have strong research agendas where research is prioritized above the teaching and service responsibilities traditionally associated with faculty work? How do such agendas protect or defer to political and economic pressures that attack academic freedom principles? Whose interests are generally served as universities take upon themselves the very values that mimic the bureaucratism inherent in corporate structures? Although these are issues that have been discussed for years, their irresolution has become increasingly problematic during times of declining resources and increasing financial uncertainty. I contend that a lack of focus upon improving undergraduate student learning is a major reason for public dissatisfaction with the academy, but even those of us who profess a commitment to this goal confront significant challenges.

I teach at a small private national liberal arts institution that is largely, although not exclusively, tuition dependent for its operational budget. As is true of many of its counterparts, the commitment to teaching and engagement in the type of inquiry that is associated with liberal education is clear within its mission statement and is widely shared among all campus constituencies. Such inquiry includes, but is certainly not limited to, the development of critical-thinking skills (i.e. distinguishing between good and bad arguments, weighing competing evidentiary claims, identifying and making appropriate textual inferences, successfully utilizing different forms of expression, and developing an understanding of the complexities of social interaction as well as the natural world of which we are a part). A commitment to liberal inquiry further compels students to examine the ways in which different forms of knowledge are related to one another and how specialized knowledge contributes to a more sophisticated understanding of broader concepts and principles. It creates the expectation that students will actively seek to learn about topics of which their knowledge is limited and will seek new experiences that can further encourage a disposition to embrace imagination and creativity.

Ambiguity of mission is not a problem for most liberal arts institutions. However, rising tuition costs and a general reticence regarding the importance of the liberal arts in contributing to students' career preparation create significant challenges in continuing to attract a capable student body over the long term. In addition, the promises of online learning and the attraction of community college curricular alternatives have created their own set of pressures that highlight comparable affordability issues. A proliferation of advanced degree programs beyond the bachelor's degree has further contributed to an undermining of the intrinsic value of the undergraduate experience. Post-undergraduate enrollments typically expand in times of job scarcity as the search for a more inexpensive undergraduate option intensifies. Indeed, it is paradoxical that at the same time that the liberal arts model is gaining greater international currency, particularly within Asian countries that have traditionally constructed centralized examination-driven educational systems (Klebnikov, 2015), the value of the United States undergraduate liberal arts experience has been subject to increasing skepticism.

None of these factors is surprising to those whose work primarily involves teaching at the undergraduate level. As teachers and scholars who work within the education field though, there are additional complexities at work that make such challenges even more daunting than they are for our colleagues trained within the arts, sciences and professional disciplines. Schools and departments of education are often viewed as service providers to their larger institutions rather than as spaces where the scholarship and teaching that is of intrinsic value to the academy that is housed. Largely associated with those teacher preparation responsibilities that give the educational unit its greatest degree of public visibility, these programs have been in recent years subjected to national criticism in the United States (Levine, 2006). The perception that prospective and novice teachers graduate from educational programs that lack quality and poorly prepare their graduates to enter the teaching profession is widespread and shared by policymakers across the political spectrum. Hence, the growth of a standards movement that has rationalized the usurpation of faculty control over teacher education curriculum on the part of state administrators, policymakers and politicians belies a trend that has been entirely predictable. At the federal level, policies embedded in the No Child Left Behind Act and the Race to the Top initiative have added support to lower-level initiatives promoting the narrowing of institutional control over the design and management of teacher education programs. Not surprisingly, the success these actors have experienced in attacking educational faculty autonomy with regard to curricular decision-making has foreshadowed even broader efforts to restrict academic freedom for the entire professoriate; efforts in Wisconsin to severely restrict and/or eliminate professorial tenure within its state public higher education institutions are an ominous example of this tendency (Davey & Levin, 2015).

Calls to shut down schools and colleges of education, and the programs they promote, are frequent, and in times of fiscal pressure these demands have to be taken seriously. At the residential liberal arts institutional level, small programs that train teachers have become increasingly expensive to operate because they are inherently labor intensive; many have become constricted or have been totally eliminated. As a result, teacher education proponents in most cases acceded to the demands of enhanced curricular standardization as an affirmation of their commitment to embrace the professionalism that the standards movement is supposed to depict (Weingarten, 2009). It is my contention that such a stance is extremely counterproductive, a claim that will be expanded upon later. In sum, the general setting in which the comparative education field is situated is contentious and problematic, even though it operates according to a logic that differs markedly from the recent efforts to manufacture and regulate a professionalized academic discipline. Nonetheless, I contend that comparative education can play an increasingly important role in reconsidering the relationship between education and the liberal arts in spite of the fact that it has traditionally been afforded ancillary status within the academic units where it has been housed (Epstein, 2007).

Comparative Education as an Academic Field

The urge to advocate in favor of policy reform as a result of investigating practices outside one's specific educational milieu was present among the early so-called founders of the comparative education field, as notions of a 'science of education' evolved and became increasingly systematic and formalized (Gautherin, 1993). Indeed, a recognition that the effects of comparative research would and should necessarily have robust policy implications for both the researcher's own country and the subject of one's investigation has been strongly present and widely accepted since the field's inception. By the early twentieth century, educational scholars trained in the humanities and the social sciences largely focused upon conducting broad-based analyses of comparative education issues, either adopting a systemic approach to the study of education in a particular country or region, or focusing upon cultural factors that supposedly influenced the formation of such systems with particularly identifiable characteristics. As western views of the social sciences evolved and adopted increasingly methodologically sophisticated and complex analytical tools, comparativists took heed, appropriating many of the same tools for their own research projects. An eclecticism of approach – from the use of large-scale survey research to the single case study, from the collection of easily quantifiable data to a reliance upon ethnographic method – has thus characterized the field over the past six decades, even as scholars have struggled with incorporating both ideographic and nomothetic methodological orientations within their work (Przeworski & Teune, 1970; Vavrus & Bartlett, 2013). Arnove (2013) has categorized the field as including scientific, pragmatic and global emphases in an analysis that further reiterates its eclecticism.

Regional specialization has also been a traditional area of emphasis within the field. Profiting from the growth of area studies centers at leading research universities in the late 1950s and 1960s, which was perpetuated with the passing of the National Defense in Education Act in 1958 at the height of the Cold War, the importance of obtaining linguistic and cultural competency in a defined region, be it Western or Eastern Europe, Africa, Latin America, East, South or Southeast Asia or the Middle East, became widely accepted. As a result, the faculty at comparative education centers, aided with funding from foundations such as Ford and Carnegie, offered doctoral degree programs that usually required their students to obtain such relevant skills prior to their embarking upon an approved research project that would define their thesis work (Kelly et al, 1980).

An additional emphasis area involved becoming conversant in and subscribing to a theoretical orientation that would provide a strong conceptual framework for one's work. While much of the research involving student learning and teacher education is loosely derived from applied psychology and educational psychology concepts, the social sciences have provided similar assistance to comparative educators. At various times, human capital theory (Anderson & Bowman, 1965), structural functionalism (Coombs, 1968), modernization theory (Adams & Bjork, 1969; Adams, 1977), Freirian consciousness raising (Morrow & Torres, 2002), dependency theory (Altbach, 1980), rational choice theory (Heyneman, 2001), Popperian notions of empirical falsification (Holmes, 1965), world systems analysis (Arnove 1980), post-structuralism (Bourdieu & Passeron, 1977), postcolonial theory (Hickling-Hudson, 2013), feminist theory (Stromquist, 2013), globalization theory (Dale & Robertson, 2009) and post-modernism (Rust, 1991; Paulston & Liebman, 1994; Carney, 2010) have been invoked by their proponents as frameworks relevant to comparative research. In the same way that the traditional social science disciplines remain split with regard to what kinds of perspectives enhance disciplinary understanding as opposed to undermining it, comparative educators have often been quite divided with regard to which perspectives best maintain the integrity of the field and whether proponents of competing viewpoints indeed talk to one another in a constructive manner (Epstein, 1983; Kelly & Altbach, 1986; Masemann, 1990). Given such diversity of perspective, the need to critically reflect upon one's own positioning and status within the field and within the academy, as well as with the subjects of one's research, has also been noted (Epstein, 1995).

Of course, comparative education in the United States has been influenced by a set of specific historical, political and social factors, made visibly evident as the United States asserted its role as the leading global political and economic power during the twentieth century in concert with its Cold War agendas that marked the 1950s and 1960s. International organizations such as the World Bank and the US Agency for International Development played a prominent role in perpetuating an international development model that served such interests, and while that model has been subject to extensive critique (Klees et al, 2012), a general nexus between education and international development was established that continues to frame a good deal of subsequent scholarship, and that remains largely uncontested even when development models are criticized. Unlike countries with a shared Commonwealth tradition, or ones with strong regional ties that are bound by culture as well as geography (Yamada, 2015), comparative education scholarship in the United States can be characterized by its encouragement of pluralism with regard to regional interest untethered to specific historic or cultural relationships, but being heavily influenced by the desire to inform and shape global educational policies *sui generis*.

Pedagogical Challenges and Opportunities

Translating the various dimensions of the comparative education field into an undergraduate course of study offers rewards and challenges to the willing instructor. On the one hand, because of the nature of the field, it is difficult to map conceptual consistency with the same degree of certainty that one might find within a traditional academic discipline. On the other hand, its multi- and interdisciplinary nature encourages interesting and creative pedagogical choices that are less available in more hierarchically constructed curricular orientations. The range of topics mentioned above is representative of the elasticity with which comparative educators have embraced issues deemed worthy of serious investigation. But the challenges instructors confront in translating the concepts and skills most commonly associated with the field involve trade-offs and choices that are not easily negotiated. For instance, we expect students who engage in comparative education study to obtain some degree of methodological expertise with regard to the collection and evaluation of evidence, an awareness of the dynamics of individual and group expression within different cultural contexts, second-language familiarity, knowledge of the institutional role of schooling and a broad understanding of social and political theory. Given such a daunting list of expectations, determining an appropriate level of skill acquisition that should be required before taking an introductory comparative education course at the undergraduate level can be problematic. Should mastery of a second language and/or familiarity with research methods be viewed as necessary prerequisites before accepting a student into one's course? To what extent does one emphasize globalization versus regionalism, survey data research versus case study analysis, or theoretical as opposed to empirical literature in one's presentation of the field? And, most crucially, does one conceive of the introductory comparative education course as a stand-alone survey experience or as a necessary building block for more focused study in a subsequent course offering? There are no formulaic answers to the issues these questions raise, but their presence is indicative of the potential for both conceptual messiness and creativity in the construction of an undergraduate comparative education curriculum that should introduce students to the nature of the field and encourage their further engagement at the graduate level.

Within the undergraduate liberal arts institutional environment, the answers to some of these questions become more easily clarified when one examines what a commitment to comparative inquiry and its affirmation of liberal education values entails. In its essence, the comparative journey is one that demands an embrace of the awareness that it is intrinsically valuable to explore ideas that are dangerous, unfamiliar and discomforting. It further compels one to acknowledge that various forms of human experience create meanings that can be shared and understood with undetermined degrees of certainty, but that the search for such meaning is a fundamental attribute of our humanity. For many 18-to-21-year-old undergraduates, jettisoning the solipsism that marks their worldview is a scary and difficult process. Engaging in comparative inquiry not only encourages them to participate in such a process, it mandates that they do so, and, as a result, they are further compelled to reflexively question the fundamental assumptions that have influenced their learning. They, of course, come to the academy understanding that there is a complex world with which they have only partially been able to engage. The courage to engage with such complexity is not easily acquired, but comparative inquiry offers the intellectual rationale to do so.

Students who are about to embark upon, or who are returning from, study abroad are looking for ways to frame the experience and are naturally attracted to undergraduate curricula with comparative, regional and global foci. International students similarly look to comparative courses as vehicles for achieving clarity with regard to the similarities and differences they encounter while adjusting to the US university or college. But of all of the various comparative courses that are accessible to undergraduates, be they situated in literature, religion, political science, sociology, economics or anthropology, the comparative education course has particular value because of the nature of its subject matter.

For obvious reasons, education is something students believe they know a great deal about. As they are beneficiaries of a system they have been successfully able to navigate, educational policy issues hold a degree of resonance as well as familiarity for them, whether they involve questions of access, equity, discrimination, school financing, testing, language policy, multiculturalism, tracking, dropout, grade repetition, teacher preparation, university entrance, or the like. Students intuitively appreciate the importance of such issues because they understand that these concerns speak to even larger questions involving identity, developmental capacity, personal expression, career aspiration, health, welfare and economic well-being – questions they themselves regularly confront. Because the teacher–student relationship in particular is inherently interpersonal, students easily understand that comparative education subject matter focusing upon curricular, pedagogical and teacher education issues adds needed context and provokes a necessary questioning of their own values and commitments with regard to the teaching role.

It is therefore not surprising that undergraduates who complete comparative education coursework or engage in ancillary experiences related to the subject matter often participate in the deeper forms of engaged learning resulting from high-impact practices that have been lauded by higher education scholars and practitioners for over a generation. Among the activities that have been noted as being most influential in supporting student learning outcomes are study abroad, internship, collaborative assignment and project work, service learning, research with or closely monitored by an instructor, and assignments that allow students to draw connections between different courses and disciplines (Kuh & Schneider, 2008). All of these activities are easily accommodated within an undergraduate comparative education curriculum. Interdisciplinary study invariably invites the construction of boundaries among various knowledge fields that are intrinsically loose and porous. It further invites students to express themselves through the use of elaborated linguistic codes, where students internalize the expectation that they clarify their communicative intentions in explicit ways (Bernstein, 1975); the inherently interdisciplinary nature of the undergraduate comparative education experience reinforces these tendencies. As a result, reliance upon high-impact curricular practice is as much a necessity as it is a virtue for the undergraduate comparative education instructor.

In order to take advantage of students' different comparative and international experiences, not to mention their varied linguistic and research capabilities, student–student collaboration, discussion and group project work are among the most effective tools of elucidating broad conceptual understandings within the field. As has been previously noted, many students who take the comparative education course do so after having studied abroad or do so with the purpose of embarking upon this experience. Upon their return, the opportunity to further pursue research involving the region, culture or country where they have lived is accommodated through coursework but also independent research, monitored with the help of a faculty member or advisor. The same possibility exists for international students as well. In addition, it is becoming increasingly clear that obtaining a quality general education at the undergraduate level involves pursuing activities that demand that the student becomes civically engaged. While there are many forms of civic engagement, it is clear that the term requires a level of intellection girding and reflective thought that extends beyond conventional notions of service learning or volunteerism per se. At the same time, the global dimensions and contexts in which civic engagement is situated have become more appreciated in recent years (Gaston, 2015). The experiences associated with but not strictly limited to formal comparative education coursework, including study abroad and mentored independent study and research, directly address these concerns. So, whether such study is pursued through the formal course or in these other ways, it can play an important role in affirming what we know to be quality pedagogical practices at the undergraduate level. Nonetheless, as has been noted, comparative education curricula do not exist in a vacuum, and in order to understand the possibilities their presence invites for extended engagement in liberal inquiry, a deeper consideration of the pernicious characteristics of the more dominant professional teacher education paradigm is warranted.

The Prevailing Educational Model

The contrast between the standards-based teacher preparation curricula, to which most education students pursuing state licensure are exposed, and the comparative education courses and ancillary activities and experiences described above, is stark. First, it is useful to note that the comparison is not simply one of disciplinary versus multi-disciplinary or interdisciplinary orientation. Teacher education is itself an artificially constructed multi-disciplinary field, selectively borrowing from literature associated with applied practice, learning theory, human development, curricular construction, planning and assessment, multicultural education, special education, reading theory, and, to a more limited degree, educational policy. When transposed into a set of standards for which all prospective teachers must demonstrate a certain expectation of understanding and mastery, a specific set of assumptions comes into play. I am most familiar with the standards implemented by the Illinois State Board of Education, and use them here as exemplars. Illinois has constructed one of the most elaborate and extensive standards-based systems in the United States, and, although specific standards vary from state to state, the basic principles in play are applicable throughout the country.

For an instructor assigned the task of preparing undergraduate students who are studying to assume the responsibilities that accompany the role of teacher, it is immensely frustrating that the Illinois Professional Teaching Standards have been designed with the purpose of articulating competencies with which *all* teachers, regardless of their experiential level, are presumed to have become conversant. Such an assumption dramatically contradicts the view of teaching as a craft, where skills are viewed as perpetually being polished as opposed to acquired. These competencies are noted within a framework that includes nine standards, whose content is enumerated by 159 indicators. However, students pursuing licensure are additionally required to successfully demonstrate mastery of standards and indicators in their specific content areas. As a result, with very few, if any, exceptions, Illinois undergraduate students who will have made the case that they are eligible for state licensure will have demonstrated some degree of mastery in over hundreds of indicators by the time they complete their teacher preparation programs, the content standards tending to mimic those that have been developed by special professional associations. One can parenthetically note that it is indeed ironic that at a time when proponents of student learning standards are moving to construct alternatives that are based upon higher levels of thinking and inquiry involving less specific content mastery (e.g. the Common Core), professional standards for teachers have not followed suit.

There are a number of conceptual problems with the way in which advocates of the standards movement have approached teacher education that go beyond micromanagement and oversubscription to detail, many of which are made clear by the extreme way in which the Illinois version has been constructed. First, the standard indicators are categorized as being knowledge or performance based. The distinction flies in the face of what we know about the nature of thinking as a series of actions that are intimately part of what we would associate with experiential encounters. While there may be some who wish to resurrect seventeenth-century Cartesian dualism, the divorce between knowledge and action as constructed within this version of the standards movement implies that knowledge acquisition is a static process and performance involves actions that need not be conceptually grounded. Such a conclusion is intellectually indefensible.

The existence of ideological bias is a second problem that is also evident in a reading of the State of Illinois Professional Teaching Standards (Illinois State Board of Education, 2013). Such bias can be seen in their homage to positivism, apparent in the assertion that the collection and analysis of data gathered from assessment measures necessarily plays an important role in determining adequate planning and instruction (as if spontaneity and creativity play no role in facilitating meaningful learning experiences).[2] The view that business interests, in addition to other community organizations and groups, play an inherently constructive role in influencing the teacher's appropriate curricular decision making is indicative of similar partiality.[3] In addition, ideological bias is visible in the contention that one can become aware of the roles different groups play in influencing educational policies without acknowledging power differentials and the existence of conflict as being natural to social interaction.[4] In the latter case, because acknowledging the institutional dimensions of racism, sexism, homophobia and disability discrimination is politically dangerous, sanitized references to the importance of understanding student diversity are expressed without any mention of the ways in which diverse groups have been oppressed or the role of educational institutions in aiding such oppression. Indeed, the assertions that are presented are framed as unqualified statements of fact that cannot be contested; as such, they ignore many of the scholarly debates within the social sciences about the framing of such content that have been present over the past seven decades.

Of course, when one examines the standards movement, the role of the assessment process, constructed for the purpose of determining degrees of compliance as well as their intrinsic efficacy, cannot be overstated, as this process is even more pernicious than the standards themselves. Instructors are required to complete elaborate matrices demonstrating how every indicator is met throughout all of the teacher education courses that are taught; course assignments are necessarily designed to demonstrate how specific standards are addressed; and internal assessment instruments, such as rubrics, must also be constructed in a compliant manner. For students, the teacher education experience involves more than passing a number of required courses – it also includes passing a battery of externally constructed tests that are expensive and demonstrate questionable relevance to the overall undergraduate curriculum, particularly when considering general education and capstone seminar and project experiences. One of the most controversial of these assessments is the edTPA, created from a partnership with Stanford University Center for Assessment, Learning, and Equity and the Pearson Publishing Company. Designed with the aim of rectifying the weaknesses of a paper-and-pencil assessment of teaching competency, the structure of the edTPA is modeled after the National Board Certification program. In the case of the latter, experienced teachers seeking confirmation of their teaching excellence create electronic portfolios that include videotapes, teaching artifacts such as assignments, lesson plans and activities, examples of student work, assessments and other evidence of teaching effectiveness, and comment upon the evidence they have presented in support of their case. Regarding edTPA, student teachers collect such evidence during their student teaching experience and submit videotape segments of their teaching. They offer extensive commentary based upon categories that include how one plans and evaluates one's own instruction, how one engages students in learning, and how one assesses student learning. The student teacher then submits her/his electronic portfolio for external scoring. It is through this system that the expectations and evaluations of the most transformative and important experiences within the teacher education program become standardized. While individual states set the passing standards for test takers, Pearson contract employees, whose qualifications, training and compensation are determined by the private company, score the portfolios. It is thus the private corporation and not the state that becomes responsible for addressing issues including scoring errors, custody and use of the videotapes after submission of the portfolios, and general confidentiality protection for participants in the process. While these issues include potentially significant ethical questions, it is the profit-making corporation and not a representative public entity that becomes moral arbitrator when such questions arise.

A final comment about the consequences of the teacher education standards movement is in order. It is not surprising that the battery of testing and the increase in course requirements and course content that addressing the standards requires, in addition to a number of other factors, have deleteriously affected student interest in entering the teaching profession (Sawchuck, 2014). The fact that these changes fail to take into consideration teacher-supply issues, or that they make alternative certification programs that require minimal teacher training comparatively more attractive, does not seem to influence movement advocates to reconsider their policies or the assumptions that frame them.

The Comparative Advantage of Comparative Education

By all accounts, the comparative education field holds a number of important advantages over the professionalized teacher education model, if one's goal is to facilitate authentic curricular and pedagogical engagement. Why, then, do its status and standing continue to be so ancillary? One could point to its traditional curricular positioning as an educational foundations/policy studies sub-field, and note that all of the foundations areas have in recent years confronted pressures manufactured by teacher education licensure requirements that have had the effect of truncating their importance. Or one might emphasize the impact of the structural conditions mentioned at the beginning of this chapter in order to fully comprehend the disparity between academic quality and status of the field. However, in so doing, it is important that we remain focused upon the larger picture regarding the political crosscurrents that are reframing the meaning of the public good, as it relates to education and education-related endeavors. The mistrust of public educators that is so pervasive in the United States has percolated within a political environment where the role of government as the foundational guarantor of public interest has been attacked. And in such a climate, the moral imperative to reform educational practice or to promote policies that can positively affect children's lives, which is present both in the calling to become a teacher and in the desire to pursue non-governmental organization (NGO) work related to comparative education training, has also been subject to unrelenting assault.

It is for this reason that the urge to construct a teacher education field based upon standards that supposedly embrace the ethic of professionalism can best be understood. Indeed, at a certain level, asserting that there are attributes common within the teaching role whose mastery is a necessary condition of future professional success can be an attractive claim, for it contradicts the assertion that anyone can teach. It further inoculates education programs against the criticism that they do little more than restrict access to the profession. However, it is my view that such a stance is doomed to fail.

Proponents of teacher education professionalism fail to correctly understand the nature of professionalism and the unique ways in which its role is defined within the education sector. There is a presumption that the quality of a program can be determined by its prestige, defined in terms of the percentage of those who are admitted to the program, its percentage of successful graduates, and its required length for completion. Medical and legal models of post-undergraduate preparation have been invoked as comparisons worthy of emulation as far back as the 1980s, with reports sponsored by the Holmes Group (Tomorrow's Teachers, 1986) and the Carnegie Foundation calling for the creation of professional development teacher education models and the extension of the length of preparation that could easily extend beyond the four-year undergraduate experience (Labaree, 1997).

However, it is clear that programmatic length or competitive admission pressures do not directly correlate to the status afforded one's professional work. With regard to programmatic length, six-year combined medical school/undergraduate degree programs that speed up the training process, in existence for over four decades, do not seem to produce graduates whose status is less highly regarded than their counterparts who pursue traditional medical school trajectories. The relatively short length of time required to obtain a master's degree in business administration gives further evidence for the proposition that length of curricular programming is in itself a poor indicator of professional status. Indeed, teachers whose training often takes place in post-baccalaureate settings, in states such as California, are no more highly respected than their counterparts who receive licenses within undergraduate programs. With respect to the competitive admission claim, although medical schools and law schools have experienced strikingly disparate enrollment trends, commensurate with national demographic changes and the increasing costs of attending school at different periods of time, one would be hard pressed to argue that the status of those entering these professions has ever been adversely affected in a direct way as a result of enrollment competitiveness.

Instead, professional status is more directly related to the conditions of one's work and the degree of autonomy one possesses in negotiating those conditions. Professions such as education, nursing, social work and police work fall within the category of street-level bureaucracies (Lipsky, 2010). In such cases, entry professionals do not have the ability to choose those whose needs they are required to meet. The teacher, as is true of other street-level bureaucrats, is additionally subject to the direction of mid-level managers who impose universalist rules and regulations one is required to follow. Adhering to such expectations while meeting the diverse and individual needs of one's clientele creates inherent contradictions within the working environment that street-level bureaucrats are expected to resolve. The freedom they exercise as they attempt to do so is what allows these professionals to thrive in spite of their circumscribed autonomy. Other factors that play a more influential role in determining teachers' comparatively low professional status include the enduring historical conditions that have created a gendered and poorly paid workforce and the lack of differentiated career options available as a classroom teacher (Ingersoll, 2004). Taking all of these factors into account when assessing the nature of professionalism and the status of teachers, it seems particularly misplaced to focus on teacher education programs as the primary source and ultimate solution to the challenges those entering or ensconced in the profession endure. Although fear can produce strange outcomes, in this case, proponents of the standards movement have in the name of skill acquisition embraced attitudes that legitimize teacher deskilling. At the very time when teachers need the freedom and support to create positive learning opportunities for all children, their nascent understandings of the nature of their work are framed by a profound mistrust in their intellectual and emotional intelligence, resulting in the promotion of bureaucratic officiousness rather than independent and creative problem-solving.

An emphasis upon teacher preparation and the attribution of its weaknesses to systemic educational failure have implications that extend beyond issues of professional status, teacher role and teacher education. Such a focus detracts from more crucial aspects of educational reform that have a larger impact upon student learning, such as the disparate funding patterns and accompanying diminution of resources available to students attending schools most in need of support – a school-to-prison pipeline exacerbated by increased testing and the narrowing of curriculum that such practices invite, as well as by the effects of systemic unemployment and poverty upon intra-family and family/school relationships. Although the importance of teacher education as a contributing factor to educational quality should not be minimized, its significance should not be exaggerated to the point whereby other factors are ignored or receive scant attention. In fact, it is because the causes of educational failure are complex, multi-faceted and inter-related, and the solutions to educational problems are difficult to discern let alone implement, that there is a prescient need for teachers who are educated with the understanding that the search for truth invites an appreciation of ambiguity, a perspective developed through comparative education.

The real comparative advantage that students who pursue a comparative-education curricular focus possess over their counterparts lies in their ability to employ inquiry as a mode of learning, acquiring the confidence that encourages them to question conventional wisdom in the process. At the undergraduate level, this expectation is communicated when nascent efforts by students to engage in meaningful comparative work are supported in a variety of settings and contexts. At the graduate level, the inquiry process is further refined and polished. However, in both settings, the field's elasticity becomes a virtue. To be fair, the criticism that comparative educators too often fail to engage with one another, particularly when they remain stuck in their advocacy in favor of different methodological and theoretical approaches, is certainly a relevant concern (Epstein, 1983). However, the fact that diversity of approach is a fundamental characteristic of the field also serves as an important model for the undergraduate student who can relate to its presumption that all conceptual frameworks can be subject to analysis and critique. That student also becomes aware of the variety of tasks that must be employed in order to address recurrent social problems and the ways in which many aspects of these problems are inherently interconnected. Whether this student decides to pursue teaching as a career either in North America or in an international setting, or decides to work for an NGO or international agency, exposure to undergraduate comparative education concepts and related practices encourages the student to embrace rather than fear contingency. Such a disposition is necessary when one works in environments where considerations of achievement, success, progress and failure become inherently fluid. It is therefore disappointing that as state-mandated teacher education programs are increasingly expanding curricular requirements, teacher education often turns into a four-and-a-half-year to five-year enterprise. As a result, the possibility of including comparative education coursework within the generic teacher education curriculum design becomes more remote.

What Needs to Be Done

In the 1970s, Uri Brofenbrenner (1979) argued in favor of an ecological model of human development that focused upon the importance of understanding the interaction between the individual and various environmental settings that constitute a series of interconnected systems affecting a person's lifespan development. One could not effectively understand the ways in which individuals developed without examining the effects of parenting, friends, teachers and significant adults *and their interactions* upon the child. But in addition, one needed to further examine the ways in which these representatives from differing social institutions connected and related to one another, and one would further need to examine the influence of environmental settings where one's engagement was decidedly passive rather than active. The social policy implications of Brofenbrenner's theory are obvious: that in understanding the needs of individual children, one cannot limit one's scope to exploring her/his modes of interaction within any one environmental setting, and it is imperative that we seek to discover the ways in which these various settings complement or negate the others' influences. Edward Zigler, founding director of Head Start, also created a School for the 21st Century program at Yale University with Matia Finn-Stevenson that has attempted to create a national network using the school as a center for family support (School of the 21st Century, n.d.). Together, the theoretical work of Brofenbrenner and Zigler's social policy activism represent the direction those committed to reforming teacher education will have to pursue if teacher education is to remain relevant within the American academy.

At the same time, it is becoming increasingly clear that the academy will have difficulty supporting professional schools and programs that define their scholarship and teaching through the manufacture and promotion of artificial curricular specialization as a means of protecting curricular turf. Twenty-first-century teachers in the United States will be forced into acquiring an understanding of the ramifications of child obesity as well as lesson-planning formation. They will need to become conversant with the effects of physical trauma and street violence upon students' mental health as well as with the mechanics of test construction. In addition, they will be expected to take appropriate action in support of students who are perpetually hungry or homeless, while also creating an effective classroom learning environment. As a result, teacher education will have to expand its focus if it is to prepare future teachers for the challenges they will inevitably confront. Such an expansion of curricular scope is in direct contradiction of current patterns that privilege enhanced specialization in the hopes of demonstrating disciplinary expertise. Those who work within schools and programs in education, social work and public health will need to discover curricular synergies and complementary conceptual approaches if they are not only to help their students successfully fulfill the obligations of their respective professional careers, but also to reassert and maintain relevance within the academy. The comparative education field offers a compelling model as to how such a transformation should proceed. At the undergraduate level, comparative education coursework and the ancillary learning activities and experiences that encourage student interest in the field (i.e. study abroad, second-language acquisition, independent research, and deep exposure to cultural, political and social similarity and difference) are popular because they promote the importance of liberal inquiry and reaffirm the utility of the liberal arts. The high-impact learning practices that sustain student interest are easily supported and promoted through exposure to an interdisciplinary and multidisciplinary field with pragmatic as well as theoretical underpinnings. Indeed, with particular reference to US students pursuing study-abroad opportunities, independent providers such as the School for International Training (in Santiago) and the Danish Institute for Study Abroad (in Copenhagen) are offering specific courses in comparative education and cross-cultural studies of childhood and youth.

From a pragmatic perspective, when undergraduate students are exposed to the work of comparative education scholars, they quickly realize that it is important that they become conversant in knowledge areas that touch upon community building and public health, as well as education. In so doing, they quickly are asked to comment upon some fundamental comparative questions. For example, when the infant mortality rate in Washington, DC is the worst of its kind among the 25 wealthiest capitals of developed nations (Results for Children Annual Review, 2015), is it fair to conclude that the conditions that create such an outcome differ little from those to which infants and newborns are exposed in the Global South? Or, is the gender discrimination apparent within educational systems throughout the world fundamentally different from that which is evident in the United States? Or, are the educational practices and therapies invoked to treat refugee children and returning child soldiers useful in addressing the trauma victims of gang violence experience in the inner city? Such are the types of questions comparative educators ask of themselves all the time, and these are the types of questions whose importance resonates with undergraduate students involved in liberal inquiry. Such questions inform the undergraduate sensibility because their resolution has profound moral consequence. These questions are grounded in the understanding that one's role as a teacher or as an education policymaker involves an ethical calling, realized through using the tools of reasoning, curiosity, reflection and empathy. It is for these reasons that the model of inquiry the comparative education field invites is worth emulating within teacher education.

Notes

[1] Research universities award a majority of their graduate degrees at the PhD level; comprehensive universities award most of their graduate degrees at the master's degree level.

[2] Standard 3 focuses upon Planning for Differentiated Instruction and states: 'The competent teacher plans and designs instruction based on content area knowledge, diverse student characteristics, student performance data, curriculum goals, and the community context. The teacher plans for ongoing student growth and achievement.' Indicator 3D further states that the teacher 'understands when and how to adjust plans based on outcome data, as well as student needs, goals, and responses'. Indicator 3G states that the teacher 'understands how research and data guide instructional planning, delivery, and adaptation'. Standard 7 involves assessment and notes that 'the competent teacher understands and uses appropriate formative and summative assessments for determining student needs, monitoring student progress, measuring student growth, and evaluating student outcomes. The teacher makes decisions driven by data about curricular and instructional effectiveness and adjusts practices to meet the needs of each student.' Indicator 7G further states that the teacher 'understands how to make data-driven decisions using assessment results to adjust practices to meet the needs of each student'.

[3] Standard 8E states that the teacher 'understands school- and work-based learning environments and the need for collaboration with all organizations (e.g., businesses, community agencies, nonprofit organizations) to enhance student learning'.

[4] Standard 1 states: 'The competent teacher understands the diverse characteristics and abilities of each student and how individuals develop and

learn within the context of their social, economic, cultural, linguistic, and academic experiences. The teacher uses these experiences to create instructional opportunities that maximize student learning.' Indicator 1A elaborates by noting that the competent teacher 'understands the spectrum of student diversity (e.g., race and ethnicity, socioeconomic status, special education, gifted, English language learners (ELL), sexual orientation, gender, gender identity) and the assets that each student brings to learning across the curriculum'.

References

Adams, D. (1977) Development Education, *Comparative Education Review*, 21(2-3), 296-310.

Adams, D. & Bjork, R. (1969) *Education in Developing Areas*. New York: D. McKay.

Altbach, P. (1980) Servitude of the Mind: education, dependency and neo-colonialism, in P. Altbach, R. Arnove & G. Kelly (Eds) *Comparative Education*, pp. 469-484. New York: Macmillan.

Anderson, C. & Bowman, M. (1965) *Education and Economic Development*. Chicago: Aldine.

Arnove, R. (1980) Comparative Education and World Systems Analysis, in P. Altbach, R. Arnove, & G. Kelly (Eds) *Comparative Education*, pp. 453-468. New York: Macmillan.

Arnove, R. (2013) Introduction: reframing comparative education, in R. Arnove, C. Torres & S. Franz (Eds) *Comparative Education: the dialectic of the global and the local*, pp. 1-26. New York: Rowman & Littlefield.

Bernstein, B. (1975) *Class, Codes and Control*, vol. 3, reprinted edn. London: Routledge & Kegan Paul. http://dx.doi.org/10.4324/9780203011430

Bourdieu, P. & Passeron, J. (1977) *Reproduction in Education, Society and Culture*, 1990 edn. London: SAGE.

Bronfenbrenner, U. (1979) *The Ecology of Human Development: experiments by nature and design*. Cambridge, MA: Harvard University Press.

Carney, S. (2010) Reading the Global: comparative education at the end of an era, in M. Larsen (Ed.) *New Thinking in Comparative Education: honoring Robert Cowen*, pp. 125-142. Rotterdam: Sense.

Cole, J. (2009) *The Great American University: its rise to preeminence, its indispensable national role, and why it must be protected*. New York: Public Affairs.

Coombs, P. (1968) *The World Educational Crisis: a systems analysis*. New York: Oxford University Press.

Dale, R. & Robertson, S. (2009) *Globalisation and Europeanisation in Education*. Oxford: Symposium Books.

Davey, M. & Levin, T. (2015) Scott Walker turns to tenure at Wisconsin colleges. *New York Times*, 4 June. http://www.nytimes.com/2015/06/05/us/politics/unions-subdued-scott-walker-turns-to-tenure-at-wisconsin-colleges.html

Epstein, E. (1983) Currents Left and Right: ideology in comparative education, *Comparative Education Review*, 27(1), 3-23. http://dx.doi.org/10.1086/446343

Epstein, I. (1995) Comparative Education in North America: the search for other through the escape from self? *Compare*, 25(1), 5-16. http://dx.doi.org/10.1080/0305792950250102

Epstein, I. (2007) Standardization and its Discontents, in C. Bjork, K. Johnston & H. Ross (Eds) *Taking Teaching Seriously*, pp. 31-49. Boulder, CO: Paradigm.

Gaston, P. (2015) *General Education Transformed: how we can, why we must.* Washington, DC: Association of American Colleges and Universities.

Gautherin, J. (1993) Marc-Antoine Jullien ('Jullien de Paris'), *Prospects*, 23(3-4), 757-773.

Heyneman, S. (2001) The Growing International Commercial Market for Educational Goods and Services, *International Journal of Educational Development*, 21, 345-359. http://dx.doi.org/10.1016/S0738-0593(00)00056-0

Hickling-Hudson, A. (2013) A Theory of Literacies for Considering the Role of Adult and Community Education in Post-colonial Change, in R.A. Arnove, C.A. Torres & S. Franz (Eds) *Comparative Education: the dialectic of the global and the local*, pp. 223-245. New York: Rowman & Littlefield.

Holmes, B. (1965) *Problems in Education: a comparative approach.* London: Routledge & Kegan Paul.

Illinois State Board of Education (2013) Illinois Professional Teaching Standards. http://www.isbe.net/peac/pdf/il_prof_teaching_stds.pdf

Ingersoll, R. (2004) Four Myths about America's Teacher Quality Problem, in M. Smiley & D. Miretzky (Eds) *Developing the Teacher Workforce: 103rd yearbook of the National Society for the Study of Education*, pp. 1-33. Chicago: University of Chicago Press.

Kelly, G. & Altbach, P. (1986) Comparative Education: challenge and response, *Comparative Education Review*, 30(1), 89-107. http://dx.doi.org/10.1086/446569

Kelly, G., Altbach, P. & Arnove, R. (1980) Trends in Comparative Education: a critical analysis, in P. Altbach, R. Arnove & G. Kelly (Eds) *Comparative Education*, pp. 505-533. New York: Macmillan.

Klebnikov, S. (2015) The rise of liberal arts colleges in Asia. *Forbes Magazine*, 3 June. http://www.forbes.com/sites/sergeiklebnikov/2015/06/03/the-rise-of-liberal-arts-colleges-in-asia/

Klees, S., Samoff, J. & Stromquist, N. (2012) *The World Bank and Education Critiques and Alternatives.* Rotterdam: Sense. http://dx.doi.org/10.1007/978-94-6091-903-9

Kuh, G. & Schneider, C. (2008) *High-impact Educational Practices: what they are, who has access to them, and why they matter.* Washington, DC: Association of American Colleges and Universities.

Labaree, D. (1997) *How to Succeed in School without Really Learning the Credentials Race in American Education.* New Haven, CT: Yale University Press.

Levine, A. (2006) *Educating School Teachers.* Washington, DC: Education Schools Project.

Lipsky, M. (2010) *Street-level Bureaucracy: dilemmas of the individual in public services*, 30th anniv. expanded edn. New York: Russell Sage Foundation.

Masemann, V. (1990) Ways of Knowing: implications for comparative education, *Comparative Education Review*, 34(4), 465-473. http://dx.doi.org/10.1086/446974

Morrow, R. & Torres, C. (2002) *Reading Freire and Habermas: critical pedagogy and transformative social change*. New York: Teachers College Press.

Paulston, R. & Liebman, M. (1994) An Invitation to Postmodern Social Cartography, *Comparative Education Review*, 38(2), 215-232. http://dx.doi.org/10.1086/447242

Przeworski, A. & Teune, H. (1970) *The Logic of Comparative Social Inquiry*. New York: Wiley Interscience.

Rust, V. (1991) Postmodernism and its Comparative Education Implications, *Comparative Education Review*, 35(4), 610-626. http://dx.doi.org/10.1086/447066

Sawchuck, S. (2014) Steep Drops Seen in Teacher-prep Enrollment Numbers, *Education Week*, 21 October. http://www.edweek.org/ew/articles/2014/10/22/09enroll.h34.html

School of the 21st Century (n.d.) Responsive Schools Initiative. http://www.yale.edu/21c/index2.html (accessed 31 July 2015).

Stromquist, N. (2013) Women's Education in the Twenty-first Century, in R.A. Arnove, C.A. Torres & S. Franz (Eds) *Comparative Education: the dialectic of the global and the local*, pp. 175-200. New York: Rowman & Littlefield.

Tomorrow's Teachers (1986) A Report of the Holmes Group. East Lansing, MI: Holmes Group.

Vavrus, F. & Bartlett, L. (2013) *Critical Approaches to Comparative Education: vertical case studies from Africa, Europe, the Middle East, and the Americas*. New York: Palgrave Macmillan. http://dx.doi.org/10.1057/9780230101760

Weingarten, R. (2009) The Case for National Standards, *Washington Post*, 16 February. http://www.washingtonpost.com/wp-dyn/content/article/2009/02/15/AR2009021501257.html

Yamada, S. (2015) The Constituent Elements of Comparative Education in Japan: a comparison with North America, *Comparative Education Review*, 59(2), 234-260. http://dx.doi.org/10.1086/680172

CHAPTER 7

Comparative Education*s*
to What Ends?

MARIA MANZON

'Aims-talk', referring to discussions about aims and purposes, has been rather marginalized in contemporary educational theory (Noddings, 2003; Siegel, 2009). In this 'age of measurement', practices of measuring educational performativity are commonly separated from the end purposes for which they are used (Webster, 2015). It is therefore timely to revive the discourse and thinking about aims and purposes not only in education but also in comparative education.

Teleology is the doctrine that the existence of phenomena may be explained with reference to the purposes they serve. This chapter will address the diverse purposes for which comparative education is pursued. The title, partly inspired by the heading of the article by Gregory Fairbrother (2005), refers to comparative educations in the plural. This harks back to the conceptual distinction made by Cowen (1982) between academic (theoretical) comparative education, professional (teacher training) comparative education, and interventionist (policy advice) comparative education, differentiated by their intellectual bases and institutional locations. This chapter mainly addresses the aims of academic and professional forms of comparative education. However, it also presents a hybrid case of a national educational institution where the academic, professional and interventionist aims of comparative education elide and even collide.

The discussion consists of three parts. Part one examines the aims of comparative education from a philosophical perspective viewed from three angles. The field of comparative education is at the intersection of education and comparative inquiry. Thus, this part initially explores the discourses on the aims of *education in general* in order to find a useful conceptual framework for evaluating the aims and purposes of comparative education. Then it examines fields of *comparative inquiry* in order to gain insights on the purposes which define them and how these resonate with comparative education. On a third plane, it reviews how comparative education scholars have defined the field by its purpose. The second part of the chapter adopts an empirical approach. It explores the case of Singapore, where comparative education is *extramural*: its professional and academic forms are almost invisible, overshadowed and curbed by a dominant interventionist purpose of education research. Borrowing the analytical lenses proposed by Nóvoa and Yariv-Marshal (2003), in Singapore, the dominant form of comparative education is as a mode of (educational) governance rather than a historical, social scientific journey. The Singapore case may be illustrative of parallel discourses about the paradoxical absence or eclipsing of comparative education in academic and teacher education programmes in highly globalized societies around the world. Thus, while the philosophical discussions seem to lead to articulate descriptions or prescriptions of the aims of comparative educations on a logical plane, the empirical case presented here makes a contrary movement. It paints a scenario that exhibits conflicts and tensions with respect to *telos*. The third part of the chapter raises questions about the worthwhile purposes of comparative education today and in the future. It suggests the importance of the moral purpose in comparative education.

Elucidating Aims and Purposes: education, comparative inquiry, comparative education

This philosophical discussion on the aims and purposes of education, comparative inquiry and comparative education requires a clarification of terms. While aims and purposes seem synonymous, they have nuances. Both 'aims' and 'purposes' are referred to in the Greek word *telos*. In English, 'aim' is used both as a noun and a verb, to denote a target result. It answers the 'what' question. By contrast, 'purpose' is a noun used to refer to the reason for which something is done or pursued. It answers the 'why' question. Using the two terms together may help illustrate the point more clearly. Take, for example, this statement: 'I study comparative education to learn what makes other countries' education systems successful (aim) *in order to* reform and improve my education system at home (purpose).' The first part of the sentence indicates the aim or target result of one's study, while the second part points to purposiveness in undertaking the study.

Aims-talk in Contemporary Educational Theory

Webster (2015) described the present era as an 'age of measurement', in which education suffers from a means–end dichotomy. Measurement practices of educational performativity (means) are separated from the purposes (ends) for which they are used. The discourse has likewise shifted from education to learning, connoting an emphasis on learning outcomes measured from a psychological perspective (see e.g. Labaree, 2014; Locke,

2015). Just as there has been a linguistic turn, this age could perhaps be called the 'performativity turn'. Lyotard (1984, p. 46) had already singled this out three decades ago when he claimed that 'the goal is no longer truth, but performativity – that is, the best possible input/output equation'. In this respect, 'aims-talk', referring to discussions about aims and purposes (Noddings, 2003), has been marginalized in recent educational theory. It is therefore timely to revive the discourse and thinking about aims and purposes not only in education but also in comparative education.

Examining the purposes of education is, however, a difficult task. Siegel (2009) claims that the most difficult problem for philosophers of education in the present day is that concerning aims. Harðarson (2012) attempted to explain why the debate about the aims of education cannot be settled. He argued that people have an imperfect knowledge of what human characteristics are worth cultivating and that one of the aims of education is intellectual independence. Based on these two premises, according to Harðarson, the purposes of education are radically open-ended and thus cannot be exhaustively described. Rather, a listing of aims of education from Aim_a to Aim_n should always include an 'Aim_k: Education should enable the student to criticise the list and propose a better one' (Harðarson, 2012, p. 233). Similarly, this discussion on the aims or purposes of comparative education needs to be viewed as open-ended and non-exhaustive. While such discussion attempts to undertake a modest meta-synthesis of the aims of comparative education as scholars and practitioners have defined them in different time–space contexts, it does not claim to be definitive and comprehensive, precisely owing to the essence of authentic education and its aims of intellectual independence. Rather, this discussion hopes to join the continuing conversations about comparative education's purposes. Rather than prescribing its aims in a close-ended way, this chapter seeks to stir the waters.

In this respect, Biesta (2009), echoing the need to reconnect with the question of educational purpose in this age of measurement, posed the question of what constitutes *good* education as distinct from effective education. Effectiveness connotes 'an *instrumental* value, a value which says something about the quality of the *processes* ... to bring about certain outcomes in a secure way' (Biesta, 2009, p. 35). By contrast, *good* education refers to *ultimate* values about the aims and purposes of education. Biesta proposed a useful conceptual framework to deliberate about what constitutes good education. He claimed that the question of the purpose(s) of education is a composite question, which can be answered by distinguishing among the three functions of education. These are qualification, socialization and subjectification. Qualification refers to providing the knowledge, skills and understanding, as well as dispositions and forms of judgment, that allow people to 'do' something, whether it be for a specific job or for general life skills. Socialization refers to the ways in which, through education, we become incorporated into particular social, cultural and political 'orders'.

Finally, subjectification refers to processes of individuation (as opposed to socialization) – to becoming a subject – and being independent from a more encompassing 'order' (Biesta, 2009).

Viewing comparative education along this conceptual framework or these dimensions of good education, we can likewise distinguish *good* comparative educations (at universities and teacher training institutions) as those which achieve these three dimensions in a qualitative way. First, they perform the function of qualification by providing students with the knowledge and skills to equip them for a teaching and/or education research career, or to work in policy-related fields. They also aim to socialize students into certain ways of seeing the world through a greater understanding of other cultures and contexts and counteracting ethnocentric biases. And finally, *good* comparative educations enable students to be constructively critical about the indiscriminate use of comparison in education without due regard to context. In this respect, the following comment of Camins (2015) on education's purposes can also be transposed to comparative education:

> Debate about the purposes of education never seems to end.
> Should young people become educated to get prepared to enter
> the workforce, or should the purpose of education be focused
> more on social, academic, cultural and intellectual development so
> that students can grow up to be engaged citizens? ... But it doesn't
> have to be either-or. Education should prepare young people for
> life, work *and* citizenship.

The above discussion has focused on the broad aims of education and its intersection with society. The following section will explore the aims of comparative studies in diverse fields with the purpose of extracting the essential purposes of comparative inquiry.

Aims and Purposes of Comparative Inquiry

In an earlier work (Manzon, 2011), I have compared some fields of comparative inquiry in the social sciences, natural sciences and humanities with comparative education. *Comparative politics* engaged in comparison for various purposes, including an explanatory/theoretical purpose (from description to scientific interpretation and testing relationships among political variables) and a meliorist/practical purpose (e.g. application to policy-making). *Comparative law* looked at different national legal systems as a laboratory to understand solutions applied to similar problems. Among the purposes of *comparative sociology* are to 'deprovincialize' sociological thought by revealing the immense diversity of social configurations; to discover systematic patterns of variations observed from social arrangements to extract 'that which was, if not universal, at least generally true of a large number of cases' (Inkeles & Sasaki, 1996, p. xi); and to systematically analyze and explain why social phenomena differ. *Comparative literature* and *comparative philosophy* aim to give a more comprehensive understanding of literature/philosophy as a whole by extending the investigation of literature both geographically and generically. Interestingly, among the purposes of *comparative anatomy* was to compare the body structures of different species in order to understand how they have evolved from common ancestors (*Encyclopaedia Britannica*, 2015). In essence, these comparative fields of inquiry, to name a few, converge in their purposes of serving as a bridge to link the national with the trans-national, or one tradition, genre, genus with another, a single discipline with multiple disciplines. This is the core of comparative interdisciplinary fields: to overcome disciplinary fragmentation and to 'de-provincialize' knowledge from ethnocentric lenses by observing diverse phenomena as in a laboratory.

These shared purposes of comparative inquiry resonate with those of comparative education. Kandel (1936, p. 406) asserted that 'the purpose of comparative education, as of comparative law, comparative literature or comparative anatomy, is to discover the differences in the forces and causes that produce differences in educational systems'. Likewise, Cowen (2015, p. 466) proposed that comparative education, concretely academic comparative education:

> is a field of study based in universities which works to understand
> theoretically and intellectually the shape-shifting of 'education' as
> it moves transnationally amid the interplay of international
> political, cultural, and economic hierarchies with domestic politics
> and forms of social power.

Moreover, for Phillips and Schweisfurth (2014, p. 22), comparative education also has the 'potential of identifying implications for policy'. To further illustrate the purposes shared by comparative education with other fields of comparative inquiry, I employ and reinterpret here the three metaphors used by Carole Hahn (2015) to elucidate the purposes of comparative inquiry in education. First, comparative education is like a *mirror* used to reflect the image of one's own education system and understand it better. Second, comparative education is like a *window* which helps to widen one's perspectives by learning from other cultures or systems. And third, comparative education is likened to a *microscope* which helps magnify our narrow or small image/understanding of educational issues and systems and their relationships with other societal configurations. These ideas are further discussed below.

Comparative Education Defined by Purpose

After examining the discourse on aims and purpose in the field of education and in fields of comparative inquiry, this section reviews how comparative education scholars have defined the field by its purpose.[1] It classifies the principal purposes of comparative education into three: theoretical, pragmatic and critical.

Arnove (2013) proposes three principal thrusts of comparative and international education: scientific, pragmatic and international/global understanding, viewing these dimensions as interrelated and intersecting. The *scientific* dimension refers to the goal of comparative education to contribute to theory building: to the formulation of generalizable propositions about the workings of school systems and their interactions with their surrounding economies, polities, cultures and social orders. The *pragmatic* dimension aims to discover what can be learned from other societies' education systems that will contribute to improved policy and practice at home. And the third thrust is to contribute to *international/global* understanding and peace, a goal that is perhaps more pertinent to international education than to comparative education. Martínez (2003) adds the *critical* dimension or aim of comparative education, important for the interpretation of educational phenomena and comparative studies. These three dimensions – theoretical, pragmatic and critical/emancipatory–echo the three cognitive interests of Habermas (1971), who is also cited by Kubow and Fossum (2007) in their discussion of the field's purposes. I therefore review the salient points of the authors who define comparative education by its purposes, which I group into three: theoretical, pragmatic and critical. Despite these classifications, these purposes overlap in reality.

- Theoretical Purpose

Several authors defend the theoretical aim of comparative education as inseparable from the practical. A clear advocate of the theoretical purpose of comparative education is Bereday (1964). He suggests that the foremost justification for comparative education is intellectual: knowledge for its own sake. Immediately following this description, however, he cites the two practical goals that comparative education serves: first, to deduce from the achievements and mistakes of school systems, other than their own, lessons for their own schools; and second, to appraise educational issues from a global rather than an ethnocentric perspective. These two practical goals could be interpreted as policy amelioration and international understanding.

Holmes (1971, pp. x-xi) echoes similar two-pronged objectives: 'One aim of comparative education is theoretical. It is to improve our understanding of education as such; and in particular of our own national problems in education. Comparative education has a practical purpose too. It should help administrators to reform their schools more effectively and efficiently.'

- Pragmatic Purpose

Arnove (2013) emphasises that the pragmatic dimension of comparative education lies in discovering what can be learned from studying other societies' education systems in order to contribute to the amelioration of

policy and practice at home. Two 'ancestors' of comparative education –
namely, Marc-Antoine Jullien (1817) and Michael Sadler (1900/1964) –
claim that the international transfer of educational policies and practices is at
the heart of the field of comparative education. Edmund King (1965, p. 148)
suggests that the implicit purpose of comparative education is 'to be useful in
the improvement of school systems', and concludes that the informative, the
analytical and the reformative aspects ought to be present in comparative
education teaching and/or research (also King, 1997).

The pragmatic purpose is also salient in the definition of the aims of
comparative education by Chinese comparativists. In the first textbook on
comparative education published after 1949, Wang et al (1982, cited in Gu,
2001, p. 238), the authors define the aim of comparative education as: 'to
discover the common educational principles and trends in educational
development in other countries, and to draw lessons from other countries'
experiences'.

- Critical Purpose

A third purpose of comparative education, according to Martínez (2003), is
to offer a critical interpretation of educational issues, as advocated by various
scholars (e.g. Altbach, 1991; Nóvoa, 2000; Ferrer, 2002). This aspect of the
field echoes Bourdieu's (1969) idea of the relative autonomy of the
intellectual field – its capacity of refracting external social power – by being
able to transform its objects of knowledge into objects of critique. McClellan
defines this 'critical' contribution of comparative education in the following
terms (1957, p. 9):

> Comparative education ... proves nothing, but what it disproves is
> of utmost importance. It is something like a gigantic magnifying
> mirror; it reveals to us our own faces pitilessly. ... [T]he study of
> comparative education protects us from resting content with
> superficial assurances while fundamental uncertainties still remain.

From another perspective defending a critical approach in a
Habermasian sense, Mason (2014, p. 253) goes further in saying that
'comparative education is best conceptualised as a critical social science,
incorporating an emancipatory interest focused on the distribution of power
and its associated attributes: economic wealth, political influence, cultural
capital, social prestige and privilege, and the like ... to the end of educational
equity'. This is probably more within the interests of international education
development rather than being a definition of comparative education per se.

By way of summary, García Garrido (1996, p. 98) lists six uses of
comparative education:

1. Comparative education helps in knowing and understanding
   educational activity in different communities, countries, nations,
   regions, etc.

2. Knowledge of others' systems enables us to have a more sufficient knowledge and better understanding of our own system.
3. Thus knowledge about others and our own educational systems can lead to an understanding of the principal trends of world education and the choice of better educational futures.
4. Comparative education is an indispensable instrument for the design and implementation of educational reforms and innovations.
5. Comparative education can decisively contribute to international understanding, peace in the world and a gradual elimination of ethnocentric attitudes.
6. It can also be a powerful instrument of educational technical assistance in less developed countries.

The discussion above has elucidated the purposes of comparative educations in its academic, professional and interventionist forms as proposed by scholars in the field. As I had argued in Manzon (2011), the academic definitions of the field are positional. Individual academics, through scholarly discourse, construct the field of comparative education intellectually by codifying the relations of power between the external social structures within which they work (from international and national, down to the local university), the various forms of capital they hold, and the intellectual traditions and criteria that govern their intellectual field.

Diverging Aims and Purposes: the case of 'extramural' comparative education

While the philosophical discussions above have articulated the aims of comparative educations conceptually, the empirical case presented here makes a contrary movement. It paints a real scenario that exhibits conflicts and tensions with respect to *telos*. It explores the case of Singapore, where comparative education is *extramural* (Manzon, 2014). It is almost invisible in academic and teacher training programmes, overshadowed and curbed by a dominant interventionist purpose of comparative education research. Adopting the analytical lenses proposed by Nóvoa and Yariv-Marshal (2003, p. 423), I argue that, in Singapore, the dominant form of comparative education is as a mode of *educational governance* rather than a historical, social scientific journey. The Singapore case may be illustrative of parallel phenomena of a paradoxical absence or eclipsing of the academic and professional forms of comparative education in highly globalized societies around the world. This section briefly describes the macro context of education and society in Singapore, the institutional context of its National Institute of Education (NIE), and the overarching purposes of education research in NIE. I draw on data collected from semi-structured interviews with five senior academics of NIE conducted in 2014, and my insider participant perspectives at the institute, for the purpose of understanding the paradoxical status of comparative education in a nation that actively engages in and with comparative discourses on education.

The Singapore Context

Singapore celebrated its fifty years of independence in August 2015. As a sovereign city-state with no natural resources, it invested in its only resource – human capital – through an excellent education system to build the nation into a significant player in international trade and finance. The priority given by the Singapore government to education is evidenced by its heavy investment in this sector. In 2014, it budgeted 20.3% of total government expenditure, equivalent to US$8.1 billion, on education (Ministry of Finance Singapore, 2015). The primary role of education in nation building is telling of the crucial role schools play in the qualification and socialization of Singapore's multiracial people (Goh & Gopinathan, 2008; Gopinathan, 2013; Chia, 2015). Thus, the delivery and governance of education is centralized under the Ministry of Education (MOE), and teacher training is solely delivered at its National Institute of Education (NIE).

The NIE is an autonomous institution of the Nanyang Technological University (NTU) of Singapore. Its highest governing body, the NIE Council, is chaired by the Permanent Secretary of the MOE. The NIE is thus somewhat a hybrid academic institution within a university system and funded by and accountable to the MOE. The NIE offers a suite of pre-service and in-service training at the undergraduate and postgraduate levels through its 12 Academic Groups. Education research has played a key function to inform policy and practice in Singapore. The NIE's Office of Education Research (OER) was established in April 2008 to forge an NIE-wide programme of research, development and innovation. It facilitates the governance, planning, monitoring, quality assurance and dissemination of education research across the NIE. The OER also administers the Education Research Funding Programme (ERFP), a pool of research funds provided by the MOE (NIE, 2015). In 2013, the OER (2015) announced its six research programmes, which were: learners' social and cognitive development; curriculum and instruction; teacher learning and professional development; leadership, organization and system studies; international benchmarking (under which falls international and comparative studies as a research niche area); and scaling, translation and knowledge management (STKM). The OER particularly seeks to encourage research in STKM that may facilitate the synthesis of research findings from projects in different disciplines, as well as to develop scalable pedagogical interventions to enable systemic improvement in the education system. The nature of the funding source substantially, though not exclusively, shapes the priorities in the research agenda of the institution.

To some extent, it can be said that there are two parallel (albeit non-exclusive) cultures or divisions of work within NIE. On the one hand, there is teacher training offered by the Academic Groups (equivalent to teaching departments). On the other, there is education research managed by the OER and undertaken by full-time research staff who are PhD holders (called research scientists and senior research scientists). Education research at the NIE is focused on K-12 education and is grouped under three research centres: the Centre for Research in Pedagogy and Practice (CRPP); the Learning Sciences Lab (LSL); and the Education and Cognitive Development Lab (ECDL).

The NIE exhibits a fairly tight tripartite relationship between teaching, policy and research. The success of its education system is attributed to this tight nexus leading to a 'unity of vision and mission of the people behind policy, research and practice' (Poon, 2012, p. 19). Poon argues that education policy formulation in Singapore is not only influenced by the nation's economic imperatives but is also informed by the careful use of research and the pragmatic knowledge of classroom practices and stakeholders' interests. Against this backdrop, education research at the NIE is thus situated at the nexus of the MOE (policy-driven), the Nanyang Technological University (academic-driven), and teacher education and professional development (NIE's core business). This gives rise to some tensions on the agenda-setting of research and related key performance indicators for research staff, among others. Within this context, comparative education – teaching and research – will be examined below.

Extramural Comparative Education in Singapore: why the paradox?

Comparative education in Singapore is *extramural*: it is invisible in teacher education, but somewhat visible in education research, albeit for limited and specific purposes. The place of comparative education in Singapore had been explored in contrast with Hong Kong in the late 1960s (To, 1970), and further developments in the early 2000s (Bray & Manzon, 2005). This pair of articles demonstrated a reversal of the status of comparative education in teacher education in Singapore, from having an important position with a Department of Comparative Studies at the then Institute of Education in the early 1970s to its virtual eclipse in the 2000s. This latter phenomenon, clearly described by Tan (2005), holds to the present day, namely:

> the total absence of comparative education courses in teacher
> education programmes in Singapore, [despite] much educational
> borrowing, official interest in foreign models, official visits
> overseas, use of foreign expertise in giving advice, many foreign
> staff teaching in Singapore, and a constant stream of foreign
> visitors who are keen to learn from what they perceive as a
> successful education system. I guess it's a paradox.

Bray and Manzon (2005) offered two explanations to the question of why comparative education is not visible in teacher education and academic research in Singapore. First, proponents of its teaching have not successfully secured a specific place for the subject in the core curriculum. Rather, comparative perspectives are infused into courses of teacher education and professional development – what Tikly and Crossley, 2001, denoted as integration in contrast to specialization. This is elucidated by data from the interviews I conducted in 2014 in which senior academics confirm the primacy of teacher education and the applied aims of comparative education.

> NIE has always been like a normal teacher training institution, it's very much *practice-oriented*, what is fit for purpose for a beginning teacher. We tend to have a very strong core, and by the time you finish, there is no time left for anything [else]. (Academic 1)

> We are not here to do academic studies. We are here to do studies to distill lessons which can be used *for application* ... within Singapore's context. (Academic 2)

> [A] lack of *official interest* has contributed to the moribund state of the field in this country. Because very often in Singapore, I think a lot has to do with official patronage of your field ... You will get people's interest and you'll get students enrolled because a lot of people take their cues from the government. (Academic 3)

While the label of 'comparative education' is absent in teacher education at the Academic Groups, it is visible in the OER's research programmes. Concretely, International and Comparative Studies (ICS) is a research niche area under the International Benchmarking research programme (see ICS, 2015). This bifurcation between teaching and research programmes is rooted in the underlying dual and parallel cultures of academic/teacher education, on the one hand, and education research on the other. Previously, a Centre for International Comparative Studies (CICS) operated within the OER but worked closely with counterparts at the MOE (from 2009 to 2013). Its main work related to secondary analyses of TIMSS, PIRLS, and PISA and their implications for Singapore (CICS, 2015). A senior academic explained the *raison d'être* of this research centre:

> The focus on this would be to bring information and knowledge that will help us *to influence policy development at the system level.* (Academic 2; emphasis added)

Another academic expounded on the role of these comparative studies in the context of Singapore:

> We are happy to be involved in PISA, TIMSS, but ... it is structured for our realities and aspirations. Singapore is very *state-centric*, and largely because of a very strong government. Singapore is also *very comparative* because it is an international city ... It's got that duality about it. (Academic 1; emphasis added)

Thus, the use of comparative education research in Singapore, even within the context of an academic institution like the NIE, is *instrumental*.

> Ours is a much more *instrumental view* of comparative education which fits in with the whole *Zeitgeist* of Singapore. (Academic 1; emphasis added)

The second explanation of Bray and Manzon (2005) for the eclipsing of comparative education in Singapore teacher education refers to academic culture and research assessment mechanisms. Walker and Bodycott (1997, p. 2) observed that 'the primary role of academics in Singapore remains focused on teaching, internal research, and service to the local community'. Contemporary patterns have slightly changed due to the practice of ranking world universities, among which Singapore universities endeavour to compete and maintain their leading edge. This has also impacted the NIE, which is nested within the NTU, albeit as an autonomous institution. Making a distinction between NIE academics and NIE researchers may help gain insights into the issue. As noted above, there are two parallel (albeit non-exclusive) cultures or possibly systems of work within the NIE. On the one hand, academic staff housed in the Academic Groups (or departments) offer teacher training programmes. On the other hand, full-time research staff, affiliated with a research centre, conduct research managed by the OER. NIE academics on the tenure track mode are evaluated following NTU's teaching and research assessment criteria. By contrast, full-time research staff under the OER are not tenure-track. Without being civil servants, their salaries come from the research funds granted by the MOE to OER to administer. These research staff thus operate within a peculiar context wherein impact on the local school system is important to the MOE. Thus, unlike researchers at Japan's National Institute for Educational Policy Research or China's National Institute of Education Sciences, where research staff are civil servants, the NIE researchers are employed on private terms yet paid from MOE funds. Their research orientations are thus not purely for academic/theoretical purposes but are also for improving schools through interventions and, whenever required, for providing research support to policymakers. These can take place through MOE-commissioned projects or by inviting MOE collaborators to form part of the research team, and the like. To some extent, the NIE is similar to teacher training institutions in other countries with an increasing research thrust. The main difference may lie in the looser coupling and alignment between other institutes of education (e.g. in Hong Kong and London) with their government compared with the situation in Singapore.

The above discussions have elucidated the nature of, and the reasons which account for, 'extramural' comparative education in Singapore. A dominant instrumental and pragmatic approach, as well as an interventionist purpose, tends to crowd out comparative education in both teaching and research spaces. Borrowing the analytical lenses proposed by Nóvoa and

Yariv-Marshal (2003), in Singapore, the dominant form of comparative education is as a mode of educational governance. Aspects of the Singapore case may find resonance in other globalized societies where comparative education is paradoxically eclipsed. Thus, while the philosophical discussions seen in the first part of this paper have formulated clear aims for comparative educations, this empirical case exemplifies more complex and dynamic interactions between structure, agency and discourse (see Manzon, 2011). It paints a scenario that exhibits conflicts and tensions with respect to *telos*. The final part of the chapter raises questions about the worthwhile purposes of comparative education today and in the future. It suggests the importance of the moral purpose.

Comparative Educations to What Ends?

As I have argued elsewhere (Manzon, 2011, pp. 225-226), 'comparative education will benefit from the recognition of the power-knowledge relations that shape it institutionally and intellectually, and thus avoid its instrumentalization'. I also queried whether an intellectual field's existence can be determined solely, if not largely, on the grounds of its usefulness. Can a field claim to be useful because it exists? Can it exist without necessarily being useful? A lack of discernment as to who defines the field, and for what purpose it is so defined, runs the risk of the field's potential instrumentalization. By elucidating the subtle power-knowledge relations that are codified in the institutional and intellectual forms of the field, this chapter hopes to have raised awareness of this potential danger not only in this field but in any endeavour creating power–knowledge relations. It also brings into focus the importance of clarifying what epistemological and axiological lenses influence the work that actors in the field do.

Peters (1981, cited by Lovat, 2012) proposed that moral education lies at the heart of all authentic education. He argued for a distinction to be made between instrumentalist education and holistic education distinguished by its values-centredness. Likewise, Habermasian epistemology challenged the authenticity of an education conceived of solely in instrumentalist terms of competencies or outcomes and argued for a values-laden pedagogy, which was not a mere option for religious schools but was suitable for public schooling (Lovat, 2012, p. 382). More specific to cross-cultural comparative education research, Mason (2014, pp. 252) has called on researchers to

> acknowledge the implicit purposes, and particularly, the moral
> and more broadly axiological purposes, that underlie their study.
> They need to ask why they are doing the study; what interests
> motivate them in carrying it out; and what values consequently
> inform the research.

For Mason (2014), comparative education's most worthwhile goal is the emancipatory cognitive interest (Habermasian sense) of a critically oriented social science: comparing across cultures to the end of educational equity. In this discussion, I do not aim to go as far as proposing the emancipatory cognitive interest as *the* end purpose of comparative education. I only seek to stir the waters and put in the forefront the primacy of *moral purposiveness* in comparative education teaching and research. If, as Edmund King said, 'education is, by nature, a purposeful act; and comparative education is a purposive study of that purposeful act' (1965, p. 157), then what is the worthwhile moral purpose of this purposive study?

This chapter has surveyed the general aims of education, of comparative fields of inquiry and of comparative education, in particular. It has also analyzed a case where an interventionist and practical purpose has tended to overshadow the field's academic ends. I conclude this chapter with more questions than answers. What, then, is the worthwhile purpose of comparative education? What is its worthwhile End (*telos*)? What is *good* comparative education? In the final analysis, I suggest that students, teachers and practitioners of comparative educations reflect on the transcendent aims of education. For comparative education to be of real value, we need to transcend such instrumentalist values as marketability, employability and practical value of application – all of which fall short of the lofty aim of authentic education, which is education in what *is* of value: in truth, goodness, beauty and unity (see e.g. Aquinas, 1256/1952).

Acknowledgement

I am grateful to Mark Bray for his comments on an earlier version of this manuscript.

Note

[1] This section draws on Chapter 5 of Manzon (2011), pp. 172-176.

References

Altbach, P. (1991) Trends in Comparative Education, *Comparative Education Review*, 35(3), 491-507. http://dx.doi.org/10.1086/447049

Aquinas, T. (1256/1952) *Disputed Questions on Truth*, trans. R. Mulligan. Chicago: Henry Regnery Company.

Arnove, R.F. (2013) Introduction: reframing comparative education, in R.F. Arnove, C.A. Torres & S. Franz (Eds) *Comparative Education: the dialectic of the global and the local*, pp. 1-20. Lanham, MD: Rowman & Littlefield.

Bereday, G.Z.F. (1964) *Comparative Method in Education*. New York: Holt, Rinehart & Winston.

Biesta, G. (2009) Good Education in an Age of Measurement: on the need to reconnect with the question of purpose in education, *Educational Assessment, Evaluation and Accountability*, 21(1), 33-46.
http://dx.doi.org/10.1007/s11092-008-9064-9

Bourdieu, P. (1969) Intellectual Field and Creative Project, trans. S. France, *Social Science Information*, 8(2), 89-119.
http://dx.doi.org/10.1177/053901846900800205

Bray, M. & Manzon, M. (2005) Comparative Education in the Education of Teachers: Singapore and Hong Kong. CESHK, *Comparative Education Bulletin*, 8, 13-28.

Camins, A.H. (2015) What's the Purpose of Education in the 21st Century?
http://www.washingtonpost.com/blogs/answer-sheet/wp/2015/02/12/whats-the-purpose-of-education-in-the-21st-century/ (accessed in August 2015).

Centre for International Comparative Studies (CICS) (2015) Centre for International Comparative Studies, National Institute of Education, Singapore.
http://www.nie.edu.sg/research-centres/centre-international-comparative-studies (accessed in September 2015).

Chia, Y.-T. (2015) *Education, Culture and the Singapore Developmental State: 'world soul' lost and regained?* London: Palgrave Macmillan.
http://dx.doi.org/10.1057/9781137374608

Cowen, R. (1982) The Place of Comparative Education in the Educational Sciences, in I. Cavicchi-Broquet & P. Furter (Eds) *Les Sciences de l'éducation: Perspectives et Bilans Européens. Actes de la Xe Conférence de l'Association d'éducation Comparée Pour l'Europe*, pp.107-126. Geneva: Section des Sciences de l'éducation, Faculté de Psychologie et de Sciences de l'Éducation, Université de Genève.

Cowen, R. (2015) Review of Education in the United Kingdom; Education in the European Union Pre-2003 Member States; Education in Australia, New Zealand and the Pacific; Education in Eastern Europe and Eurasia; Education in North America, *Comparative Education*, 51(3), 464-467.
http://dx.doi.org/10.1080/03050068.2015.1047151

Encyclopaedia Britannica (2015) Comparative Anatomy.
http://global.britannica.com/science/comparative-anatomy (accessed on 8 September 2015).

Fairbrother, G. (2005) Comparison to What End? Maximizing the Potential of Comparative Education Research, *Comparative Education*, 41(1), 5-24.
http://dx.doi.org/10.1080/03050060500073215

Ferrer, F. (2002) *La educación comparada actual*. Barcelona: Ariel.

García Garrido, J.L. (1996) *Fundamentos de educación comparada*. Madrid: Editorial Dykinson S.L.

Goh, C.B. & Gopinathan, S. (2008) The Development of Education in Singapore since 1965, in S.K. Lee, C.B. Goh, B. Fredriksen & J.-P. Tan (Eds) *Toward a Better Future: education and training for economic development in Singapore since 1965*, pp. 12-38. Washington, DC: World Bank.

Gopinathan, S. (2013) *Education and the Nation State: the selected works of S. Gopinathan*. New York: Routledge.

Gu, M.Y. (2001) Comparative Education in China: name and reality, *Education in China and Abroad: perspectives from a lifetime in comparative education*, pp. 236-242. Hong Kong: Comparative Education Research Centre, University of Hong Kong. Originally published in Chinese in *Journal of Foreign Education Studies*, 1 (1991).

Habermas, J. (1971) *Knowledge and Human Interests*, trans. J.J. Shapiro. Boston: Beacon Press.

Hahn, C. (2015) Citizenship Education Pedagogy: a comparative perspective. Keynote address for the 11th CitizED conference, National Institute of Education, Singapore, 4 June.

Hardarson, A. (2012) Why the Aims of Education Cannot Be Settled, *Journal of Philosophy of Education*, 46(2), 223-235. http://dx.doi.org/10.1111/j.1467-9752.2012.00847.x

Holmes, B. (1971) Foreword, in *Comparative Education: purpose and method*, pp. ix-xi. St. Lucia, Queensland: University of Queensland Press.

Inkeles, A. & Sasaki, M. (1996) Preface, in A. Inkeles & M. Sasaki (Eds) *Comparing Nations and Cultures: readings in a cross-disciplinary perspective*, pp. xi-xv. Englewood Cliffs, NJ: Prentice Hall.

International and Comparative Studies (ICS) (2015) International and Comparative Studies, National Institute of Education, Singapore. http://www.nie.edu.sg/office-education-research/research-and-development-framework/ICS (accessed in September 2015).

Jullien, M.-A. (1817) *Esquisse et vues préliminaires d'un ouvrage sur l'éducation comparée*. Paris: Société Établie à Paris pour l'Amélioration de l'Enseignement Elémentaire. Reprinted in 1962. Geneva: Bureau International d'Éducation.

Kandel, I.L. (1936) Comparative Education, *Review of Educational Research*, 6(4), 400-416. http://dx.doi.org/10.2307/1167463

King, E.J. (1965) The Purpose of Comparative Education, *Comparative Education*, 1(3), 147-159.

King, E.J. (1997) A Turning-point in Comparative Education: retrospect and prospect, in C. Kodron, B. von Kopp, U. Lauterbach, U. Schäfer & G. Schmidt (Eds) *Vergleichende Erziehungswissenschaft: Heraus-forderung, Vermittlung, Praxis: Festschrift fur Wolfgang Mitter zum 70. Geburtstag*, pp. 81-90. Frankfurt am Main: Bohlau Verlag.

Kubow, P.K. & Fossum, P.R. (2007) *Comparative Education: exploring issues in international context*, 2nd edn. Upper Saddle River, NJ: Pearson Education/Merrill Prentice Hall.

Labaree, D.F. (2014) Let's Measure What No One Teaches: PISA, NCLB, and the shrinking aims of education, *Teachers College Record*, 116, 1-14.

Locke, K. (2015) Performativity, Performance and Education, *Educational Philosophy and Theory*, 47(3), 247-259. http://dx.doi.org/10.1080/00131857.2013.857287

Lovat, T. (2012) Values Education, in J. Arthur & A. Peterson (Eds) *Routledge Companion to Education*, pp. 380-388. New York: Routledge.

Lyotard, J.-F. (1984) *The Postmodern Condition: a report on knowledge*, 10th edn, trans. G. Bennington & B. Massumi. Manchester: Manchester University Press. (Originally published in 1979.)

Manzon, M. (2011) *Comparative Education: the construction of a field*. Hong Kong: Comparative Education Research Centre, University of Hong Kong, and Dordrecht: Springer. http://dx.doi.org/10.1007/978-94-007-1930-9

Manzon, M. (2014) Comparative Education *fuori le mura*: why the Singapore paradox? Paper presented at the Comparative Education Society in Europe (CESE) conference, Freiburg, 11 June.

Martínez, M.J. (2003) *Educación Comparada: nuevos retos, renovados desafíos*. Madrid: Editorial La Muralla, S.A.

Mason, M. (2014) Comparing Cultures, in M. Bray, B. Adamson & M. Mason (Eds) *Comparative Education Research: approaches and methods*, 2nd edn, pp. 221-257. Hong Kong: Comparative Education Research Centre, University of Hong Kong, and Dordrecht: Springer.

McClellan, J.E. (1957) An Educational Philosopher Looks at Comparative Education, *Comparative Education Review*, 1(1), 8-9. http://dx.doi.org/10.1086/444745

Ministry of Finance Singapore (2015) Budget 2014 Singapore. http://www.singaporebudget.gov.sg/budget_2014/revenueandexpenditure/Revenue andExpenditureEstimates.aspx (accessed in January 2015).

National Institute of Education (NIE) (2015) Fast Facts on NIE. National Institute of Education, Nanyang Technological University, Singapore. http://www.nie.edu.sg/about-nie/general-information/fast-facts-nie (accessed in August 2015).

Noddings, N. (2003) *Happiness and Education*. Cambridge: Cambridge University Press. http://dx.doi.org/10.1017/CBO9780511499920

Nóvoa, A. (2000) Estat de la qüestió de l'educació comparada: Paradigmas, avanços i impassos, *Temps d'Educació*, 24, 101-123.

Nóvoa, A. & Yariv-Marshal, T. (2003) Comparative Research in Education: a mode of governance or a historical journey? *Comparative Education*, 39(4), 423-438. http://dx.doi.org/10.1080/0305006032000162002

Office of Education Research (OER) (2015) Research and Development Framework, Office of Education Research, National Institute of Education, Singapore. http://www.nie.edu.sg/office-education-research/research-and-development-framework (accessed in August 2015).

Peters, R.S. (1981) *Moral Development and Moral Education*. London: George Allen & Unwin.

Phillips, D. & Schweisfurth, M. (2014) *Comparative and International Education: an introduction to theory, method, and practice*. London: Bloomsbury.

Poon, C.L. (2012) Fourth Way in Action: translation of research into policy and practice, *Educational Research for Policy and Practice*, 11(1), 19-25. http://dx.doi.org/10.1007/s10671-011-9113-x

Sadler, M. (1900/1964) How Far Can We Learn Anything of Practical Value from the Study of Foreign Systems of Education? *Comparative Education Review*, 7(3), 307-314.

Siegel, H. (2009) Introduction: philosophy of education and philosophy, in H. Siegel (Ed.) *The Oxford Handbook of Philosophy of Education*, pp. 3-10. Oxford: Oxford University Press.

Tan, J. (2005) Personal communication to Mark Bray. National Institute of Education, Nanyang Technological University, Singapore.

Tikly, L. & Crossley, M. (2001) Teaching Comparative and International Education: a framework for analysis, *Comparative Education Review*, 45(4), 561-580. http://dx.doi.org/10.1086/447692

To, C.Y. (1970) Comparative Education in the Education of Teachers: Singapore and Hong Kong. Paper presented at the First World Congress of Comparative Education Societies, Ottawa, Canada. Republished in *Comparative Education Bulletin*, 8 (2005).

Walker, A. & Bodycott, P. (1997) Academic Cultures in Singapore and Hong Kong: some personal impressions, *International Higher Education*, 7, 1-3.

Wang, C., Zhu, B. & Gu, M. (Eds) (1982) *Comparative Education*. Beijing: People's Education Press [in Chinese].

Webster, R.S. (2015) Valuing and Desiring Purposes of Education to Transcend Miseducative Measurement Practices, *Educational Philosophy and Theory*. Published online 23 June. http://dx.doi.org/10.1080/00131857.2015.1052355

CHAPTER 8

Comparative Education, Globalization and Teaching with/against the Nation-State

NOAH W. SOBE

The nation-state is an accomplishment whose rise, it can be argued, parallels the emergence of the social or human sciences – comparative education among them – in the nineteenth century. From the nation-centered studies proposed by Marc-Antoine Jullien in the 1810s to the World's Fair exhibits of the turn of the twentieth century, the nation and educational comparison have been inextricably bound. Indeed, through the Cold War and presently with the Programme for International Student Assessment (PISA) and other international educational assessments, it is clear that the nation-state and educational comparison have continued to be strongly linked.

The nation-state as the ultimate horizon of reference for 'society' has long been the ultimate 'unit' of analysis in sociology, something reflected in the field of comparative education in both structural functionalist and many political economy approaches. Whether conceived of as an organic unity of forces and factors or as internally differentiated and conflict-ridden, there is a striking persistence to the idea of the nation-state as a unit container. At the same time, globalization theory and currents of transnationalism invite us to question the nation-state. Ulrich Beck's (2002) notions of a cosmopolitan sociology also ask us to rethink our standard notions of units of analysis and develop conceptual and methodological resources for understanding the world that is undergoing what Beck refers to as a cosmopolitan transformation.

The problem of sorting out the salience of the nation-state thus presents challenges both for comparative education research and for the teaching of comparative and international education. As a contribution to a book dedicated to teaching in the field, the present chapter concerns itself more with the latter; however, some of the arguments advanced bear on the design of comparative and international education research as well.

In an era where concerns about globalization traverse both academic and popular debates, it seems particularly pressing that courses in comparative and international education devote some attention to grappling with the ways in which schools are situated in, and in relation to, global processes and phenomena. Even a cursory review of leading textbooks and syllabi collections shows that this occurs widely. Nonetheless, this essay calls for a more careful rethinking of the ways that both nation-state and globalization concerns are integrated into our field. And even though its primary aim is to offer suggestions for how to teach 'with and against' the nation-state in the setting of today's world, my arguments extend back to diagnose and problematize how things national and things global or world-level have been treated in our field.

The Foundations of Teaching Comparative Education

Let us begin with an observation from the French science studies scholar Bruno Latour, who has proposed that:

> Most of the social sciences were invented, a century ago, to short-cut political processes after many years of insufferable civil wars and revolutionary strife. If we have a society that is *already composed as one single whole* and which can be used to account for the behavior of actors who do not know what they are doing, but whose unknown structure is visible to the keen eyes of a social scientist, it then becomes possible to embark on the huge task of social engineering in order to produce the common good, without having to go through the painstaking labour of composing this commonality through political means. (Latour, 2000, pp. 117-118; emphasis in original)

Latour is speaking of a historical moment when society was seen as coextensive with the territory of the nation-state. And important here for our purposes are his observations on what was 'achieved' through this conceptual legerdemain and what this means for the habitus and training of the social scientist as one who was to enjoy a privileged position in bringing about reform. The project of studying and teaching of comparative education manifested across the nineteenth and most of the twentieth century very much in these same terms. Kaloyannaki and Kazamias (2009) have described a 'meliorist' strand of comparative education study marked by a focus on lesson-learning and an emphasis on leveraging research for purposes of reform and improvement. Their characterization of certain technical strands of comparative and international education research certainly rings true on many levels. However, it is also important not to lose sight of the fundamentally normative nature of social science *ipso facto*. Even in its more phenomenological, humanistic, critical, and *Verstehen*-oriented variants, social science is a project of social engineering. Teaching comparative education is bound up in the teaching of social engineering.

Latour's (2000) observations on social science and the nineteenth-century imagining of societies as *constituted as a single whole to begin with* are also relevant to the ways that globalization is often discussed in contemporary social science – and in the field of comparative and international education specifically. Quite often the existence of a 'globalized world' is presented as an orienting fact, a fait accompli, as the starting point of analysis. And, indeed, one might rework and rewrite Latour's analysis as follows: if we have *a globalized world* that is already *composed as one single whole* and which can be used to account for the behavior of actors who do not know what they are doing, but whose unknown structure is visible to the keen eyes of a social scientist, it then becomes possible to embark on the huge task of social engineering in order to produce the common good.

In many globalization-analysis frameworks, the requirement of 'keen eyes' and the illumination of structures purportedly 'unknown' to those enmeshed in them enshrines the contemporary social scientist as a mandarin every bit as privileged as the nineteenth- and twentieth-century sociologists who studied their own and others' societies with an eye seeing what others could not and making improvements where others could not. Stäheli (2003) describes attribution to 'the global' of an overarching explanatory power as 'a pervasive totalizing gesture which tries to make the outside of the global unthinkable' (p. 2). Stäheli also observes that even those who exalt the subversive power of the 'local' tend to reify the global as a pre-existing whole. The prevalence (and perhaps obduracy) of this tendency to take globalization as a set-piece is partly evidenced by many recent challenges to it. These include many calls to shift analytic focus onto the construction of the global. Collier and Ong (2005) and Sobe (2014) have called for the study of the making of 'global assemblages'. In like manner, Dale and Robertson (2009) have called for an emphasis on the constitution of social and political processes and phenomena, analysis of how different sets of relations are formed, and a rejection of reliance on ossified and static categories of analysis.

The challenge for teaching comparative and international education is to avoid taking 'the nation-state' and 'a globalized world' as two already-constituted facts whose purported reality and potential conflict with one another demarcate the terrain of analysis.

Imagining Locals and Globals

One avenue of addressing this challenge is suggested by the work of the late Benedict Anderson, whose scholarship on 'imagined communities' has had a paradigm-shifting impact on the ways that scholars across the social sciences and the humanities study nationalism; ethnic, social and cultural belonging; and social identities broadly considered. From Anderson's work, both in terms of how he does *and doesn't* discuss education, we can draw some important guidelines and insights for teaching comparative and international education.

To begin, permit me to note that when reading Anderson's *Imagined Communities: reflections on the origin and spread of nationalism* (1983, 1991, 2006), I sometimes imagine him to be addressing comparative education's inappropriately overquoted 'Sadlerian dictum'. With Jamie Kowalczyk (Sobe & Kowalczyk, 2012), I have argued that turn-of-the-twentieth-century British comparative education advocate Michael Sadler's (1900/1964) recommendation that education reformers not 'wander at pleasure among the educational systems of the world, like a child strolling through a garden, and pick off a flower' (p.310) is a dangerous and colonialist way of conceptualizing educational 'context'. Sadler's recommendation echoes the colonialist science of 'acclimatization' (Osborne, 1994, 2000) that investigated which agricultural crops and animals could and couldn't be transported to what parts of the world in the interest of resource exploitation. And it also egregiously inscribes principles of difference that enable different curricula, pedagogical methods and forms of schooling to be applied to particular 'kinds' of people based on outsiders' perceptions of worth, aptitude and potential. Moreover, Sadler's organicist argument about so-called native soil is also an example of the dubious assumption that a unique 'national spirit' is inscribed in the philosophy and institutions of particular national education systems. The error is not just Sadler's. For most of its history, the field of comparative and international education has been entirely incorrect when analyzing the relation between schools and nations – the critical error being to treat the nation-state as an explanatory independent variable from which most of the salient aspects of schools and school systems flow. Instead, the nation needs to be taken as something that needs to be explained, more than it explains (Sobe, 2014).

Robert Cowen (2014) has argued that the nation-state appears in many contemporary political and academic conversations about international educational comparisons as the 'reverse translation of a political category into a research-technical category', with the result being a black-boxing of the 'nation' into a set of so-called variables. In like manner, Lynn Fendler has recently discussed the ways that 'ghosts of the nation-state haunt educational histories when nations are treated as independent variables, frozen in time and exempt from critical investigation' (2013, p. 227). In comparative education too, this has ironically led to the contents of national education traditions being left unexamined and more unchallenged (Welch, 2009) than the tradition (and critique) of methodological nationalism would actually seem to predict. When the nation is black-boxed and treated as if it were an independent variable, there is an unfortunate side effect of short-changing educational research by not exploring the ways that schools fabricate national identities, national imaginaries and national practices.

Given that Anderson approaches the nation as a created, enacted imagined community, it is surprising how little mention there is of schooling in his work. In one of his chapters that is most often cited (and taught), Anderson (1991, 2006) discusses the 'Census, Map and Museum' as three 'institutions of power' (p. 163) that bring to light key elements of the 'grammar' of imagined communities. He recounts that in the first edition of the book (1986), he wrote that one can see the 'instilling of nationalist ideology through the mass media, the educational system, administrative regulations, and so forth' (p. 114) but that in the 1991 revised edition he then saw things differently. It is thus interesting to ponder why in both the second and the later editions schooling drops out of his formulation for how nationalist sentiments are imparted and national communities imagined.[1]

On my reading, Anderson offers an extremely persuasive analysis of how census-taking, mapping and museum practices generate a structural grammar through which national sentiments can come to operate as social facts (Appadurai, 1990). Anderson explains that he turned to census, map and museum as part of revising his earlier assumption that official nationalisms in Asia and Africa emulated the nationalisms of Europe. Instead of this 'superficial' (Anderson's word) reading, he sees the operations of the colonial state as setting the stage for national imaginaries through the three aforementioned institutions of power. Regarding schooling, it is notable that Anderson's earlier view on the inculcation of nationalist ideologies includes educational systems as part of an 'and so forth' list of various communication/dissemination technologies. This is emblematic of an unfortunate tendency within academic scholarship to assume that schools are merely one of many sites of social reproduction and to not treat them as sites of cultural production that are contingent, contested and consequential in their own right (Sobe, 2009). In fact, I would propose that students of comparative and international education need to be made well aware of the drawbacks and limitations to assuming that schools and what happens at schools are *derivative* of tensions and social compacts that have been worked out in other social arenas. Schools are the sites of major political, cultural and social flashpoints, and one of the major contributions of our field has been to show schools as less stable and less authoritative sites for disseminating social and political ideals than they are sometimes taken to be.

Anderson's *Imagined Communities* appropriately remarks on the European/North American cultural specificity of the age-graded classroom model as part of a proposal that the very provision of classrooms as part of a sequenced progression helped to foster colonial nationalisms. He describes the regimented and standardized features of schools as creating 'a self-contained, coherent universe of experience' (1991, 2006, p. 121), though he does not extensively elaborate on the consequences of this. He notes that the tiered, hierarchical features of school systems brought a series of pilgrimages into being in many settings. Middle schools and secondary schools brought students out of smaller villages and towns and into regional centers, and then those who advanced on to higher education necessarily traveled to colonial capitals, or – in rare circumstances – to the colonial metropoles themselves. Anderson writes:

> the tender pilgrims made their inward, upward way, meeting fellow-pilgrims from different, perhaps once hostile, villages in primary school; from different ethnolinguistic groups in middle-school; and from every part of the realm in the tertiary institutions of the capital. And they knew that from wherever they had come they still had read the same books and done the same sums. They also knew ... that all these journeyings derived their 'sense' from the capital, in effect explaining why 'we' are 'here' together. (1991, 2006, pp. 121-122)

The pyramid-like structure of an education system, by virtue of the very mechanics of its operation, thus might assist greatly in developing the horizontal comradeship that is so fundamental to the imagined community of a nation. In other words, even leaving the potential 'national'-specific content of curricula and textbooks out of the picture, one can contend that the institution of modern schooling lends to the creation of the imaginaries of nation-states. A clear and obvious extension of this insight would be to analyze the ways that the materiality and repetition of international student mobility helps to construct global sensibilities and imaginaries.[2]

In sum, there seems to be a pressing need to orient the teaching of comparative and international education towards a study of educational assemblages (Webb, 2009; Ball, 2012; Sobe, 2015). When we study educational borrowing and lending, it becomes imperative to think about the formation, coordination and extension of networks and discursive formations through which heterogeneous, disparate objects are brought into relation. Collier and Ong's argument that rather than examining 'the changes associated with globalization in terms of broad structural transformations or new configurations of society or culture', attention should be paid to 'the specific range of phenomena that articulate such shifts' (2005, p. 3) is useful advice for teaching in our field. Learning to analyze the materialities (Lawn & Grosvenor, 2005; Coole & Frost, 2010), embodiments (Epstein, 2007) and apparatuses (Agamben, 2009) of schooling is a worthy endeavor for the keen eyes and keen minds of our students.

Teaching with the Nation-State

How best to articulate the salience of a single-case study is a recurrent question in the field of comparative and international education. Editors of journals in our field sometimes express concern at the surprisingly small number of studies that are actually *comparative*. I see this reflection as a useful exercise, if only because it helps to articulate numerous and varied arguments for embracing the heterogeneity of scholarship that falls under the broad umbrella that is the field of comparative and international education. How, why and when to identify a 'national case' remains a question worth asking in our teaching. Ample are the introductory (and advanced) courses that spend considerable time having students grapple with transnational actors, institutions, processes and phenomena – and yet then require a single nation-centered final paper, with little comment on the juxtaposition. (And indeed, at times my own courses certainly fit this model.) The convincing critiques of 'methodological nationalism' (Dale, 2005) notwithstanding, it is still important not to abandon the nation-state in our teaching. Building off my previous arguments, this section aims to raise additional considerations for what it can mean to teach 'with' the nation-state, particularly in an era of heightened sensitivity to globe-spanning relations, processes and phenomena.

The field of comparative and international education has advanced well beyond thinking about the nation-state and the global in an either/or binary manner. Some have moved to recast this as a 'dialectic' (Arnove et al, 2012) or as a 'nexus' (Schriewer, 2003). Yet, thinking in transactional terms along these lines seems to needlessly pre-judge any particular scenario and may be more a diversion and distraction than generative of productive new analytic insights. The assemblage approach that I have urged above focuses instead on 'the formation, coordination and extension of networks and discursive formations through which heterogeneous, disparate objects are brought into relation' (Sobe, 2014, p. 2). When studying schools in national and/or global terms, students in comparative and international education need to grapple with the contingent bundling together of heterogeneous elements and not struggle to match these contingent assemblages to any prefigured 'cultural models' or reified ideological platforms.

Teaching with the nation-state thus means taking context seriously and actually giving it its due. Too much comparative education research approaches contextualization as a preliminary front-end research activity when the problem of context is more usefully seen as a 'matter of concern' across a research project (Sobe & Kowalczyk, 2014). An analytic focus on contexts as sets or bundles of relations also helps us think about the research challenge presented by globalization, particularly as it heightens our ability to capture localizations and the strategic moves that comparative and international education scholars analyze so well. As an example, consider Dickhaus' (2010) work on 'accountability regimes' in a comparative study of quality assurance initiatives in the South African and Argentinean higher education sectors. She points to the historical accretion of modes of higher education governance in each setting as helping to explain how new accreditation initiatives played out. Nonetheless, Dickhaus argues that transnationally circulating quality assurance policies have become a hegemonic tool for reorganizing the higher education sector, in part *because of* the variety of meanings that can be attached to them and the selectivity that goes into the contested process of appropriation and meaning creation. The challenge of teaching with the nation-state is the challenge of equipping our students with tools and strategies for understanding mobility, mutability and heterogeneity at ephemeral moments.

Teaching with the nation-state also means devoting serious attention to discursive constructions of nations and the ways that national imaginaries come to operate as social facts. Drawing off Ferguson and Gupta's (2002) work on state practices of spatiality, comparative and international education would do well to give significant thought to the ways that 'verticality' and 'encompassment' are at play in education policies and practice. The performative nature of accountability policies (Webb, 2006) is often remarked upon and is a useful reminder that scholars need to pay heed to 'what else' is occurring via education policy enactments in addition to the putative or aspirational regulation of schools, teachers, children and families. Looking at the ways that nation-states construct a sense of being 'above' society and of 'enveloping' their localities is useful for teaching with the nation-state in comparative and international education. This means not taking nations as pre-given a priori 'containers', but instead, foregrounding strategies of 'containment' as ongoing social, cultural and political projects.

Teaching against the Nation-State

Unsettling the pre-given and deconstructing the taken-for-granted brings the nation-state form itself into question. In this final section of the chapter, I argue that teaching 'against' the nation-state flows naturally and concurrently from teaching 'with' it. Hence, the backslash of with/against in my chapter's title should be taken not as an expression of binary opposition (one either teaches for or against), but rather should be taken as more of an ambivalent gesture that simultaneously inclines in two directions.

Alongside examinations of encompassment and verticality technologies as well as discursive fabrications of nation-ness, it is clearly essential to recognize the heterogeneity located within nations (Lingard & Rawolle, 2011; Robertson, 2012). This may mean that intra-national comparisons need more attention in the field of comparative and international education than they tend to receive, particularly, perhaps, in our teaching. Different groups may exhibit dramatically and subtly different ways of understanding the 'educated person' (Levinson et al, 1996), something that necessitates intra-national comparative scholarship accompanying any transnational analyses of the purposes and aims of schooling.

Teaching against the nation-state also means bringing into question the sincerity with which the 'national' component of education policies is enunciated. While political elites in many locales have often shared cosmopolitan convictions and commitments, it is only recently that we find such a density of operations that, as Saskia Sassen (2007) writes, 'take place within national institutional settings but are geared to non-national or transnational agendas' (p. 298). Sassen makes a strong case for recovering the significance of place in the global economy; however, a key feature of her argument about 'global cities' is that urban space often becomes de-nationalized. And, indeed, research examining education reform in cities like Chicago (Lipman, 2004) shows how a national collective frame can easily vanish from the picture. International organizations, both non-governmental organizations (NGOs) and inter-governmental organizations, also come into the picture by providing non-national sites for legitimate claim-making, all of which is arguably linked to a possible transformation of nation-based citizenship into rights-based citizenship.

The final dimension of teaching against the nation-state that I will review here deals with unsettling the politics of scale that so often frames inquiry in the field of comparative and international education. On what grounds ought we to maintain that something *global* is 'larger' and something *local* is 'smaller', and that the *nation* is most likely somewhere in between? Having brought encompassment practices into question in the previous section, we seem required also to question any vision of pre-arrayed concentric circles showing one layer of social reality necessarily enveloping and surrounding another. In place of taking the local as necessarily contained within the global – and also rejecting the idea that the two can be usefully distinguished by their valence or concrete potential for action (as in the chess analogy of the *global* moving like a queen and the *local* moving like a king) – Guy (2009) suggests that they are two opposite sides of the same distinction and more important as varieties of self-description than anything else. We can investigate the nation-state also as self-description, and while we should clearly attend to scalar relations, we should work off the assumption that spatialities and the politics of scale have unique situational contours. And these are the very things that the field of comparative and international education needs to make central as subjects of inquiry.

Throughout this piece I have frequently discussed the intellectual activity of questioning or putting-into-question. To question is not to repudiate. It is simply to say that these are questions that we as teachers and our students as learners should seek to answer. In this chapter I have proposed that learning how to teach with/against the nation-state holds promise for making known structures better known. It requires a certain kind of alacrity of vision for the social scientist, and it might allow us to contribute to producing common good through solidly political means.

Notes

[1] The discussion in this and the subsequent two paragraphs is drawn from Sobe (2014).

[2] This is a charge that applies both to our present moment and to historical analyses (Sobe, 2008; Goodman, 2015).

References

Agamben, G. (2009) *'What Is an Apparatus?' and Other Essays*. Palo Alto, CA: Stanford University Press.

Anderson, B. (1983, 1991, 2006) *Imagined Communities: reflections on the origin and spread of nationalism*. London: Verso.

Appadurai, A. (1990) Disjuncture and Difference in the Global Cultural Economy, *Theory, Culture and Society*, 7(2), 295-310. http://dx.doi.org/10.1177/026327690007002017

Arnove, R.F., Torres, C.A. & Franz, S. (Eds) (2012) *Comparative Education: the dialectic of the global and the local*. Lanham, MD: Rowman & Littlefield.

Ball, S.J. (2012) *Global Education Inc: new policy networks and the neo-liberal imaginary*. London: Routledge.

Beck, U. (2002) The Cosmopolitan Society and Its Enemies, *Theory, Culture & Society*, 19(1-2), 17-44.

Collier, S.J. & Ong, A. (2005) Global Assemblages, Anthropological Problems, *Global Assemblages: technology, politics, and ethics as anthropological problems*, 3-21.

Coole, D. & Frost, S. (Eds) (2010) *New Materialisms: ontology, agency, and politics*. Durham, NH: Duke University Press. http://dx.doi.org/10.1215/9780822392996

Cowen, R. (2014) With the Exception of Switzerland...: thoughts about the nation and educational research, *International Journal for the Historiography of Education*, 2, 216-227.

Dale, R. (2005) Globalisation, Knowledge Economy and Comparative Education, *Comparative Education*, 41(2), 117-149. http://dx.doi.org/10.1080/03050060500150906

Dale, R. & Robertson, S. (2009) Beyond Methodological 'ISMS'in Comparative Education in an Era of Globalisation, in *International Handbook of Comparative Education*, pp. 1113-1127. Dordrecht: Springer.

Dickhaus, B. (2010) The Selectivity of Translation: accountability regimes in Chilean and South African higher education, *Globalisation, Societies and Education*, 8, 257-268. http://dx.doi.org/10.1080/14767721003780090

Epstein, I. (2007) *Recapturing the Personal: essays on education and embodied knowledge in comparative perspective*. Charlotte, NC: Information Age Publishing.

Fendler, L. (2013) There Are No Independent Variables in History, in T.S. Popkewitz (Ed.) *Rethinking the History of Education: transnational perspectives on its questions, methods, and knowledge*, pp. 223-244. New York: Palgrave Macmillan.

Ferguson, J. & Gupta, A. (2002) Spatializing States: toward an ethnography of neoliberal governmentality, *American Ethnologist*, 29(4), 981-1002. http://dx.doi.org/10.1525/ae.2002.29.4.981

Goodman, J. (2015) Gender, Cosmopolitanism, and Transnational Space and Time: Kasuya Yoshi and girls' secondary education, *History of Education*, 1-17. http://dx.doi.org/10.1080/0046760x.2015.1076066

Guy, J.-S. (2009) What is Global and What is Local? A Theoretical Discussion around Globalization, *Parson's Journal of Information Mapping*, 1(2), 1-16.

Kaloyannaki, P. & Kazamias, A.M. (2009) The Modernist Beginnings of Comparative Education: the proto-scientific and the reformist-meliorist administrative motif, in *International Handbook of Comparative Education*, pp. 11-35. Dordrecht: Springer.

Latour, B. (2000) When Things Strike Back: a possible contribution of 'science studies' to the social sciences, *British Journal of Sociology*, 51(1), 107-123. http://dx.doi.org/10.1080/000713100358453

Lawn, M. & Grosvenor, I. (Eds) (2005) *Materialities of Schooling: design, technology, objects, routines*. Oxford: Symposium Books.

Levinson, B., Foley, D. & Holland, D. (1996) *The Cultural Production of the Educated Person: critical ethnographies of schooling and local practice*. Albany: State University of New York Press.

Lingard, B. & Rawolle, S. (2011) New Scalar Politics: implications for education policy, *Comparative Education*, 47(4), 489-502. http://dx.doi.org/10.1080/03050068.2011.555941

Lipman, P. (2004) *High Stakes Education: inequality, globalization, and urban school reform*. Hove: Psychology Press. http://dx.doi.org/10.4324/9780203465509

Osborne, M. (1994) Acclimatizing the World: a history of the paradigmatic colonial science, *Osiris*, 15, 135-151. http://dx.doi.org/10.1086/649323

Osborne, M. (2000) *Nature, the Exotic, and the Science of French Colonialism: science, technology, and society*. Bloomington: Indiana University Press.

Robertson, S. (2012) Researching Global Education Policy: angles in/on/out..., in A. Verger, M. Novelli, & H.K. Altinyelken (Eds) *Global Education Policy and International Development: new agendas, issues, and policies*, pp. 33-53. London: Bloomsbury.

Sadler, M. (1900/1964) in G. Bereday, Documents: Sir Michael Sadler's 'Study of Foreign Systems of Education', *Comparative Education Review*, 1964, 307-314.

Sassen, S. (2007) Theoretical and Empirical elements in the Study of Globalization, in I. Rossi (Ed.) *Frontiers of Globalization Research*, pp. 287-305. New York: Springer.

Schriewer, J. (2003) Globalisation in Education: process and discourse, *Policy Futures in Education*, 1(2), 271-283. http://dx.doi.org/10.2304/pfie.2003.1.2.6

Sobe, N.W. (2008) *Provincializing the Worldly Citizen: Yugoslav student and teacher travel and Slavic cosmopolitanism in the interwar era*. New York: Peter Lang.

Sobe, N. (2009) Educational Reconstruction 'By the Dawn's Early Light': violent political conflict and American overseas education reform, *Harvard Educational Review*, 79(1), 123-131. http://dx.doi.org/10.17763/haer.79.1.p863j2h538570442

Sobe, N.W. (2014) Textbooks, Schools, Memory and the Technologies of National Imaginaries, in J.H. Williams (Ed.) *(Re)constructing Memory: school textbooks and the imagination of the nation*, pp. 313-318. Rotterdam: Sense.

Sobe, N.W. (2015) All That is Global is Not World Culture: accountability systems and educational apparatuses, *Globalisation, Societies and Education*, 13(1), 135-148. http://dx.doi.org/10.1080/14767724.2014.967501

Sobe, N.W. & Kowalczyk, J. (2012) The Problem of Context in Comparative Education Research, *Journal for Educational, Cultural and Psychological Studies*, 6, 55-74.

Sobe, N.W. & Kowalczyk, J. (2014) Exploding the Cube: revisioning 'context' in the field of comparative education, *Current Issues in Comparative Education*, 17(1), 6-12.

Stäheli, U. (2003) The Outside of the Global, *New Centennial Review*, 3, 1-22. http://dx.doi.org/10.1353/ncr.2003.0030

Webb, P.T. (2006) The Choreography of Accountability, *Journal of Education Policy*, 21, 201-214. http://dx.doi.org/10.1080/02680930500500450

Webb, P.T. (2009) *Teacher Assemblage*. New York: Sense.

Welch, A. (2009) The Triumph of Technocracy or the Collapse of Certainty? Modernity, Postmodernity, and Postcolonialism in Comparative Education, in R. Arnove & C.A. Torres (Eds) *Comparative Education: the dialectic of the global and the local*, pp. 25-50. Lanham, MD: Rowman & Littlefield.

CHAPTER 9

Teaching Comparative Education: the dialectics of the global and the local

CARLOS ALBERTO TORRES

Introduction

In quoting others, we cite ourselves. (Cortázar, 1986)

This chapter discusses teaching comparative education in the context of global citizenship education as an emerging focal point of the field. First I shall explain my philosophy of teaching, already presented in a previous publication (Torres, 2015a). This teaching philosophy will serve as an introduction and will perhaps even problematize teaching, for some comparativists may disagree with a teaching philosophy based on Paulo Freire's work and the contributions of critical theory and feminism (Malsbary & Way, 2014).

My second claim is that our readers will be well served in that, in addition to pointing out the political philosophical and methodological principles of my teaching, I focus on the theoretical constructs undergirding one of the most successful textbooks in comparative and international education. So, as one of the editors of *Comparative Education: the dialectic of the global and the local*, a textbook which is in its fourth edition and published in several languages, let me speak about this book and how it may help in teaching comparative and international education. As said in many places, a fundamental premise of my work and that of true critical theorists is that we teach and conduct research to change the world, not simply to observe as detached alchemists experimenting with different products in social engineering or scientific voyeurs enjoying at a distance the intricacies of social behavior and the agonies of everyday life (Torres, 2009).

A central thesis of my work calls into question whether it is possible to fully dissociate the normative from the analytical in the construction of scientific thought. This issue raises the importance of the notion of a good society guiding the intellectual, theoretical, meta-theoretical and empirical analysis. Today, the 'politicity' of education is recognized in ways that will surprise even one of its principal advocates, Paulo Freire, who argued in the late 1960s about the nature of this relationship (Torres, 2009, 2014). Yet, it is important to recognize that this new narrative finds it 'impossible to avoid the historicity of thought and the policy prescriptions that emanate from a particular mode of theorizing. After all, not all social constructions are equally powerful in their logical configuration, methodological rigor or solid empirical proof, hence the need for serious analytical and scientific work' (Torres, 2011, p. 180).

Teaching to Change the World[1]

It really must be stressed that it is precisely the first elements, the
most elementary things, which are the first to be forgotten.
(Gramsci, 1971)

We are all traveling scholars. We travel through cultural and social constructions, through theoretical and meta-theoretical narratives, and through empirical analyses. No critical theorist can reach the best of his or her contribution without serious empirical analysis. At the same time, I am cognizant of the fact that some technocrats, who call themselves scholars, compile, analyze, even 'torture' data until they tell them exactly what they want to hear or expect to get.

We travel, but we do so framed by the politics of location and the politics of identity. This positionality should lead us not only to understand our sources of wisdom but also, as for any critical theory–oriented traveling scholar, to locate our own positionality and politics of identity against the proverbial racism, sexism, religious absolutism, homophobia or classism of our societies. Therefore, to separate analysis from advocacy is a very difficult process.

The best way of rationalizing teaching as a philosophy is to establish our own philosophy of teaching. Drawing from my own teaching experience over four decades and the influence of Freire (1971), critical theory à la Marcuse and Habermas (e.g. Habermas, 1992), feminism and the pedagogues of liberation (e.g. Belenky et al, 1986; Hale, 2007), what follows are some of the principles of teaching comparative and international education in what I consider rigorous ways: (a) to teach is to engage students in rigorous consideration of the key intellectual questions discussed in our courses; (b) to challenge students to consider the substantive (i.e. theoretical, normative and ethical issues involved in education, both at the level of theory and in terms of methods of inquiry); (c) to challenge graduate students in education to take advantage of the classic texts of philosophy, as they have informed the work of Freire, and the variety of social sciences available to them – particularly history, political science, sociology, political economy and anthropology – in order to develop an intellectual framework that is broadly interdisciplinary and comparative; (d) to involve students in independent analysis and writing, and eventually to publish with them, thereby helping them to establish their own research agendas; and (e) to allow undergraduate and graduate students to experiment with the techniques to radically change classrooms proposed by Paulo Freire, Orlando Fals Borda and the founders of participatory action research (PAR) [2], together with the contributions of feminist pedagogy, bringing the promises of democracy from an ideal to a true reality in the lives of their students.

One of the key elements that new scholars ponder is what constitutes academic rigor and excellence in their classrooms. Without attempting to provide an exhaustive list, I would like to identify nine components that I believe are essential in thinking about rigor and excellence, and that will help the pedagogical task in the classroom (Torres, 2014).

The first is respect for students' knowledge and experiences. From a Freirean perspective, this is the starting point of any serious academic engagement and community building. The second is respect for the classics properly deconstructed. If teaching and research is a never-ending process of deliberation and analysis, the classics of social theory and pedagogy cannot be ignored or brushed aside. They are central to our teaching and research endeavors. The dictum of C. Wright Mills is very appropriate. Speaking about the classics of sociology, Wright Mills stated:

> The important thing about the classic sociologists is that even when they have turned out to be quite wrong, and inadequate ... even then, by their work and by the way in which they did it, they reveal much about the nature of society, and their ideas remain directly relevant to our work today ... In general, our immediate generation of social scientists are living off their ideas. (1960, pp. 3-4)

The third component is data emphasis. Without creating a fetish out of using data to document any and every aspect of our teaching and research, and knowledge content, the proper utilization of data is important in our teaching. Likewise, without falling into the epistemological trap that by resorting to methods we will achieve scientificity, it is imperative that we address data as much as we can in dealing with epistemology, methods, meta-theories and theories in the classroom. Fourth is the importance of sound methods of inquiry. Classroom activity should be based on a multitude of strategies linking sound methods of inquiry with a healthy dose of analytical skepticism. Defining precisely what 'sound methods of inquiry' means and how to integrate them into our practice, and avoiding heavy reliance on certain methods to the exclusion of others, is part of the art of teaching.

The fifth component is relational analysis. Perhaps it is my own obsession, but when one begins to analyze a specific problem and places specific focus on the different dimensions of the problem, it is imperative to do so relationally, relating that analysis to the other dimensions that we typically deal with in education. To be brief, I would argue that we are constantly relating the economic, political and cultural domains or spheres of praxis and knowledge to questions connected with ethnicity, race, gender, sexuality, class and many other 'variables' of the analysis. Thus, adopting a relational analysis is fundamental to teaching. Sixth, the distinction between what is normative and what is analytical should be preserved in our teaching. I have already stated that critical theorists teach to change the world, not to simply reproduce it (Rexhepi & Torres, 2011).

The seventh component to guide comparative pedagogy is respect for contradictions and tensions. For a long time, one of the key axes of definition in sociology was considered the distinction between a sociology of conflict and a sociology of consensus. However, both conflict and consensus take place constantly in our classrooms. We should pay attention to, and respect, the degree of contradictions and the tensions that all of us, teachers and students together, experience in a given class.

Eighth, our teaching should also address the connections between theory, praxis and transformation. This is part of the moral commitment of teaching. With the pervasive presence of a 'value-free science' approach in universities, the question of moral commitment in our teaching becomes a lynchpin in linking the normative and the analytical moments of scientific work. Alvin Gouldner, in his presidential address at the annual meeting of the Society for the Study of Social Problems on 28 August 1961, said it very well, and I would like to quote him extensively, making his observations my own:

> If today we concern ourselves exclusively with the technical
> proficiency of our students and reject all responsibility for their
> moral sense, or lack of it, then we may someday be compelled to
> accept responsibility for having trained a generation willing to
> serve in a future Auschwitz. Granted that science always has
> inherent in it both constructive and destructive potentialities, it
> does not follow that we should encourage our students to be
> oblivious to the difference. Nor does this in any degree detract
> from the indispensable norms of scientific objectivity; it merely
> insists that these differ radically from moral indifference.
> (Gouldner, 1964, p. 216)

Finally, ninth, in the long classical tradition of academic engagement, it is imperative to promote critique, criticism and dissatisfaction in the treatment of the material and classroom analysis. Over the years, it has become evident to me that the advocacy role inherent in good teaching and scholarship is ever present in the scholarship and pedagogy of feminism, critical theory and Freire's work.

Following these principles, a central tenet of my political philosophical perspective in teaching validates one of the oldest forms of teaching:

storytelling. By storytelling I mean telling stories and vignettes of your own life, and of other people's lives, and letting students do the same – listening and learning from these vignettes and life stories and making these stories problematic from an epistemological perspective. This is one of the oldest pedagogies in the world, practiced by the elders in many communities, and certainly the type of pedagogical love we may have experienced when we were children listening to family stories or world stories from our grandmothers and grandfathers. To bring storytelling into the classroom is to validate the 'lived experience' of individuals and communities, another extremely important source of knowledge.

While teaching my annual course as a Visiting Professor at the Universidade Lusófona de Humanidades e Tecnologias in Lisbon a few years ago, in one of my sessions, Professor Antonio Teodoro, coordinator of the graduate program in education, argued that teaching is an appetizer to open the palate. His suggestion is useful. When we teach, we cannot offer a complete meal. There are too many obstacles against that – for instance, the quarter or semester systems that allow for few contact hours; the multiple demands that graduate and undergraduate students have on their time, including coping with a variety of readings covering multiple fields of knowledge; the bureaucratic rules of undergraduate and graduate studies; and the fact that teaching may be undermined by the 'publish or perish' dictum forcing professors to concentrate more on their research than on their teaching.

In this context, to think of teaching as an appetizer that opens the palate makes a lot of sense. We have all experienced that sensation of arriving to a restaurant for dinner but not having much of an appetite. In the Ibero-American tradition, the servers will immediately bring some appetizers with the drinks, and *voilà tout*, we are ready to have a wonderful dinner. We are suddenly hungry. The appetizers opened our palate, and we are ready to explore other flavors, colors, smells and shapes in the iconography of a liturgy of dining. That is in essence the role of teaching: to open the palate, to tease the students, to open new avenues for students to continue their own processes of education through being exposed to readings, themes, questions, experiences and problems that make sense, excite, preoccupy or challenge them. Teaching is one of the landmarks, but only one of many in a lifelong learning experience.

At this juncture, let me summarize the three claims I have made thus far. One, any form of teaching should respect the students, their knowledge and experience that they bring with them into the classroom. In doing so, however, if we want to change the world, we should rely on a fundamental principle that it is almost impossible to fully dissociate the normative from the analytical in our teaching. The notion of the good society will always guide teaching, learning and research of critical theorists (Rexhepi & Torres, 2011). Two, teaching comparative and international education requires that we whet the appetite of our students because no professor could ever be able to offer a full meal in our classrooms, perhaps not even in our lifeworld *oeuvre*. Moreover, the field is so diverse, so deeply interdisciplinary, regionally bound and at the same time regionally dispersed, microscopic and yet macroscopic, metacentric and yet multi-centric – that is, all of the above at the same time – that no professor could ever offer a synthetic theory that embraces all possible dimensions and nuances of the topics at hand, or provide a theory that will explain once and for all the universe of this multidiscipline. No professor would be able to offer a theory which is completely *abrangente* (comprehensive), as the Brazilians would say. And three, textbooks are useful didactic resources and should be carefully chosen. However, choosing didactic resources to guide the teaching and research of our students is a difficult task because we are confronted with the task of translation in a field as interdisciplinary, multidisciplinary and international as this one.

The following section explains how a major textbook in comparative and international education, in its four distinct and singular editions, has been constructed, and how it could help the work of teachers and researchers in comparative and international education. I then address some questions about translation and intelligibility across languages regarding meaning-making patterns.

Every Book has a History

My words itch at your ears till you understand them. (Walt Whitman, 'Song of Myself')[3]

Every book, like every piece of craft or art, is, by design, an intellectual construction; every good book by its very same nature should whet our appetite for more. Yet, once the archeology and architecture of the book is accomplished, any book becomes a social construction. In a fascinating way, the intellectual and social constructions reflect each other through multiple rays of light enhancing the analysis of the reality people try to understand. Over the last two decades, our book *Comparative Education: the dialectic of the global and the local* has sought to shed light on complex relationships, while accepting the darkness of the shadows still with us. The book by Arnove and Torres (1999) (with Franz in the fourth edition [Arnove et al, 2013]) has made a modest contribution to educational theory, analysis and praxis. The reasons behind writing or editing any book could be many. For us, it was that social change is a possible dream, and a possible dream for today, not for tomorrow.

When Robert Arnove and I discussed the project of this book in the mid-1990s at one of the Comparative and International Education Society (CIES) conferences, we were convinced that we were witnessing a phenomenal change in our lives and in the lives of our families, students, communities, nations and institutions. The multiple processes of globalization that we were experiencing then, what some have termed the first wave of globalization, or the '1.0 globalization process', was impacting our consciousness as much as it was impacting our universities, teaching, research and political-pedagogical action.

We thought of editing a book that would help teaching comparative and international education by tackling most of the pressing issues of the time – specifically, the process of transformation that we were experiencing and that would help empower children, youth, adults, teachers and parents. To accomplish these goals, we brought together a senior generation of comparativists from around the world. The diversity of locations, gender, ethnicities, languages and political-pedagogical commitments, and the plurality of methods and theory employed in the book, brought multiple voices and ways of enriching our understanding of what was occurring. Four editions and 15 years later[4], we are convinced that it was a wonderful dream which became a reality.

Bringing this book to fruition was a process that merged collective history and individual stories. It intentionally consisted of a pedagogical process involving our colleagues and students in navigating the growing complexity of comparative education as a field of teaching and research – a field coming to age after more than 100 years from its initial inception in universities.[5] But, as I have anticipated above, any textbook involves a process of translation, which is not merely a linguistic artifact.

Translations as Border Crossing

I am the poet of the Body and I am the poet of the Soul, The
pleasures of heaven are with me and the pains of hell are with me,
The first I graft and increase upon myself, the latter I translate
into a new tongue. (Walt Whitman, 'Song of Myself')[6]

Different editions of our book *Comparative Education: the dialectic of the global and the local* have been translated into several languages, including Chinese, Japanese, Portuguese and Spanish. The editors could not be more pleased that the fourth edition of the book is now available in English as well as other languages – a book which has become the textbook of choice in many of the English-speaking programs and courses of comparative education in the world. Translations bring it into the hands of different scholars, teachers, students and members of the general public who may prefer to read the book in their mother tongue, enjoying all the subtle rhetorical codes and linguistic devices of the vernacular language which obviously are not to be found in the English edition.[7] Susy Harris (2011) has argued that:

different issues to do with language and questions of translation ...
are pertinent to the contemporary situation in higher education.
Translation is normally understood in relatively simple terms – as
the transfer of meaning from one language to another – and to see
it primarily as a technical matter, albeit one that can raise

considerable difficulties. It is argued that this way of thinking is limited and does not allow us to see other important things about language and translation. In order to do so we need to consider the student experience and the language of international policy in order to explore more profound aspects of translation. (p. 14)

Translation, as Harris so carefully points out, is the response to the biblical dilemmas of the Tower of Babel: 'It was named Babel therefore, because there Yahweh confused the language of the whole earth. It was from there that Yahweh scattered them over the whole face of the earth' (Genesis 11: 1-9). Despite the double jeopardy of translating any material, a scholarly translation is a fundamental chore in our intellectual lives. Despite the difficulties of translating the power of expression from one language to another, and the difficulties of truly understanding the subtle meanings of one language in the linguistic patterns of another, translating becomes a central element in the life of international scholarship. Yet, translations are occasionally impossible, and, instead of translation, we have adaptation.

Not long ago, I received a kind invitation to write an article for a distinguished Chinese peer-reviewed journal. I wrote in English about neoliberalism's new common sense in education following the arguments of my previous work on the matter (Torres, 2011, 2013). The translator very skillfully and patiently explained to me that the concept of 'common sense' in the way I was using it in the article does not exist in Chinese. Hence she offered me, with very analytical descriptions, close to twelve alternative concepts to convey the meaning of my theoretical analysis. Though I was perplexed because I was using the concept of common sense in a Gramscian way and the substance of this concept was central to the intellectual construct of the articles that I have written, I had to live under the present conditions of untranslatability of the master concept of 'common sense' anchoring my analysis and choose one of the options offered by the translator!

The key point is that translations are border crossings. We move from one location with its intellectual, epistemological and logical universe, including its cornucopia of disciplinary concepts, images and values, to a different set of similar domains but articulated in different geographies, histories and, more importantly, identities of subjectivities and otherness. The two questions posed by Harris are forever relevant: how translation impacts student experience, and how translations impact international policy. To some extent, we tried to address these two questions in the architecture of the book; however, I believe there is a combination of factors responsible for its success.

First and foremost is the approach taken to the ecology and intellectual architecture of the book. The dialectics of the global and the local is not merely a rhetorical device – the concepts speak to subtle and open, intimate as well as universal processes deeply impacting our lived experience, the ecology of the social sciences, and certainly the thinking about, and practice of, education worldwide. Second, the success of the book should be attributed to the quality of its contributors, most of them truly world authorities in their fields and areas of specialization. Moreover, the impact of the book is well documented when one considers that the theme of the XVI World Congress of Comparative Education Societies, which will take place in China in August 2016, will focus on 'The Dialectics of Education: the global and the local'.[8]

As a Freirean, and from a very personal perspective, I am pleased to note that the publication of the fourth edition of this book in 2013 invited also a celebration of another landmark in the history of world education – the fiftieth anniversary of the experience of literacy training in Angicos, Rio Grande do Norte, Brazil – an experience conducted by Paulo Freire and a group of idealist and radical students and young scholars who considered it their mission to link popular education via literacy training to popular culture, research and praxis seeking to teach to change the world. Most authors of *Comparative Education: the dialectic of the global and the local* share this view about the transformative power of education. We believe in education as empowerment of children, youth, adults and communities searching for peaceful, just, egalitarian and equitable global and national societies – geographical territories but also imagined communities which are becoming more diverse and multicultural (Torres, 2014).

The translations of *Comparative Education: the dialectic of the global and the local* come at a very propitious time, a time to think globally and act locally, but also a time to consider the emerging perspective of global citizenship education as an alternative narrative transforming educational research, teaching and praxis. The next section focuses on teaching global citizenship education as a new narrative in comparative and international education.

Teaching Global Citizenship Education

Do I contradict myself? Very well then I contradict myself, (I am large, I contain multitudes.) (Walt Whitman, 'Song of Myself')[9]

The world of comparative education was taken by surprise by, but very much welcomed, the 2012 initiative of the UN Secretary-General, Ban Ki-moon, entitled 'The Global Education First Initiative'. Launched on 26 September 2012, the Global Education First Initiative is a five-year program built on three key principles: education for all; quality of education; and global citizenship. In the Secretary-General's own words, 'when we put Education First, we can reduce poverty and hunger, end wasted potential – and look forward to stronger and better societies for all.'[10]

This is the first time that a UN Secretary-General has launched such an ambitious project on education in the UN system. Because it focuses on education, UNESCO is playing a major role in designing and implementing the initiative. As I said, there are three pillars in this initiative: putting every child into school; improving the quality of learning; and fostering global citizenship. While the first and second pillar are essential to the work of comparative education as a field of teaching, research and practice, the third pillar, fostering a global citizen education, is particularly relevant for the goals and purposes of *Comparative Education: the dialectic of the global and the local.*

Granted, to be feasible and successful, this ambitious project of global citizenship needs serious theoretical refinements. Other scholars and I have discussed in many places why global citizenship as opposed to other forms of citizenship, and how comparative education may contribute to advancing global citizenship education (Abdi & Shultz, 2008; Shultz et al, 2011; Torres, 2015b).

Moreover, I will argue that the concept of global citizenship education needs to be framed in the context of a new narrative about education, or, perhaps, to follow the critique of neoliberalism that I had advanced in other places (Torres, 1998, 2011, 2013). The Global Education First Initiative should be framed as a new common sense in education. This new common sense will be able to transform the traditional canons of culture and civics, citizenship education, as well as global education concepts that have become shifting signifiers – implying different things to different people – into a new horizon yet not fully clarified. I am cognizant of the fact that the concept of common sense, with its Gramscian overtones, may not be acceptable to everybody. There is a suspicion that 'common sense' represents an ontological position that lacks an explicit sense of reflexivity. I have discussed these conundrums in one of my articles on neoliberalism and do not need to repeat it here (Torres, 2011).

The third pillar of the Global Education First Initiative is now being negotiated within the intellectual and institutional space of UNESCO and the UN system. Like any negotiation, the concept of global citizenship is subject to polarizing forces, diverse and divergent interests and ideologies, and, by implication, contestation. Tensions, conundrums, paradoxes and contradictions will signal the complex configuration of any project of this magnitude. It is a project that will be negotiated in the globalized environments of the world system and international organizations. The negotiation involves a constant dialectical interplay of national, state or provincial, regional and municipal governments – in short, the ecology of the local heavily compounded with the presence of national and transnational social movements. At least one element seems to be very clear: the need to remove theoretical ambiguities in the definition of the concept.

In more than one presentation in the UNESCO Forums on Global Citizenship Education, I have argued that global citizenship education seems to be an intervention in search of a theory. Fortunately, this conversation is taking place with new voices and new narratives – and a possible new common sense – emerging in education (Torres, 2015b). In other words, teaching comparative and international education has become a formidable challenge for those professing knowledge, skills and commitment in this brutally interdisciplinary field, particularly if we pay attention to and honor culture, language and area studies. Conducting teaching and research in comparative and international education in the first quarter of the twenty-first century requires an understanding and a praxis of a new educational narrative, setting apart this epoch of comparative education from previous ones (Torres, 2013). Let me focus on the importance of global citizenship education and the changes that are connected with the regime of human rights.

Human rights, as a worldwide social movement sponsored by the UN and particularly UNESCO, is one of the most visible faces of the multiple globalizations we are experiencing. As such, human rights are crucial to fostering global citizenship. Yet, it is imperative to decouple human rights from imperialist behavior. With the end of the Cold War in 1989, we have some of the a series of most important military interventions enacted in the name of human rights. The first Gulf War in 1991, the wars that resulted from conflicts in the breaking up of the former Yugoslavia, including the Serbo-Croatian and Bosnian wars, the implications of the Kosovo war, the Iraq invasion, and the war in Afghanistan, by now the longest war fought by the United States in the twentieth century and twenty-first century, or the rumblings about intervention in Syria, all of them identify military interventions using troops on the ground or 'smart bombs' as a moral responsibility to preserve human rights.

Alas, interpreting the here and now of human rights, and how to intervene to prevent a genocide, often relates specifically to geopolitical interest of the western powers involved. Otherwise, how does one justify these interventions, which have resulted in a devastating bloodshed with great loss of lives, while ignoring the Rwandan genocide of 1994? A genocide not prevented by the western powers, resulting in between 500,000 and one million deaths (i.e. 20% of the population) in less than 100 days of bloodshed. Critical theorists know that political calculation always plays a role in international relations, but it is imperative that the ethics and morality of human rights, if it is going to preserve its moral authority, be clearly separated from political interference and interventions by the mighty powers that struggle to run the world system. This failure to resolve issues, as evidenced by the Rwandan genocide, is indicative of an important democratic deficit with regard to the protection of human rights which needs to be remedied.

In other words, there are multiple debates and diverse ideologies about human rights. I will claim, however, that no global citizenship can be accomplished without preserving human rights as a framework and linking global citizenship to economic citizenship. No global citizenship can be achieved without bare essentials, including the right to a job, education, medical care, housing or retraining over the course of one's life. Some of the basic principles of a global citizenship education include not only respect for human rights, but also new models of social justice education and a planetarian citizenship for sustainability. Acknowledging the roles of migration and diversity, of cognitive democracy, and of enhancing the proliferation of public spheres are truly preconditions for school reform promoting global citizenship education and new perspectives in lifelong learning that move beyond simply the premises of competition in growing globalized markets.

Other aspects of citizenship should be incorporated in this new narrative. For example, the right to live free of violence (i.e. considering the rising levels of violence against women in its many forms across the world); the right to conduct important unpaid work in the home, which should be appreciated and recognized (e.g. caring work); the right to live free of oppressive regimes such as 'compulsory heterosexuality'; and all of the above with the need to be ever more conscious of our delicate relationship with our world and environment.

Given the challenges, new generations of comparative educators have to become more knowledgeable in traditional fields such as educational foundations and ethnic, class, race, gender or area studies, but they also need to delve into the new domains of political sociology of education, educational anthropology, political science and political philosophy. Becoming more knowledgeable also means being able to create better connections between facts, data, theory and methods to seek models of explanation of the dilemmas of comparative education. Such models, theories and theses can be assessed and evaluated jointly with our students in our classrooms.

Teaching from a New Educational Narrative?

A call in the midst of the crowd, My own voice, orotund sweeping and final. (Walt Whitman, 'Song of Myself')[11]

The time is ripe to launch a new narrative in our comparative teaching and research. Any astute observer will agree that there are powerful forces at play in rethinking educational sciences. At the same time, current hegemonic ideological models that we have observed in the recent past are being challenged. This contestation contributes to forging a new consensus and new policy directions in education. The dominance of positivism has been challenged over more than three decades by a variety of models. Despite the tenets of positivist epistemology, there is little resemblance between the logic of the natural sciences and the logic of the social sciences (Torres, 2009). More recently, a tension has become evident between conventional scientific research oriented toward hypothesis testing and theory development (dominant in universities) and evidence-based research oriented toward informing action and policy (dominant in international organizations such as the Organisation for Economic Co-operation and Development [OECD], the World Bank and the like) – not to mention the tensions with other methodologies that emerge from critical perspectives, such as feminist and postcolonial methodologies. Not surprisingly, these contrasting paradigms collide. The tensions between the policy and the research communities (perhaps an insurmountable tension) have not prevented causal analysis from remaining the dominant model of scientific work, though this model is under heavy attack by other epistemologies.

Similarly, over the last two decades, there has been an extraordinary effort to focus on test scores in international comparisons, making cognitive learning the essential mission of schools. In a formidable rebuttal to this perspective, Henry Levin (2012) argues:

> Around the world we hear considerable talk about creating world-class schools. Usually the term refers to schools whose students get very high scores on the international comparisons of student achievement such as PISA or TIMSS. The practice of restricting the meaning of exemplary schools to the narrow criterion of achievement scores is usually premised on the view that test scores are closely linked to the provision of a capable labor force and competitive economy. In fact, the measured relationships between test scores and earnings or productivity are modest and explain a relatively small share of the larger link between educational attainment and economic outcomes. What has been omitted from such narrow assessments are the effects that education has on the development of interpersonal and intrapersonal skills and capabilities that affect the quality and productivity of the labour force. (p. 269)

Not surprisingly, in light of the economics of education evidence reported by Levin (2012) and other scholars, the emphasis on achievement scores and cognitive learning has been called into question in the new narrative that seems to be emerging in international quarters and some universities. What is at stake is that other forms of human life, beyond paid labor, should be seriously considered when designing and implementing policy and pedagogy.

Occasionally, comparative educators reach a scientific impasse with scholars and policymakers, unable to communicate across their paradigmatic fortresses. A most welcome outcome of this tension is a growing methodological plurality where dominant stochastic (i.e. random processes usually involved in the collection of random variables) and conventional statistical models are being challenged, or at least contrasted or supplemented, by alternative methodologies such as observational models, exploratory data analysis, action research and phenomenological or qualitative research of diverse orientations.

Another outcome of this tension is the growing perspective of intersectional studies, linking diverse 'variables' and spheres of social action while simultaneously bringing together qualitative and quantitative methods, or at least mixed methods of some sort to aid in the explanation of phenomena. This inter-sectionality, coupled with heavy doses of inter-sectional analysis and inter-disciplinary work now more consolidated in distinguished disciplinary departments of social sciences and education, is leading the field closer to an understanding of relational analysis in education (Ross, 2002).

Perhaps it is my own obsession, but when one begins to analyze in our teaching and/or research a specific problem with a specific focus on the different dimensions of an issue, it is imperative to do so relationally, relating that analysis to the other dimensions that we typically deal with in education. We are constantly relating the economic, political and cultural domains or spheres of praxis and knowledge to questions connected to ethnicity, race, gender, sexuality, class and many other 'variables' of the analysis, including structural and cultural inequalities (McCarthy & Apple, 1998). Thus, adopting a relational analysis is fundamental to teaching and research and obliterates, by definition, specialization as the only basic attribute of good science, 'bean counters' [12] as the only strategy to understand reality, and instrumental rationality as the only viable course of policy action.

The hegemony of statistics and research from above, often based on what feminists call 'soft' objectivity, particularly in studies of opinions, expectations and aspirations, has been challenged via models of standpoint theory that guide toward a logic of inquiry 'from below' (Harding, 2008). While male-centric models of inquiry have not been fully debunked, particularly in international organizations enamored with metrics of any kind, technocrats cannot run the show as easily as they did in the past. *Pari passu*, in a male-centric, andro-centric, logo-centric and Euro-centric dominated world, governments tend to have a strong dose of statistical fetishism in their policy making – though I suspect – and allow me to speak very personally – that statistical data and, for the sake of the argument, research findings of any kind only reach policy-making implementation when they get to the right hands of the right person in the right decision-making position.

Nobody will object to the need for empirical data and empirical studies in comparative education. What is objectionable is the predominance of rational choice and the testing movement, with the fetishism of achievement scores which have affected education in different ways. There is a discourse of science that needs to be carefully inspected. One of them is giving 'numbers' the ability to 'speak for themselves' and hence playing a key role in the new 'science of education'. A critical book argues against the 'culture of science' currently dominating education discourse, instead favoring a more critical understanding of various modes of inquiry (Baez & Boyles, 2009; de Sousa Santos, 2007). According to Baez and Boyles (2009),

> The entire discourse on education science reflects a number of distinct, but mutually constitutive, political forces or movements using science to shape what we can think, and thus, what we can become in the so-called postmodern age. These forces or movements are briefly (1) the movement to professionalize educational researchers, (2) the attempts to restrict democracy via scientism, (3) the uses of academic classification for organizing the

world into social groups, (4) the imperatives of the informational society, which seek precision in order to convert the world into 'data' for governing, and (5) the effects of transnational capitalist exchanges, which convert everything into a cost-benefit analysis and make us all complicit in ways we do not fully grasp. (p. vii)

This culture of scientism, which could also be termed 'scientificism', separates culture from knowledge, dissociating also power from human interest. Science then emerges as a powerful and unchallenged principle of social rationalization, which serves only analytical goals, though eventually could be implemented in specific policies. Science seems then narrowly defined as a mixture of positivism and instrumentalism and is defended on the grounds of statistical rigor and objectivity (Torres, 2013).

A new research rationality – with growing importance to phenomenology, dialectics, grounded theory, mixed methods and several forms of qualitative methods – and new narratives such as eco-pedagogy, postcolonialism, subaltern theories, critical theory, socialist theories of racism, or cultural-sensitive pedagogies, to name a few, are gaining ground in educational research, departing drastically from educational patterns that we have witnessed and that are associated with top-down neoliberal models of globalization. Still public education has been called upon to develop a new labor force to meet the rapidly changing economic demands, presenting policy dilemmas on issues concerning the privatization and decentralization of schools (Arnove & Torres, 1999). This movement includes raising educational standards and placing stronger emphasis on testing and school accountability. Decisions based on economic changes have espoused new visions for school reform in universities as well. These reforms, associated with international competitiveness, are also known as 'competition-based reforms' (Carnoy, 1999; Torres, 2009).

It would be remiss of me not to conclude this chapter with a few remarks about the importance of teaching planetarian citizenship. At the same time the Arnove, Torres, and Franz book went to press in its Japanese edition (2014), there was radiation still leaking from the Fukushima plant after the massive earthquake and tsunami, and Japanese fish exports had been banned in some countries. The environment matters, and comparative educators should consider moving the background to the foreground when teaching global citizenship education, which dovetails so nicely with education for sustainable development.

The urgency to design, implement and make viable a model of sustainable development for the planet cannot be denied. Education has a major role to play in preventing our civilization design from failing to preserve the environment. The expected environmental catastrophe that I could term, to use Gabriel Garcia Márquez's Nobel prize-winning book title, *Chronicle of a Death Foretold*, cannot ever be ignored in any serious conversation about the principles and strategies needed to achieve a good society. The first encyclical of Pope Francis of 24 May 2015, *Laudati Si*, or

'The Care of Our Only Home', is a sobering reminder of what is at stake in preserving the environment and the planet (Pope Francis, 2015). If we endorse a model of inter-disciplinarity connected with relational theories, the discussion in our classrooms will address the environment and education for sustainable development; therefore, a model that aligns well with global citizenship education cannot be absent.

By its intellectual ecology and architecture, the Arnove, Torres and Franz book (Arnove et al, 2013) engages the reader in the conversation about global citizenship in multiple ways, and it is a resource for the new three pillars advanced by the much-welcomed UN Global Education First Initiative. Comparative education as a field of theory, research and practice has gained a unique momentum and importance for the future preservation of human civilizations, the planet and its species. The field and its practitioners, particularly those professing comparative and international education in classrooms and lifelong learning environments, should pause, wait and hear Walt Whitman when he implores us:

> Stop this day and night with me and you shall possess the origin of all poems... You shall listen to all sides and filter them from your self.[13]

Acknowledgements

I would like to thank Robert Arnove, Ratna Ghosh, Penny Jane Burke and the editors of this book for their comments on previous versions of this chapter.

Notes

[1] This section draws selectively from Carlos Alberto Torres, *The Art of Teaching* (brief commentary accepting the Distinguished Teaching Award in recognition of outstanding dedication in teaching and mentoring by the Department of Education, Graduate School of Education and Information Studies, UCLA, Convocation, 25 September 2012) (Torres, 2015a).

[2] 'PAR stands on the epistemological grounds that persons who have historically been marginalized or silenced carry substantial knowledge about the architecture of injustice, in their minds, bodies, and souls; in ways that are conscious and floating; individual and collective' (Cammarota & Fine, 2008, p. 223).

[3] Walt Whitman, 'Song of Myself'.
http://www.poetryfoundation.org/poem/174745

[4] Now with the contribution of Stephen Franz as third editor in the fourth edition (Arnove et al, 2013).

[5] Professor Miguel Pereyra reminded of this history in his lecture entitled 'Cosmopolitanism, History and Schooling in the Late Modern World: the

origins of the study of educational systems in teacher education' (Pereyra, 2013).

[6] Walt Whitman, 'Song of Myself'.
http://www.poetryfoundation.org/poem/174745

[7] The editors of the book are deeply indebted to Professor Yotaka Otsuka, former president of the Japan Comparative Education Society (JCES), for translating the book into Japanese.

[8] See wcces.com. Perhaps one may ask if this choice is more reflective of the fact that I am, at the moment of writing this article, the WCCES president, and therefore shaping the agenda. Just for the record, the title and organizers were chosen months before I was elected president of WCCES in 2013. In my opinion, the title reflects the importance of both concepts, so well captured in the title of Arnove, Torres and Franz's book (Arnove et al, 2013), impacting the current teaching and research in comparative and international education.

[9] Walt Whitman, 'Song of Myself'.
http://www.poetryfoundation.org/poem/174745

[10] http://www.unesco.org/new/en/education/global-education-first-initiative-gefi/

[11] Walt Whitman, 'Song of Myself'.
http://www.poetryfoundation.org/poem/174745

[12] 'A person, such as an accountant or financial officer, who is concerned with quantification, especially to the exclusion of other matters' (http://www.thefreedictionary.com/bean+counters).

[13] Walt Whitman, 'Song of Myself'.
http://www.poetryfoundation.org/poem/174745

References

Abdi, A. & Shultz, L. (Eds) (2008) *Educating for Human Rights and Global Citizenship.* Albany: SUNY Press.

Arnove, R. & Torres, C.A. (Eds) (1999) *Comparative Education: the dialectic of the global and the local.* Lanham, MD: Rowman & Littlefield. (2nd edn, 2003; 3rd edn, 2007; 4th edn [with Stephen Franz], 2013.)

Baez, B. & Boyles, D. (2009) *The Politics of Inquiry: education research and the 'culture of science'.* Albany: New York Press.

Belenky, M., Clinchy, B., Goldberger, N. & Tarule, J. (1986) *Women's Ways of Knowing: the development of self, voice, and mind*, pp. 217-219. New York: Basic Books.

Cammarota, J. & Fine, M. (2008) *Revolutionizing Education: youth participatory action research in motion.* New York: Routledge.

Carnoy, M. (1999) *Globalisation and Educational Reform: what planners need to know.* Paris: UNESCO/IIEP.

Cortázar, J. (1986) *Around the Day in Eighty Worlds.* San Francisco: North Point Press. (Originally published in 1967).

de Sousa Santos, B. (Ed.) (2007) *Cognitive Justice in a Global World: prudent knowledges for a decent life.* Lanham, MD: Lexington Books, Rowman & Littlefield.

Freire, P. (1971) *Pedagogy of the Oppressed.* New York: Seaview.

Gouldner, A. (1964) Anti-minotaur: the myth of a value-free sociology, in I. Horowitz (Ed.) *The New Sociology: essays in social science and social theory in honor of C. Wright Mills*, pp. 196-217. New York: Oxford University Press.

Gramsci, A. (1971) *Selections from the Prison Notebooks*, trans. & ed. Q. Hoare & G. Nowell Smith. New York: International Publishers.

Habermas, J. (1992) *Autonomy and Solidarity*, ed. Peter Dews. London: Verso.

Hale, S. (2007) Appreciating and Critiquing Freire: the connections between education and power in the feminist classroom. Paper presented at *Paulo Freire at UCLA. A Dialogue on His Contributions 10 years after his Death*, Paulo Freire Institute, Graduate School of Education and Information Studies, UCLA, 6 November. Unpublished paper.

Harding, S. (2008) *Sciences from Below: feminisms, postcolonialities, and modernities.* Durham, NC: Duke University Press. http://dx.doi.org/10.1215/9780822381181

Harris, S. (2011) *The University in Translation: internationalizing higher education.* London: Continuum.

Levin, H. (2012) More Than Just Test Scores, *Prospects*, 42(3), 269-284. http://dx.doi.org/10.1007/s11125-012-9240-z

Malsbary, C. & Way, W. (2014) The Scholarship of Carlos Alberto Torres: a dialectic of critique and utopia, in S. Totten & J. Pederson (Eds) *Educating about Social Issues in the 20th and 21st Century: critical pedagogues and their pedagogical theories*, vol. 4. Charlotte, NC: Information Age.

McCarthy, C. & Apple, M. (1998) Race, Class and Gender in American Education: toward a nonsynchronous parallelist position, in L. Weiss (Ed.) *Class, Race, and Gender in American Education*, pp. 9-39. Albany: SUNY Press.

Pereyra, M. (2013) Cosmopolitanism, History and Schooling in the Late Modern World: the origins of the study of educational systems in teacher education. Keynote to the XV World Congress of Comparative Education Societies, Buenos Aires, 25 June.

Pope Francis (2015) *Laudato Si.* http://w2.vatican.va/content/francesco/en/encyclicals/documents/papa-francesco_20150524_enciclica-laudato-si.html (accessed on 29 August 2015).

Rexhepi, J. & Torres, C.A. (2011) Reimagining Critical Theory, *British Journal of Sociology of Education*, 32(5), 679-698. http://dx.doi.org/10.1080/01425692.2011.596363

Ross, H. (2002) The Space between Us: the relevance of relational theory to re-imagining comparative education (presidential address), *Comparative Education Review*, 46(4), 407-432. http://dx.doi.org/10.1086/345417

Shultz, L., Abdi, A. & Richardson, G. (Eds) (2011) *Global Citizenship Education in Post-secondary Institutions: theories, practices, policies.* New York: Peter Lang.

Torres, C.A. (1998) *Democracy, Education and Multiculturalism: dilemmas of citizenship in a global world.* Lanham, MD: Rowman & Littlefield.

Torres, C.A. (2009) *Globalizations and Education: collected essays on class, race, gender, and the state*. Introduction by Michael W. Apple, afterword by Pedro Demo. New York: Teachers College Press.

Torres, C.A. (2011) Public Universities and the Neoliberal Common Sense: seven iconoclastic theses, *International Studies in Sociology of Education*, 21(3), 177-197. http://dx.doi.org/10.1080/09620214.2011.616340

Torres, C.A. (2013) Neoliberalism as a New Historical Bloc: a Gramscian analysis of neoliberalism's common sense in education, *International Studies in Sociology of Education*, 23(2), 80-106. (Special Issue: Neoliberal Common Sense in Education, Part One, ed. C.A. Torres & G. Jones.)

Torres, C.A. (2014) *First Freire: early writings in social justice education*. New York: Teachers College Press.

Torres, C.A. (2015a) The Art of Teaching, in S. Totten (Ed.) *The Importance of Teaching Social Issues: our pedagogical creeds*, pp. 127-140. New York: Routledge.

Torres, C.A. (2015b) Global Citizenship and Global Universities: the age of global interdependence and cosmopolitanism, *European Journal of Education*, 50(3), 262-279. http://dx.doi.org/10.1111/ejed.12129

Whitman, Walt, *Song of Myself.* http://www.poetryfoundation.org/poem/174745 (accessed on 29 August 2015).

Wright Mills, C. (1960) *Images of Man: the classical tradition in sociological thinking*. New York: George Braziller.

CHAPTER 10

Teaching Comparative and International Education: bridging social demands for practical performance-based competencies with critical reflectivity

MARCELO PARREIRA DO AMARAL & SABINE HORNBERG

Introduction

Education research and teaching in higher education have been influenced by a number of international developments and trends with socio-political and cultural implications during the past decades. In particular, comparative and international education (CIE) has devoted substantial attention to these topics and, in some cases, CIE itself has spearheaded some of these trends and developments. For instance, CIE scholarship, on the one hand, was among the first to discuss widely the implications and challenges brought about by globalization and internationalization processes, thus both introducing the topic to students and to other subfields of education and further popularizing the phenomena in academia. On the other hand, CIE was – directly and indirectly – impacted by 'global' processes for instance, in terms of renewed political and media attention to 'international standards' and to comparative arguments at large. However, in the same breath, an approach to comparative research became dominant among policy and practice circles, but also students, thereby influencing how CIE is viewed and what its contributions should be. We discuss some important issues and trends affecting CIE teaching and learning in German universities. In this chapter, we focus on socio-political and cultural themes and trends that helped shape research foci in the field, but also, importantly, public and policy attention to the field during the past years, which in turn has important implications for CIE teaching at higher education institutions. The aim of this chapter is first to deliberate on how these issues and trends are influencing the field of CIE in Germany and how they impact teaching and learning of CIE in the academy. Second, this contribution aims at reflecting on the potential (side) effects of these socio-political and cultural trends on the (self-) understanding of CIE as a field of scholarly inquiry in education as well as on CIE teaching and learning.

Drawing on Cowen and Kazamias's (2009) statement that there are several CIEs, not just one, the chapter begins with a brief discussion of the CIE field in Germany, describing historical events and recent ongoing developments that have shaped and are still impacting the field. By relating them to more general trends and issues – in particular, to globalization and Europeanization processes, to the discourse on the 'knowledge-based economy' and to processes related to the (international) governance of education – the chapter discusses how CIE teaching is currently being influenced.

The CIE Field in Germany:
past and recent events, developments and trends

There is no final consensus on defining CIE, and the terminology used to denominate this field is accordingly heterogeneous. In the past, many comparativists defined CIE with reference either to its method or to its research object; however, more often than not they described and justified the field along the lines of their own understanding of science (e.g. Noah & Eckstein, 1969) or in terms of programmatic intention (Schneider, 1931/32). Comparative and international education is difficult to define with regard to its object of research and teaching; attempts to define CIE by pointing to constitutive questions or problematiques – as is common in studies of theory of science – rather illustrate the blurriness of boundaries and other differentiating criteria. This has implications not only for research, but also for teaching. In their introduction to CIE, David Phillips and Michele Schweisfurth quoted a student who expressed the difficulty of grasping CIE as follows: 'The problem with the comparative and international course ... was that it was about all aspects of education in every country of the world throughout all time' (2008, p. 11). The problem – that 'the comparison' or 'comparing' has become almost ubiquitous in educational science – also applies to Germany, while those entering CIE are faced with the difficulty of getting an overview of its complex field.

A common understanding of CIE in Germany is that it is a pluri-disciplinary field of research and teaching rather than a clearly contoured scientific discipline (Waterkamp, 2006; Adick, 2008; Parreira do Amaral & Amos, 2015b). This understanding emphasizes the spatio-geographic situatedness and historicity of any definition of the field and is rather inclusive than exclusive in nature in acknowledging the diversity of approaches, identities and different understandings of CIE and their projects. It also makes clear that the field is constituted by diverse disciplinary, theoretical and methodological traditions and that those working in the field have to deal with various tensions among research/theory and practice/policy. This definition is also mirrored in the self-understanding of the German Section for Intercultural and International Comparative Education of the German Association for Education Research (SIIVE-DGfE) and its three commissions – namely, 'Education for Sustainable Development', 'Intercultural Education' and 'Comparative and International Education'. In its mission statement, SIIVE-DGfE emphasizes attention to issues of education in a globalized world. All three commissions aim at examining both the global and the national/regional specificities of education processes (e.g. related to internationalization or migration processes) and at inquiring into their relevance for the sustainable development of regions and societies (SIIVE-DGfE, n.d.).

In sum, rather than a flaw, diversity, complexity and plurality are constitutive characteristics of the field, and this may be seen as one major attractor of CIE. Indeed, CIE is at present a highly productive and intellectually stimulating terrain. CIE constructs its objects through an inherent and specific form of perspectivity and conceptualization by means of comparative and international approaches. Very generally, CIE has always to deal with the issue of contingency of education, because it shows that education, as it is practised and institutionalized in country A, may look very different in country B, C or D. Thus, there are many different answers to questions as to how education processes, practices and institutions are understood, designed and organized (Parreira do Amaral & Amos, 2015b). While policymakers and students alike often expect CIE scholarship and its teaching in higher education institutions to contribute more practical (reform) knowledge – a CIE tradition Andreas Kazamias (2009) termed melioristic and which focuses on 'learning from abroad' – scholars rather emphasize its contribution to enhancing the level of reflectivity among students and future educational professionals by calling attention to the contingency of what is habitually seen as 'normal'. In this light, CIE teaching is inherently related to reflecting, analyzing and criticizing the very same socio-political and cultural developments impacting education.

The next section briefly presents and discusses selected events and developments that have had enduring influence on CIE in Germany.

Socio-political and Cultural Developments Shaping CIE in Germany

Germany has experienced major societal, political and cultural changes since the 1950s, which have exerted an important influence on educational theories and concepts, didactic approaches and the organization of state-run compulsory education systems. These transformations have to be taken into consideration when trying to better understand CIE as an academic field of research and teaching at German universities. In what follows, we will refer mainly to the Federal Republic of Germany, as it is beyond the scope of this chapter to fully discuss the developments in CIE also in the German Democratic Republic (for a concise discussion, see Steiner-Khamsi, 2013). We will concisely and selectively focus on immigration since the 1950s, on German reunification in 1990, and on more recent Europeanization processes and relate these more generally to globalization and Europeanization processes, to the discourse on the 'knowledge-based economy' and to processes related to the (international) governance of education.

Discussions about the changes brought about by globalization processes revolve around economic and financial flows, information and communication technologies, as well as social and cultural implications of these processes for nationally bounded societies (see e.g. Dale, 2015). Although the focus has usually been placed on its economic dimension, global or transnational migration has been widely discussed as one main trend impacting education systems worldwide. In Germany, the debate over the implications of migration, however, places its focus on the 'national' history of migration in the host country and its implication for education. That is, rather than addressing issues of international migration and their *trans*national dynamics,[1] this discussion strand has predominantly focused on migration from a host-country perspective, namely, by focusing on the development of labour migration in Germany.

Due to a severe shortage of workers during the years of the *Wirtschaftswunder* (economic miracle) in the post–World War II period, the Federal Republic of Germany signed several bilateral labour recruitment agreements from the mid-1950s to the early 1970s.[2] These agreements included a rotation scheme that required foreign workers to leave the country after a maximum of two years. When in 1973 labour recruitment was stopped, several millions of labour migrants already lived in Germany, both workers and their family members, which ultimately transformed Germany from a country of emigration into a country of immigration (Bade, 1983; Auernheimer, 2007). In reaction to the growing numbers of students from immigrant background in schools, education researchers and practitioners developed various pedagogical concepts such as *Ausländerpädagogik* (pedagogy for foreign students) or intercultural education, which later developed into quite a broad strand in education research. While working from different theoretical foundations and concepts, they all focused on the effects of migration and the resulting ethnic, cultural and linguistic heterogeneity for society, institutions, organizations and individuals in Germany. One reason why intercultural education has grown in importance in the CIE field in Germany is that it offered national policy-makers, ministries of education and pedagogical institutions important practical knowledge – for instance, by thematizing pressing educational issues of the day such as heterogeneity, multiculturalism and educational equity (Steiner-Khamsi, 2009). For this reason, it is especially this strand of CIE scholarship that is currently quite strongly involved in academic teacher education.

A further historical event related to political globalization has had crucial implications for CIE's thematic foci and academic infrastructure: German reunification. The years 1989 and 1990 mark a further major transformation that substantially changed the CIE field in Germany. After the dissolution of the Soviet Union and the German reunification in 1990, the field of CIE in Germany underwent an important shift in focus. As Waterkamp (2007) writes, the development of CIE in Germany was related in a twofold way with Eastern Europe: first, many of the most influential scholars in the field had grown up in Eastern Europe (e.g. Leonhard Froese, Sergius Hessen and Wolfgang Mitter), and second, due to political reasons, this region became an important focus in CIE scholarship in the Federal Republic of Germany.[3] With the end of the Cold War and reunification, 'the East' as a central theme for German CIE collapsed, and it was not until the end of the 1990s that other thematic foci took its place. During this period, globalization ascended to a prominent theme in CIE in the country, and especially the relationship between the global and the national/local has been widely discussed.[4] Other important topics, such as international development, remained, however, rather marginal among German CIE scholars.

More recent developments related to Europeanization and a more pronounced role of education in European integration, as a means of creating and harmonizing a 'European Educational Space' but also of becoming 'the most dynamic and competitive knowledge-based economy in the world' (EU Lisbon Strategy), brought about important social and cultural changes to CIE scholarship. Whereas the original treaties which laid the foundations for the European Community during the 1950s only included some aspects of vocational education and left the bulk of educational responsibility under the subsidiarity clause, the current Maastricht Treaty that came into force in 1992 establishing the European Union put far more emphasis on general and higher education (Nóvoa & Lawn, 2002). Specifically, the first paragraph in Article 126 of the Treaty [5] provided the basis for extensive changes in the field of education in general, and in CIE scholarship in particular. While there are also a number of other developments related to Europeanization that could be discussed here – for instance, the so-called Bologna Process in higher education, issues and initiatives related to lifelong learning and many others – one of the most important shifts in focus impacting CIE scholarship is arguably concerned with educational quality and performance monitoring. Amid discussions about the opportunities and requirements of a 'knowledge-based economy', education governance stood out as a priority for creating high-performing education systems.

For the past two decades, discourses on education policy and research, especially those concerned with compulsory schooling, have been dominated by a focus on quality assurance and improvement of competencies, which in turn has been furthered by recurrent international large-scale comparative studies of educational achievement such as the Programme for International Student Assessment (PISA), the Progress in International Reading Literacy Study (PIRLS), and the Trends in Mathematics and Science Study (TIMSS).[6]

The socio-political and cultural developments sketched above have had a lasting impact on CIE in the country, and it is against this background that more recent developments and trends are shaping research and teaching practice of CIE, as will be discussed next.

Recent Developments and Current Trends Impacting Research and Practice of CIE

In this section, we will briefly present and discuss recent developments and current trends impacting the research and practice of CIE in Germany by drawing from extant literature on the topic. The current state of CIE in Germany may be characterized as a rather paradoxical situation: while there are clear signs of intensified interest in comparative and international knowledge – both from policy and from academic circles, as illustrated by external indicators such as publications and research commissioned by policy – the institutional basis of the field is shrinking, and a dominant understanding of the definition and uses of 'international comparison' has substantially narrowed the scope for CIE scholarship.

In terms of external indicators, CIE seems to be enjoying a renaissance, for, since the turn of the millennium, we can observe a growing number of publications on the state of the art or on the condition of CIE in the country (e.g. Kotthoff, 2015; Parreira do Amaral & Kotthoff, forthcoming 2016). These publications include edited books and monographs on the state of comparative and intercultural education in Germany (e.g. Gogolin et al, 2003; Hornberg et al, 2009), encyclopaedia articles on selected aspects or topics of CIE (e.g. Allemann-Ghionda, 2010; Caruso, 2010; Baumann, 2011), and introductory textbooks to the field (e.g. Waterkamp, 2006; Adick, 2008, 2013; Parreira do Amaral & Amos, 2015a). Furthermore, there is also a growing number of German-language journals, such as *Tertium Comparationis*, *Zeitschrift für Internationale Bildungsforschung und Entwicklungspädagogik* [Journal of Research in International and Development Education] and *Bildung und Erziehung* [Education and Upbringing], and several established CIE book series, such as *Studien zur International und Interkulturell Vergleichenden Erziehungswissenschaft* [Studies on Intercultural and International Comparative Education Research], *Historisch-vergleichende Sozialisations- und Bildungsforschung* [Historical Comparative Socialization and Education Research] and *New Frontiers in*

Comparative Education (Waxmann) or *Komparatistische Bibliothek* [Comparative Studies Series] (Peter Lang) (Parreira do Amaral & Kotthoff, forthcoming 2016). Likewise, in terms of policy attention, CIE seems to be on the rise, as illustrated by increased policy interest in international comparisons in education in the aftermath of the publication of several comparative large-scale assessment studies (among others, TIMSS and PISA). Also, during the past years, a number of state-commissioned comparative studies focusing on the reasons for the success in PISA of selected countries (e.g. Finland and Canada) have been carried out by an International Comparative Study Working Group financed by the Federal Ministry of Education and Research (see e.g. Arbeitsgruppe Internationale Vergleichsstudie, 2004, 2007). However, as will be discussed below, these visible signs of renewed and increased interest in CIE scholarship are not mirrored by the institutional infrastructure of the field.

A second trend is related to an increasing diversification and pluralization of CIE in Germany. As noted above, the German Section for Intercultural, International and Comparative Education consists of three different commissions – namely, 'Education for Sustainable Development', 'Intercultural Education' and 'Comparative and International Education' – which hints at the different intellectual and practical orientations and projects of CIE scholarship in the country. It is against this background that Steiner-Khamsi (2009) argued that there are intellectual and practical reasons for creating synergies and coherence as well as for pooling research capacity of the CIE field in Germany. In intellectual terms, we may note that, while the three represent distinct and specific perspectives and approaches to issues related to education in contemporary societies that are marked by global-scale processes (e.g. internationalization, transnational flows of people, finance, technology, media, ideas, sustainable development in ecological and economic terms, and the like), they also respond to, focus, analyze and criticize common or closely related trends. In pragmatic terms, in times of scant resources for staff and research activities, further fragmenting the field seems counterproductive and actually goes against developments in other parts of the world. In sum, it can be argued that the diversification of the field in Germany has not kept pace with developments elsewhere in terms of disciplinary, geographical and practical orientations. To a certain extent, the three different CIE branches in Germany remain isolated, precluding important synergies in terms of intellectual development and research infrastructure.

Third, as already mentioned above, since the early 2000s there has been growing significance and reception of large-scale international comparative assessment studies (e.g. Kotthoff, 2015; Parreira do Amaral & Kotthoff, forthcoming 2016). This represents a major development in CIE and is currently the most prominent trend and perhaps also the most challenging development for CIE as a field of study in Germany. Here, it might suffice to refer to the reception of PISA results in the country. Ever since the first publication of PISA results in Germany in 2001, there has been a growing body of texts investigating the reception of PISA results in the country (e.g. Ertl 2006; Gruber, 2006; Tillmann et al, 2008; Waldow 2009, 2010). At the same time, education policy-making, administration, school leaders and teacher training institutions in Germany have predominantly been preoccupied with reforming the German education system in reaction to Germany's low scores in PISA and other studies. In this context, reference is constantly made to more successful education systems, according to their ranking in international large-scale comparative studies of educational achievement. Among many circles, this form of 'comparison' has become the standard understanding of what CIE does, whereby mistakes or misinterpretations occur because comparative results are stripped of their specific contexts. In addition to frequent misinterpretations of PISA results ensuing from superficial and decontextualized comparison, the discussion is characterized by a highly selective policy-borrowing orientation (Steiner-Khamsi & Waldow, 2012). Policies borrowed were mainly concerned with reforming school governance and included evaluation and monitoring instruments, such as systematic and regular national school evaluation (e.g. central exit exams, standardized tests, school inspections and self-evaluation), increased autonomy of schools, educational standards, and the development of professional agencies for the evaluation of educational processes and outputs.

Accordingly, in terms of thematic priorities, themes related to quality improvement and educational governance have been emphasized by education and research policy (and funding). For a number of years, research and policy debates in Germany have been dominated by a specific type of comparative research oriented towards questions such as: 'What are the reasons for the differences in student achievement which we can observe from international comparisons?' 'What features characterize a successful school system?' 'What kinds of correlations can be determined for student achievement, socio-cultural contexts and the governance of school systems by taking into account the special conditions of a federal state structure?' (e.g. Arbeitsgruppe Internationale Vergleichsstudie, 2007). To some extent, this research focus has impacted mainstream education research, where now comparison is mainly seen as a means of analyzing the *causes* of differential achievement and of identifying governance features that explain 'success' in performance testing. Also, the emphasis on international large-scale comparative studies of educational achievement and the introduction of national or regional studies on educational achievement in schools have brought about important changes to CIE. Germany has taken part in large-scale assessment studies for more than twenty years, and will continue to do so, according to the policy of the Standing Conference of the Ministers of Education and Cultural Affairs (KMK) of the Länder in the Federal Republic of Germany. For this purpose, the KMK founded the Institute for Educational Quality Improvement (IQB) [7] hosted at the Humboldt

University Berlin. The IQB is responsible for regularly monitoring the extent to which Germany's schools are achieving educational standards.

In turn, this has had an important impact on the infrastructure of the CIE field, since this emphasis on performance testing and evidence-based policy has created a specific 'need' for comparative knowledge (i.e. empirical quantitative research and know-how for designing, carrying out and interpreting large-scale empirical studies of the PISA type). The result was a thorough realignment in academic education and research. Currently, most scholars working in CIE hold professorships not explicitly dedicated to comparative and international education.[8] In addition, many professorships formerly dedicated to CIE have been redesignated to school development, competence assessment or, more generally, to 'quantitative-empirical research' (*Empirische Bildungsforschung*). Consequently, in Germany the majority of those working in CIE in Germany are not, or are not exclusively, affiliated with CIE, which, while not detrimental in itself, diverts attention away from the field and has the potential to substantially change the self-understanding of CIE, as the field has rapidly diversified and fragmented since scholars in all fields of expertise in education (e.g. school or social pedagogy, adult education, etc.) have increasingly produced comparative work, often commissioned by policymakers and narrowly oriented towards 'performance' and 'productivity/success' of education systems.

These last trends are related to central changes in school governance over the past two decades, often referred to in Germany as a paradigm shift from input to output orientation. Among these changes, data-driven teacher training was introduced, implying that students in education studies and in teacher education now have compulsory courses on 'empirical' research methods in order to be able to understand the main findings of reports on competence-assessment studies. While in many cases this was introduced at the cost of themes and courses related to the foundations of education (i.e. courses discussing the ideological, philosophical, psychological, socio-economic and historical foundations of education), of which CIE has traditionally been a central part, we may see this not only as a challenge, but also as an opportunity for CIE to address these themes from a more holistic comparative and international perspective. The latter requires both profound knowledge of the social and cultural embedding of education and social-scientific methodologies to produce coherent, systematic and contextualized comparative knowledge.

Thus, the vitality and visibility of CIE in Germany, as suggested by external indicators, seem to indicate that the field is thriving. However, with this increased attention, especially from the policy realm, has also come a highly specific but dominant understanding of what constitutes – or should constitute – CIE scholarship. In parallel to this, a diversification and compartmentalization of approaches to CIE has further fragmented the field. Moreover, CIE in Germany has been impacted by ever-increasing attention to international comparative assessment studies, which, due to the way that they are used, does not necessarily help increase the salience and reputation of CIE as an academic discipline in Germany, since comparison is seldom explicit and is mostly decontextualized. Importantly, questions as to the intellectual implications and/or side effects of these trends to CIE as a field of research and teaching have not yet been sufficiently tackled. We shall return to this issue in the concluding section of the chapter.

Two Examples of CIE Teaching and Learning in Germany: tensions, challenges and opportunities

In what follows, we briefly illustrate the implications of these trends by referring to our own teaching activities at the Technical University Dortmund and at the University of Münster.[9] Some brief information on the main structures and contents of education studies in higher education in Germany might be useful for the contextualization of the examples we discuss here. Education studies in Germany is usually pursued in three-year bachelor's and two-year master's degrees, either as a main subject (*Erziehungswissenschaft* or *Pädagogik*) or in teacher education programmes. The latter are divided into two stages: initial teacher education in higher education institutions and in-service training in schools. Students in teacher education programmes study at least two compulsory subject areas and educational sciences, which is analogous to 'social foundation' courses in the United States. Universities in Germany usually offer one summer and one winter term each year, each lasting about 15-18 weeks, during which lectures and seminars are offered weekly in 1½-hour sessions. Lectures and seminars at the bachelor or master's level cater to students in main subjects, as well as in teacher education. In the course of implementing the so-called Bologna Reform that introduced a common bachelor's/master's/doctorate study structure across European countries, one important aspect relates to stricter organization of course catalogues and examination practices, as well as less scope for individual choice of themes and subjects for students. Some critics have also pointed to the shortening of programmes, which led to students hurrying from course to course simply collecting their credits, and to rote learning becoming the main competence developed (Schramm, 2010).

The first CIE example is an elective seminar at the master's level in a teacher education programme at the Technical University Dortmund. The seminar 'Education Systems in International Comparative Perspective' in a broader sense is aimed at the students developing an understanding of the complex interplay at work in education systems. In this respect, the gains and limitations of international large-scale assessment studies are the objectives for identifying and critically analyzing conditions of 'good practice' against the background of national education systems, by taking into consideration their histories and societal contexts, policies, school practice and pedagogy. One aim of the seminar is for teacher students, who traditionally concentrate on the national education system they intend to work in, to practise taking a wider international perspective on educational developments and national education systems, and to learn and practise how to read and carefully interpret information gained from international large-scale assessment studies against the aforementioned background. Thus, the emphasis of the seminar is not so much on the aspect of identifying good practice to learn from, but on making students aware of, and able to reflect critically on, the complex global, international and national developments, actors and pedagogies shaping the conditions and practices in education systems.

These broader aims were broken down into the following seminar goals: (1) making students aware of international and global trends and institutions impacting national education systems; (2) raising students' awareness of the meaning of national histories and societal contexts in the development of education systems, policy, and school practice, as well as pedagogy; and (3) practising the 'reading' of international large-scale school assessment studies (i.e. reflecting on what can be learned from them and identifying their limitations). In the first phase of the seminar, students read selected sections from a textbook on comparative education developed by Dietmar Waterkamp (2006) with, and for, students in teacher education. The parts of the book introduced and discussed in the seminar dealt with the 'constitution of the subject of comparative education by referring to legislation and the nation' (pp. 17-34) and a demonstration of how a pedagogical perspective can be applied to the subject 'education systems of the nations' (pp. 35-66). These discussions relate to two main aspects of particular interest to students in teacher education: first, the historical origins and societal contexts of national education systems, which includes national as well as international developments and dimensions of education systems; and second, characterizing education systems historically with reference to influential politicians, institutions (e.g. a religious congregation), societal circumstances (e.g. nation-building processes), educator(s) or pedagogies, administrative and/or pedagogical features of a national educational system, and the like.

At the end of the seminar's first phase, a table was introduced to the students with categories on various aspects of education systems, such as political system (e.g. democracy) and organization (e.g. central or federal), ethnic minorities, official state language(s), language(s) used in schools, state expenditure on education, percentage of students attending state/private schools, structure of the education system, teaching methods, achievement according to international large-scale assessment studies in the subjects tested, and information gained by the reports on other variables. The second phase of the seminar consisted of group work and was dedicated to exploring selected national education systems, covering one example of a southern, northern, western and eastern European country, as well as Latin America, North America and Asia. Students worked in groups assigned with the task of preparing, documenting and presenting one education system to the seminar by referring to the aspects included in the table prepared. The last session of the seminar required participants to reflect on the seminar's aims.

It is important to note that students, especially in teacher education in Germany, often do not display an outspoken international orientation and focus. In particular, when referring to educational science courses, they often show a rather instrumental attitude and tend, for example, to attribute relevance only to courses where practical knowledge and 'learning how to teach' are anticipated. This orientation, which is focused more on practice than on theory/research, from an individual perspective is quite rational, in view of the strict selection practices in entrance to service in schools where much attention is given to teaching practice. Furthermore, it reflects policy and public discussions where the need for quality and performance improvement is widely emphasized, which in turn is addressed to teachers and teacher students. In our view, while acknowledging the students' orientation, CIE has the potential and obligation to take the students' motivation as a starting point for widening their rather instrumental attitude so as to support their critical thinking and analysis.

Against this background, information on the reasons for students to elect CIE courses in teacher education programmes is quite instructive. When asked why they chose to take the seminar 'Education Systems in International Comparative Perspective', many students stressed that in an increasingly globalized world 'it is important for a teacher to know something about the differences in education systems'. Others referred to their previous knowledge of school systems gained, for example, in courses on American literature, to language acquisition (e.g. French, Spanish, etc.), or to their plans to write their master's thesis on a national education system. When asked what they learned from the seminar, the following answer of one student is quite representative: 'I learned that there is not one ideal school system, but that there are many roads leading to Rome.' Another student stated, 'It was interesting to see that pedagogies may differ according to the national education system, its historical and societal development.' When further asked as to what they would take with them from the seminar for their future work as teachers, a typical student response was that 'one should more often "think outside the box" and learn from others, while bearing in mind that every system has its weaknesses and strengths'. This example illustrates how, in a context where students generally are not 'rewarded' for being internationally oriented and are usually directed to 'evidence-based competence teaching', CIE courses succeed in providing room for reflection and in countering parochialism.

The second CIE example is from an introductory lecture entitled 'Introduction to International and Comparative Education' at the University of Münster. The course catered both to students pursuing studies in education as a main subject and to students in teacher education programmes at the bachelor's level. The lecture aimed at providing students with insights into the conceptual, theoretical and methodological issues in CIE. The first four sessions shed light on different aspects and themes of education from different perspectives: intercultural, international and comparative. The basic aim was to introduce participants to the specific conceptual, theoretical and methodological perspectives associated with each of the three CIE branches. While these three may be viewed as distinct in approach and outlook, the lecture underlined that they may also be regarded as focusing, analyzing, scrutinizing and critiquing the social, political and cultural frameworks of education at various levels (i.e. local, national and global). A second block of the course included research presentations by several guest speakers. The research presentations addressed the following projects: 'Transnational Migration and Education: a research project between Brazil and Europe' by Sara Fürstenau and Javier Carnicer (University of Münster); 'The Educational Situation of Roma: a theme for CIE' by Sabine Hornberg (Technical University Dortmund); 'Holocaust Education as a Theme of CIE' by Wolfgang Meseth (University of Marburg); and 'Education in the Life Course from International Comparative Perspective' by Andreas Walther (University of Frankfurt). Three concluding sessions rounded out the lecture, during which students were required to transfer knowledge gained during the lecture by elaborating on how exactly the three disciplinary perspectives discussed in the course focused, analyzed, scrutinized and critiqued the social, political and cultural frameworks of education that were illustrated in the presentation of the different research projects.

In particular, during the concluding sessions of the lecture, several tensions became visible between programme requirements, student behaviour and policy/public discourse on comparative research. In terms of programme requirements, the competences to be acquired in accordance with programme regulations, including knowledge of the societal and cultural frameworks of education, of inequality, of social change and the like, demand a high degree of reflectivity and autonomy in arguing, reading and writing about a subject. The acquisition of these competences needs time and requires dedication in terms of deliberating and thinking critically about societal/political/cultural conditions of education. This, in large part, contradicts study programmes that are highly fragmented (modularized), that are rather strict in terms of choice, and that do not require attendance, as is the case in North Rhine-Westphalia, and, on the side of students, that do not leave enough time for elaboration and reflection. Related to the last point, student behaviour is arguably 'pre-conditioned' by these study structures and exacerbated by time pressure and the sense that only cognitive knowledge and rote learning ('evidence-based competences') count, which is reinforced in public and policy discourses.

To be sure, these are arbitrary examples of teaching CIE at two institutions. At the same time, they offer insights into the tensions, challenges, but also opportunities for CIE teaching in higher education in Germany. One important insight refers to how CIE teaching still contributes to expanding the horizons of students, even in programmes that generally do not foster an international orientation and that usually direct students to practical knowledge, such as briefly discussed in the first example. Here, CIE courses offer opportunities for crucially needed reflection on the social/cultural embedding of education, thus uncovering the contingency of what is otherwise seen as 'normal'. Also, the discussion above hints at the current challenge of productively integrating CIE in higher education teaching. The main issue relates to bridging the requirements of CIE scholarship, programme structures and policy expectations, as hinted at in the example above. In terms of the requirements of CIE scholarship, there is need to respect and support conceptual and methodological diversity, pluralism and complexity, which demands a high degree of reflectivity and intellectual autonomy in arguing, reading and writing about a subject. The acquisition of these competences requires time and a high level of dedication. Pursuing these competences in the context of programmes that leave only little time and room for deliberation, while at the same time demanding 'evidence-based competences', represents one of the greatest challenges for CIE scholarship at present. The scope for CIE scholarship is further narrowed because in public and policy discourses an understanding of CIE is favoured that is cast in the mould of current international large-scale assessment studies and primarily interested in practical knowledge for improving quality and performance.

Concluding Remarks

The aim of this chapter was to discuss and deliberate on how social, political and cultural issues and trends are influencing the field of CIE in Germany and how they are impacting teaching and learning of CIE in the academy. We emphasized the contribution of CIE scholarship to enhancing the level of reflectivity among students and future educational professionals by calling attention to the contingency of what is habitually seen as 'normal' and by countering parochialism and a pure melioristic orientation. CIE teaching, it was argued, is inherently related to reflecting, analyzing and criticizing the very same socio-political and cultural developments impacting education. The chapter has described selected past events, as well as recent and ongoing developments, that have shaped and are still affecting the field in the country. Discussing more recent developments such as Europeanization processes, it was argued that amid these developments a strong focus on quality and performance as well as on education governance became dominant, which in turn reinforced a specific approach to comparative research – namely, international comparative large-scale assessment studies. Moreover, the two examples from our own teaching activities at German universities briefly illustrated the tensions and challenges for CIE scholarship in German universities – for instance, the difficulties of bridging the requirements of CIE scholarship and programme structures.

This chapter also reflected on the ways CIE still contributes to academic teaching and learning that go beyond the narrow scope of decontextualized international comparisons of education systems and educational achievement, by enhancing students' reflective capacity for contextualized critical thinking and analysis. While the German tertiary education system still provides scope for such CIE seminars and lectures, the impact of the socio-political and cultural trends discussed above – which explain the current strong focus on large-scale assessments and international test scores – and the accompanying output orientation, educational standards and evidence-based-competences continue to have palpable consequences for CIE teaching and learning. Likewise, the trends discussed above have potentially important implications for CIE as a field of scholarly inquiry in education. Having suggested a rather positive outlook for perspectives of CIE in teaching at the tertiary level, the visible signs of renewed and increased interest in CIE scholarship identified here are not mirrored by the institutional infrastructure of the field. On the contrary, there has been a substantial impact on the CIE institutional infrastructure, with several professorships formerly dedicated to CIE being redesignated to school development, competence assessment or generally to quantitative-empirical research. The ensuing developments have contributed to curtailing the scope for contextualized comparative research due to the dominance of large-scale assessment testing as the preferred form of comparison. To be sure, these are not inner scientific debates but are related to education and science policy. There is nothing intrinsically wrong or less important about large-scale quantitative forms of comparisons; the issue is rather connected to how policy-making has used (and abused) them. Further, the focus on 'lessons learned from elsewhere', or the demand for practical knowledge and 'evidence-based competences', has substantially drawn attention away from educational foundation courses. As the examples from teaching CIE above show, attempts are still made to reconcile programme requirements and study circumstances with CIE scholarship. The tensions felt, however, indicate that in the long run, the implications of these developments for (self-)understanding CIE as a field of scholarly inquiry in education, as well as for understanding CIE teaching and learning, deserve vigilant attention.

Notes

[1] For instance, Levitt and Jarkowsky (2007) summarize the literature on transnational migration along different domains – namely, economic, political, social, cultural and religious.

[2] Italy (1955), Spain and Greece (1960), Turkey (1961), Portugal (1964), Morocco and Tunisia (1965), and the former Republic of Yugoslavia (1968).

[3] This is linked to the political climate dominated by the separation of Germany and by the Cold War, but is also due to the sources of financing of research (Steiner-Khamsi, 2013) and the personal experiences of scholars (see also Waterkamp, 2007; Kotthoff, 2015).

[4] But even then, at least in Germany, emphasis was placed on theory development in CIE, not on the practical, social and cultural dimensions of globalization processes.

[5] 'The Community shall contribute to the development of quality education by encouraging cooperation between Member States and, if necessary, by supporting and supplementing their action, while fully respecting the responsibility of the Member States for the content of teaching and the organisation of education systems and their cultural and linguistic diversity' (Maastricht Treaty, 1992, Article 126, § 1).

[6] PISA is conducted by the Organisation for Economic Co-operation and Development (OECD), and both PIRLS and TIMSS are led by the International Association for the Evaluation of Educational Achievement (IEA).

[7] IQB is the German acronym for 'Institute for Educational Quality Improvement' (Institut zur Qualitätsentwicklung im Bildungswesen) (https://www.iqb.hu-berlin.de/bista [accessed on 25 July 2015]).

[8] Currently, the only professorships with explicit denominations to 'comparative and international education' are at the universities of Berlin, Bochum, Hamburg, Cologne, Leipzig, Münster and Magdeburg. Not counted here are those institutions that hold chairs for intercultural education.

[9] Both examples discussed are from the State of North Rhine-Westphalia; due to the federal organization of the country, differences may apply in other German Länder. For more details, see: http://www.kmk.org/fileadmin/doc/Dokumentation/Bildungswesen_en_pdfs/te achers.pdf (accessed on 25 June 2015).

References

Adick, C. (2008) *Vergleichende Erziehungswissenschaft. Eine Einführung* [Comparative Education. An Introduction]. Stuttgart: Kohlhammer.

Adick, C. (Ed.) (2013) *Bildungsentwicklungen und Schulsysteme in Afrika, Asien, Lateinamerika und der Karibik* [Educational Systems and Trends in Africa, Asia, Latin America and the Caribbean]. Münster: Waxmann.

Allemann-Ghionda, C. (2010) Methodologische Ansätze der Vergleichenden Erziehungswissenschaft – Die Operation des Vergleichs [Methodological Approaches of Comparative Education – the Operation of Comparison], in D. Waterkamp (Ed.) *Enzyklopädie Erziehungswissenschaft Online. Fachgebiet: Vergleichende Erziehungswissenschaft VE, Der Vergleich in der VE*, pp. 1-35. Weinheim: Juventa Verlag.

Arbeitsgruppe Internationale Vergleichsstudie (International Comparative Study Working Group) (Eds) (2004) *Features of Successful School Systems: a comparison of schooling in seven countries.* Münster: Waxmann.

Arbeitsgruppe Internationale Vergleichsstudie (International Comparative Study Working Group) (Eds) (2007) *Schulleistungen und Steuerung des Schulsystems im*

Bundesstaat. Kanada und Deutschland im Vergleich [School Performance and Control of the School System in the Federal State. Canada and Germany Compared]. Münster: Waxmann.

Auernheimer, G. (2007) *Einführung in die Interkulturelle Pädagogik* [Introduction to Intercultural Pedagogy], 5th edn. Darmstadt: Wissenschaftliche Buchgesellschaft.

Bade, Klaus J. (1983) Vom Auswanderungsland zum Einwanderungsland? Deutschland 1880-1980 [From a Country of Emigration to a Country of Immigration? Germany 1880-1980]. Berlin: Colloquium.

Baumann, U. (2011) Die Vergleichende Erziehungswissenschaft an deutschen Universitäten, Forschungsinstituten und in wissenschaftlichen Vereinigungen, in D. Waterkamp (Ed.) *Enzyklopädie Erziehungswissenschaft Online. Fachgebiet: Vergleichende Erziehungswissenschaft VE, Die VE in der Hochschullehre*, pp. 1-33. Weinheim: Juventa Verlag.

Caruso, M. (2010) Die Vielfalt der vergleichenden Bildungsforschung: Forschungsdesigns und Textgattungen [The Diversity of Comparative Educational Research: research design and text genres], in D. Waterkamp (Ed.) *Enzyklopädie Erziehungswissenschaft Online. Fachgebiet: Vergleichende Erziehungswissenschaft VE, Der Vergleich in der VE*, pp. 1-24. Weinheim: Juventa Verlag.

Cowen, R. & Kazamias, A. (Eds.) (2009) *International Handbook of Comparative Education*. Dordrecht: Springer. http://dx.doi.org/10.1007/978-1-4020-6403-6

Dale, R. (2015) Globalisierung in der Vergleichenden Erziehungswissenschaft re-visited [Globalization in Comparative Education re-visited], in M. Parreira do Amaral & K. Amos (Eds) *Internationale und Vergleichende Erziehungswissenschaft. Geschichte, Theorie, Methode und Forschungsfelder* [International and Comparative Education. History, Theory, Method and Research Fields] (Vol. 2 of *New Frontiers in Comparative Education*), pp. 171-187. Münster: Waxmann.

Ertl, H. (2006) Educational Standards and the Changing Discourse on Education: the reception and consequences of the PISA study in Germany, *Oxford Review of Education*, 32(5), 619-634. http://dx.doi.org/10.1080/03054980600976320

Gogolin, I., Helmchen, J., Lutz, H. & Schmidt, G. (Eds) (2003) *Pluralismus unausweichlich? Blickwechsel zwischen Vergleichender und Interkultureller Pädagogik* [Pluralism inevitable? Change of perspective between comparative and intercultural pedagogy]. Münster: Waxmann.

Gruber, K.H. (2006) The German 'PISA-shock': some aspects of the extraordinary impact of the OECD's PISA study on the German education system, in H. Ertl (Ed.) *Cross-national Attraction in Education: accounts from England and Germany*, pp. 195-208. Oxford: Symposium Books.

Hornberg, S., Dirim, I., Lang-Wojtasik, G. & Mecheril, P. (Eds) (2009) *Beschreiben – Verstehen – Interpretieren: Stand und Perspektiven International und Interkulturell Vergleichender Erziehungswissenschaft in Deutschland* [Describing – Understanding – Interpreting: State and Perspectives in International and Intercultural Comparative Educational in Germany]. Münster: Waxmann.

Kazamias, A.M. (2009) Forgotten Men, Forgotten Themes: the historical-philosophical-cultural and liberal humanist motif in comparative education, in

R. Cowen & A. Kazamias (Eds) *International Handbook of Comparative Education*, vol. 1, pp. 37-58. Dordrecht: Springer.

Kotthoff, H.-G. (2015) Zwischen Renaissance und Bedeutungslosigkeit. Aktueller Stand und Perspektiven der Vergleichenden Erziehungswissenschaft in Deutschland [Between Renaissance and Irrelevance. Current State and Perspectives of Comparative Education in Germany], *Tertium Comparationis*, (21), 1, 6-26.

Levitt, P. & Jarkowsky, B.N. (2007) Transnational Migration Studies: past developments and future trends, *Annual Review of Sociology*, 33, 129-156. http://dx.doi.org/10.1146/annurev.soc.33.040406.131816

Maastricht Treaty (1992) Treaty of Maastricht on European Union. http://eur-lex.europa.eu/legal-content/EN/TXT/HTML/?uri=URISERV:xy0026&from=EN (accessed on 24 August 2015).

Noah, H. & Eckstein, M. (1969) *Towards a Science of Comparative Education*. London: Macmillan.

Nóvoa, A. & Lawn, M. (Eds) (2002) *Fabricating Europe: the formation of an education space*. Dordrecht: Kluwer. http://dx.doi.org/10.1007/0-306-47561-8

Parreira do Amaral, M. & Amos, K. (Eds) (2015a) *Internationale und Vergleichende Erziehungswissenschaft. Geschichte, Theorie, Methode und Forschungsfelder* [International and Comparative Education. History, Theory, Method and Research Fields] (Vol. 2 of *New Frontiers in Comparative Education*). Münster: Waxmann.

Parreira do Amaral, M. & Amos, K. (Eds) (2015b) Introduction, in *Internationale und Vergleichende Erziehungswissenschaft. Geschichte, Theorie, Methode und Forschungsfelder* [International and Comparative Education. History, Theory, Method and Research Fields] (Vol. 2 of *New Frontiers in Comparative Education*), pp. 7-13. Münster: Waxmann.

Parreira do Amaral, M. & Kotthoff, H.-G. (forthcoming 2016) *Comparative and International Education in Germany: a discussion of current trends*, in A.W. Wiseman & E. Anderson (Eds) *Annual Review of Comparative and International Education 2015*. International Perspectives on Education and Society (IPES) series. Bingley: Emerald Group.

Phillips, D. & Schweisfurth, M. (2008) *Comparative and International Education: an introduction to theory, method, and practice*. London: Continuum.

Schneider, F. (1931/32) Internationale Pädagogik, Auslandpädagogik, Vergleichende Erziehungswissenschaft. Geschichte, Wesen, Methoden, Aufgaben und Ergebnisse [International Education, Foreign Education, Comparative Education Science. History, Nature, Methods, Tasks and Results], *Internationale Zeitschrift für Erziehungswissenschaft*, 1, 15-39, 243-257, 392-407.

Schramm, K. (2010) *Erziehungswissenschaft im Bologna-Prozess. Zwischen Professionalisierung und Deprofessionalisierung* [Education Science in the Bologna Process. Between Professionalization and Deprofessionalization]. Marburg: Tectum.

SIIVE-DGfE (n.d.) Homepage. German Section for Intercultural, International and Comparative Education of the German Education Research Association (DGfE). http://www.siive.de/ (accessed on 24 August 2015).

Steiner-Khamsi, G. (2009) The Politics of Intercultural and International Comparison, in S. Hornberg, I. Dirim, G. Lang-Wojtasik & P. Mecheril (Eds) (2009) *Beschreiben – Verstehen – Interpretieren: Stand und Perspektiven International und Interkulturell Vergleichender Erziehungswissenschaft in Deutschland* [Describing – Understanding – Interpreting: State and Perspectives in International and Intercultural Comparative Educational in Germany], pp. 39-61. Münster: Waxmann.

Steiner-Khamsi, G. (2013) The Case Study in Comparative Education from an International Historical Perspective, in S. Hornberg, C. Richter & C. Rotter (Eds) *Erziehung und Bildung in der Weltgesellschaft* [Education in the World Society], pp. 51-73. Münster: Waxmann.

Steiner-Khamsi, G. & Waldow, F. (Eds) (2012) *Policy Borrowing and Lending in Education. World Yearbook of Education 2012.* London: Routledge.

Tillmann, K.-J., Dedering, K., Kneuper, D., Kuhlmann, C. & Nessel, I. (2008) *PISA als bildungspolitisches Ereignis: Fallstudien in vier Bundesländern* [PISA as an Education Policy Event: case studies in four federal states]. Wiesbaden: VS Verlag. http://dx.doi.org/10.1007/978-3-531-91127-4

Waldow, F. (2009) What PISA Did and Did Not Do: Germany after the 'PISA-shock', *European Educational Research Journal*, 8(3), 476-483. http://dx.doi.org/10.2304/eerj.2009.8.3.476

Waldow, F. (2010) Der Traum vom 'skandinavisch schlau Werden' – Drei Thesen zur Rolle Finnlands als Projektionsfläche in der gegenwärtigen Bildungsdebatte [The dream of becoming as 'smart as the Scandinavians' – three theses on the role of Finland as a projection screen in the current debate on education], *Zeitschrift für Pädagogik*, 56(4), 497-511.

Waterkamp, D. (2006) *Vergleichende Erziehungswissenschaft. Ein Lehrbuch* [Comparative Education: a textbook]. Münster: Waxmann.

Waterkamp, D. (2007) The Section for International and Intercultural Comparative Education in the German Society for Education (SIIVE-DGfE), in V. Masemann, M. Bray & M. Manzon (Eds) *Common Interests, Uncommon Goals: histories of the World Council of Comparative Education Societies and its members*, pp. 139-154. Hong Kong: University of Hong Kong, Comparative Education Research Centre.

AFTERWORD

Teaching Comparative Education: a personal afterword

DAVID PHILLIPS

Like many academics of my generation whose specialism is the study of education, I initially trained as a teacher. After that I taught for a total of eight years in a grammar (academic secondary) school and, as a senior teacher, in a comprehensive school in England. The way in which to gain qualified teacher status after completing an undergraduate degree was to study for what then (the late 1960s) was called the Diploma in Education, a one-year postgraduate course. In my day that course in Oxford combined training in a teaching subject, including a whole term of teaching practice in a grammar school, with study of the contributing disciplines of education: philosophy and history, psychology, and sociology. Various optional 'special subjects' could also be studied in the final third of the course, and included in the list of possibilities was comparative education. I chose philosophy, and have wondered ever since what the content of the course in comparative education would have been like.

A clue is to be found in the three 3-hour written examination papers which students were required to sit at the end of the course.[1] Here are some of the questions with which candidates were faced in Paper III of the examination:

> Compare the role and status of the teacher in England with that in *either* Germany and the United States *or* any developing country.

> Comment on the view that in Britain and in developing countries the schools concentrate so hard on helping their pupils to acquire qualifications that they neglect the development of many of the qualities needed for success in adult careers.

Compare the religious agreement achieved in the educational systems of either Germany or France with that achieved in England.

Review the present position of voluntary agency schools in a developing country known to you. How far does experience in any of the more developed countries suggest possible solutions?

'French education is predominantly intellectual in character, English is non-intellectual, and American anti-intellectual.' Discuss.

Compare recent developments in English higher education with those in France.

Discuss to what extent the British or the American idea of a university is relevant to the needs of a developing country.

What is interesting here is the range of knowledge expected of students during a taught course in Oxford of two terms (only one term of eight weeks in the case of a 'special subject'). Alongside this high expectation in covering topics in comparative education, of course, there were two terms (16 weeks) of study in philosophy and history, in psychology, and in sociology. Here candidates were faced with questions such as:

What did Matthew Arnold understand by 'culture'?

What did the public [='independent'] schools of the nineteenth century owe to Dr Arnold?

Discuss the educational relevance of our knowledge of processes of social interaction.

Discuss how far educational thought needs a clear concept of 'human nature'.

What is meant by saying of a man [*sic*] that he is highly trained but not educated?

What is meant by a 'theory of education?'

Is it possible to define the scope of the sociology of education?

Discuss the significance for classroom instruction of *either* studies of incentives *or* the concept of 'cognitive needs'.

Write briefly on *three* of the following: learning sets; reinforcement schedules; distributed practice; level of aspiration.

'The teacher might well be wary of anyone who suggests some change in educational practice on the basis of his knowledge of learning psychology.' Discuss.

It is comforting to know that the answers to such questions are destroyed at some point following the examination, so that they no longer exist to haunt the candidates.

The questions on comparative topics suggest a focus on the philosophical/historical tradition, with answers expected to engage in argument based on a secure knowledge of countries or regions. The comparative education course was taught by Dr W. D. (Bill) Halls, an urbane and sophisticated scholar who was later to be my doctoral supervisor. Bill Halls was an expert on the history of education in France and so that country and the others about which he was deeply knowledgeable (the United States, Canada, Germany, Belgium among them) would have formed a prominent part of his teaching. I am sure that the approach would have been to examine the nature of education systems and to extrapolate themes from the example of a series of country studies, an approach – with its origins in the earliest traditions of comparative studies in education, exemplified by the work of Michael Sadler – which is nowadays quite rare and often summarily dismissed. And yet, one of the basic problems in designing any introductory course in comparative education is to balance the need to know about contexts (countries, regions) with the desire to gain a perspective on themes (the role of the state, equity issues, attainment, etc., etc.). How can a student of comparative education have a proper understanding of comparative themes without a detailed knowledge of the contexts in which they are exemplified and through which they might be analysed and explained? And how can such detailed knowledge be acquired without residence in other countries and – as necessary – fluency in at least one other language (as called for by George Bereday)?

When designing the course that Colin Brock and I started in Oxford in 1994, we wanted first to avoid a split between traditional comparative inquiry on the one hand and development studies on the other. All too often, it seemed to us, postgraduate courses were either of one kind or the other, with little interrelationship between the two. Some British universities had courses only in one of these domains, with no exchange of ideas across their boundaries. At the same time we wished to make it clear that the Oxford course was an *academic* course of study, not a training course that would equip its graduates to become fieldworkers in a developing country, or policy analysts in an international organisation. We were always fortunate in having far more applicants than there were places available, and so we always had a truly international intake of well-qualified graduates, speaking many languages between them and bringing to the course a very wide range of personal experience and expertise based on a variety of basic disciplines.

As the course progressed during its early years, checklists of expectations were drawn up by those teaching the syllabus: by the end of the one-year course it was expected that students should:

- have an understanding of the nature of comparative studies in education;
- have knowledge of some theories of comparative education and their exponents;
- be familiar with the education systems of a number of industrialised and developing countries and be able to analyse those systems critically;
- be able to devise schemes to make basic comparisons of educational issues in any two or more countries;
- be familiar with several key research studies in comparative and international education;
- have a particular knowledge of educational developments in key areas of western and eastern Europe, including familiarity with the education and training policy of the European Union;
- have detailed knowledge of major issues affecting education at all levels in developing countries;
- be familiar with the work of various non-governmental agencies concerned with educational planning, research and development.[2]

The course content in comparative and international education was as follows in 2005-06:

I Theoretical, Methodological and Systemic Studies

- Historical development of Comparative Education
- Theories and research methods
- Use and misuse of comparative data
- Selected educational issues in comparative context
- Methods of large-scale international data collection
- The role of international organisations in education
- Systemic and thematic studies, including the UK, USA, Japan, Germany, France
- Education in countries in transition
- EU education and training policy
- Historical origins of education systems

II Education in Developing Countries

- Development theories and the educational dimension
- Colonialism and education: legacies and links
- Education and national development
- Education for All – the post-Jomtien era
- Urbanisation, migration and education

- Gender, development and education
- Selected issues, trends and cases from Africa, Asia, Latin America and the tropical island zones

Students were required to write a 20,000-word dissertation and to undertake a common core course in educational research methods, the content of which changed frequently to accommodate the needs of students with other specialisms. Towards the end of the taught components the course moved to Paris for specially designed seminars at UNESCO (including separate sessions at UNESCO's Institute for International Educational Planning) and at the Organsiation for Economic Co-operation and Development.

The chapters in this present collection raise many issues that resonate with my experience of the creation and evolution of this introductory postgraduate course in comparative and international education as it existed until 2012. The challenges described by the contributors demonstrate the full range of problems of course design for such a complex field of inquiry, but they also indicate its inherent richness, a richness embedded in its inherent diversity of approaches. The challenges include definition of the field, especially the unravelling of what is meant by 'comparative' and 'international' in the titles of courses, together with fundamental aims and purposes, with the range of course coverage, with the focus in terms of theoretical underpinnings, with research approaches, and with the integrated participation and contributions of course members (who themselves constitute a strength, since they inevitably come from such diverse backgrounds).

In 1965, shortly before my initial training as a secondary school teacher, a conference was held at the University of Reading on 'The Place of Comparative Education in the Training of Teachers'. From that conference emerged the British comparative education society (now known as BAICE). The contributors included Joseph Lauwerys, Vernon Mallinson, Brian Holmes, Edmund King, and W. D. Halls, and the topics covered ranged from comparative education as a discipline, through techniques, 'area', 'field' and 'problem' studies, to the needs of overseas students and the status of the field in the context of teacher training.[3] Some fifty years on the field has developed in ways that those original contributors could scarcely have imagined. This present collection demonstrates the sophistication of comparative inquiry and its place in undergraduate and graduate courses and serves as a stimulus for further development of a field whose value should be beyond dispute.

Notes

[1] University of Oxford: 'Examination in the theory, history and practice of education, 1967'.

[2] Quoted from the 2003-04 course handbook.

[3] P. J. Mercier (Ed.) (1966) *The Place of Comparative Education in the Training of Teachers*. Reading: University of Reading Institute of Education.

Notes on Contributors

ROBERT F. ARNOVE is Chancellor's Professor Emeritus of Educational Leadership and Policy Studies at Indiana University Bloomington. He is an Honorary Fellow and past president of the Comparative and International Education Society. He has written extensively on education and social change. His latest publications include *Talent Abounds: profiles of master teachers and peak performers* and the co-edited volume, *Comparative Education: the dialectic of the global and the local* (4th edn). *Correspondence*: arnove@indiana.edu

KAREN L. BIRAIMAH is a tenured professor of comparative education and Director of International and Special Programs at the University of Central Florida. She has served as a Fulbright Senior Scholar at the University of Malaya, Kenyatta University, Nairobi, and the University of Namibia. Prior to these experiences, Biraimah served as a Peace Corps volunteer teacher in Ghana and as a member of the Faculty of Education at the University of Ife, Nigeria. She is past-president of the Comparative and International Education Society, and her research interests focus on the effects of race/ethnicity, class, language and gender on educational equity within a comparative context. *Correspondence*: karen.biraimah@ucf.edu

ALLISON H. BLOSSER holds a PhD in Cultural and Educational Policy Studies from Loyola University Chicago. In the fall of 2016 she will be joining the School of Education at High Point University in North Carolina as an Assistant Professor of Educational Studies, Policy, and Culture. She also serves as co-chair of the Teaching Comparative Education Special Interest Group for the Comparative and International Educational Society. Her research examines the teaching of comparative education, multicultural education, diversity in private schools, and the global spread of market-based educational reforms. *Correspondence*: ablosser@highpoint.edu

BARRY L. BULL is Emeritus Professor of Philosophy of Education and Education Policy Studies at Indiana University Bloomington. His research and teaching focus on the moral and political justification of public policies in education. He has published on such subjects as standards-based school reform, government control of schools, school finance, civic education, teacher professional development, the professionalization of teaching, and education for the gifted and talented. His books include *The Ethics of*

Multicultural and Bilingual Education, Learning Together: professional development for better schools and *Social Justice in Education: an introduction.* *Correspondence*: bbull@indiana.edu

MICHAEL CROSSLEY is Professor of Comparative and International Education, a former Director of the Doctor of Education Programme (Bristol and Hong Kong), Director of the Centre for Comparative and International Research in Education at the Graduate School of Education, and Director of the Education in Small States Research Group (www.smallstates.net), University of Bristol, UK. Professor Crossley is a former editor of the journal *Comparative Education* and former chair of the British Association for International and Comparative Education (BAICE). He is currently Adjunct Professor of Education at the University of the South Pacific, and is an elected Fellow, FAcSS, of the British Academy of Social Sciences. *Correspondence*: m.crossley@bristol.ac.uk

ERWIN H. EPSTEIN is Professor Emeritus at Loyola University Chicago. He is a former president of the Comparative and International Education Society and of the World Council of Comparative Education Societies, and is a past editor of the *Comparative Education Review*. He is editor of *Crafting a Global Field: six decades of the Comparative and International Education Society*, scheduled for publication in 2016 by Springer/Comparative Education Research Centre at the University of Hong Kong. *Correspondence*: eepstein@luc.edu

IRVING EPSTEIN is the Ben and Susan Rhodes Professor of Peace and Social Justice at Illinois Wesleyan University, where he chairs the Department of Educational Studies and directs the Center for Human Rights and Social Justice. He has written widely on children's rights and youth-related issues and has most recently edited *The Whole World is Texting: youth protest in the information age* (Pittsburgh Studies in Comparative and International Education; Rotterdam: Sense, 2015). *Correspondence*: iepstein@iwu.edu

SABINE HORNBERG, Dr. phil. habil., is Professor in School Pedagogy and General Didactics in the Context of Heterogeneity and Director of the Institute for General Didactics and School Pedagogy at the Technical University of Dortmund, Germany. She has been active in comparative and international education for many years and was president of the section 'International and Intercultural Comparative Education' (SIIVE) in the German Association of Educational Research (GERA)/(Deutsche Gesellschaft für Erziehungswissenschaft (DGfE). Her research interests focus on education and schools in the process of internationalization, transnational educational spaces, intercultural education, teaching and learning in the context of heterogeneity, and empirical research. *Correspondence*: sabine.hornberg@tu-dortmund.de

PATRICIA K. KUBOW is Professor in Educational Leadership and Policy Studies and Curriculum and Instruction at Indiana University. She is also director of the Center for International Education, Development and Research (CIEDR) in the Indiana University School of Education. Her research interests focus on the comparative study of global-local constructions of democracy, citizen identity and formal education in sub-Saharan Africa and the Middle East. Her scholarship has received distinguished research awards from the American Educational Research Association and the Association of Teacher Educators. Kubow's co-authored textbook with Paul R. Fossum, *Comparative Education: exploring issues in international context*, is used in schools of education around the world. Kubow is co-chair of the Teaching Comparative Education Special Interest Group of the Comparative and International Education Society (CIES) and is also a member of the CIES Publications Committee. *Correspondence*: pkubow@indiana.edu

MARIA MANZON is a research scientist at the National Institute of Education (NIE), Nanyang Technological University, Singapore, where she is Research Convenor of NIE's International and Comparative Studies Task Force. She is chair of the Admissions and New Societies Standing Committee of the World Council of Comparative Education Societies (WCCES). She is also an associate member of the Comparative Education Research Centre at the University of Hong Kong. Her research interests and publications focus on the theory, history and methodology of comparative education, as well as on parent involvement in education. She was co-editor of a volume of histories of comparative education societies (2007), and of another volume about comparative education in universities worldwide (2008). Her 2011 book entitled *Comparative Education: the construction of a field* has been acclaimed for its comprehensive approach and path-breaking conceptualisation. *Correspondence*: maria.manzon@nie.edu.sg

MARCELO PARREIRA DO AMARAL is Professor of International and Comparative Education at the University of Münster. He is also president of the German Section for Intercultural, International and Comparative Education Research of the German Association of Education Research (SIIVE-DGfE). His main research interests include international comparative education, education policy, and international educational governance and its implications for educational trajectories, in particular issues of access to and equity in education. Among his latest publications is the edited volume *Shaping the Futures of Young Europeans: education governance in eight European countries* (Symposium Books). *Correspondence*: parreira@uni-muenster.de

DAVID PHILLIPS is Emeritus Professor of Comparative Education, University of Oxford, and an emeritus fellow of St Edmund Hall, Oxford. He is a fellow of the UK Social Sciences Academy and of the Royal Historical Society. A past chair of the British Association for International Education (BAICE), he has also served on the board of directors of the Comparative and International Education Society (CIES). He is the founder editor of the journal *Research in Comparative and International Education*, series editor of *Oxford Studies in Comparative Education*, and currently edits *Comparative Education*. He served for twenty years as editor of the *Oxford Review of Education*. His latest book is *The German Example: English interest in educational provision in Germany since 1800* (Continuum/Bloomsbury). His book with Michele Schweisfurth, *Comparative and International Education: an introduction to theory, research, and practice* (Bloomsbury, 2nd edn, 2014) is used in comparative education courses around the world. *Correspondence*: david.phillips@education.ox.ac.uk

NOAH W. SOBE is Associate Professor of Cultural and Educational Policy Studies at Loyola University Chicago where he also directs the Center for Comparative Education. He is Vice-President (2015-16), President-Elect (2016-17) and President (2017-18) of the Comparative and International Education Society (CIES). His research examines the global circulation of educational policies and practices, and he takes a particular interest in the ways that schools function as contested sites of cultural production for the making up of people, peoples, societies and worlds. He also works on research methodologies in comparative education, specifically around how notions of context, the nation, transnationalism and globalization/the global can be reconceptualized. His work has appeared in journals such as *Harvard Education Review*, *Current Issues in Comparative Education (CICE)*, *Educational Theory* and *Paedagogica Historica*. *Correspondence*: nsobe@luc.edu

CARLOS ALBERTO TORRES is Distinguished Professor of Education in the Graduate School of Education and Information Studies at the University of California-Los Angeles. He is also UNESCO Chair in Global Learning and Global Citizenship Education, Director of the Paulo Freire Institute, and President of the World Council of Comparative Education Societies (WCCES). His book *First Freire: early writings in social justice education* (New York: Teachers College Press, 2014) received the 2015 prestigious Cyril O. Houle Award for Outstanding Literature in Adult Education from the American Association of Adult and Continuing Education. *Correspondence*: catnovoa@aol.com